Ashley Mallett is a born storyteller.

aimed to play Test cricket and his amb ...... 100 Test wickets – a feat he achieved in his twenty-third match (an identical match strike rate as Shane Warne, Glenn McGrath and Graham McKenzie). During his career, Ashley played 38 Tests, taking 132 wickets at an average of 29. In his time, the Sheffield Shield competition was widely regarded as the strongest domestic cricket in the world. The Test players competed regularly and, often, games were red-hot battles of international standard. Ashley's Sheffield Shield record compares favourably with two of the game's greatest bowlers: England and WA left-arm spinner Tony Lock and WA and Australian legendary fast bowler Dennis Lillee. In 66 matches, Lock took 302 wickets at 23.87; Lillee, in 75 matches, took 338 wickets at 23.83; and Mallett, in 77 matches, took 344 wickets at 23.75.

Along with fellow off-spinners, Indian great Erapalli Prasanna and West Indian Lance Gibbs, Ashley was globally acclaimed as a world-class Test spin bowler. During the Australian tour of Indian in 1969, Ashley took 28 wickets at an average of 19. In December 1972, he took 8/59 for Australia versus Pakistan – the best single innings bowling analysis for any bowler in a Test match at Adelaide Oval in the twentieth century.

Ashley is a consultant for Cricket Australia's National Cricket Centre, in Brisbane, and he runs an internationally recognised coaching program, Spin Australia, working closely with such luminaries as England's off-spinner Graeme Swann and Sri Lanka's left-handed slow man, Rangana Herath.

A successful writer, Ashley wrote the definitive history of the 1868 Aboriginal Australian cricket tour of England, *The Black Lords of Summer* (2002), as well as 14 children's books and the biographies of Victor Trumper, Clarrie Grimmett, Ian Chappell, Jeff Thomson, Doug Walters and Dr Donald Beard, legendary medical man of Australian cricket and the battlefields of Korea and Vietnam. Ashley writes regularly for *Cricinfo*, the internet's foremost cricket website.

Great Australian Test Cricket Stories is his thirty-third book.

LIFE OF A SPINNER

Left: Ashley, three years old, with his mother, in Sydney, 1948.

Below At the age of 12, Ashley won his first state blazer for Western Australia.

Meeting Queen Elizabeth II, at Lord's, 1968.

Above: South Australia's winning Sheffield Shield team, 1970–71.

Above: WA's John Iverarity trapped plumb lbw by Ashley Mallett, Adelaide Oval, 1971–72.

Right: Ashley Mallett bowling for Australia versus Northamptonshire in May 1968, finishing with match figures of 10/106.

Also by Ashley Mallett

Autobiography

Rowdy

Spin Out

Biography

Clarrie Grimmett: The
*   Bradman of Spin*

Trumper: The Illustrated
*   Biography*

Chappelli Speaks Out

One of a Kind: The Doug
*   Walters Story*

Thommo Speaks Out

Nugget: Man of the Century

Scarlet: Clarrie Grimmett,
*   Test Cricketer*

No Beating About the Bush

The Digger's Doctor

Historical

The Black Lords of Summer:
*   The Story of the 1868*
*   Aboriginal Tour of England*
*   and Beyond*

The Catch that Broke a Bank

Master Sportsman Series
(for children)

CRICKET

Doug Walters

Dennis Lillee

Rodney Marsh

The Chappell Brothers

Allan Border

Kim Hughes

Geoff Lawson

Don Bradman

AUSTRALIAN RULES FOOTBALL

Mark Williams

Tim Watson

Robert Flower

Wayne Johnston

SOCCER

John Kosmina

TENNIS

Evonne Cawley

GREAT
AUSTRALIAN
TEST CRICKET
STORIES

ASHLEY MALLETT

ABC
Books

The ABC 'Wave' device is a trademark of the Australian Broadcasting Corporation and is used under licence by HarperCollins*Publishers* Australia.

First published in Australia in 2017
by HarperCollins*Publishers* Australia Pty Limited
ABN 36 009 913 517
harpercollins.com.au

HarperCollins*Publishers*
Level 13, 201 Elizabeth Street, Sydney NSW 2000, Australia
Unit D1, 63 Apollo Drive, Rosedale, Auckland 0632, New Zealand
A 53, Sector 57, Noida, UP, India
1 London Bridge Street, London, SE1 9GF, United Kingdom
2 Bloor Street East, 20th floor, Toronto, Ontario M4W 1A8, Canada
195 Broadway, New York NY 10007, USA

National Library of Australia Cataloguing-in-Publication entry:

Creator: Mallett, Ashley, 1945- author.
Title: Great Australian test cricket stories / Ashley Mallett.
ISBN: 9780733337956 (paperback)
ISBN: 9781460707821 (ebook : epub)
Notes: Includes index.
Subjects: Mallett, Ashley, 1945-
Cricket players – Australia.
Cricket matches – Australia.
Test matches (Cricket) – Australia.
Cricket stories.

Cover design by Luke Causby, Blue Cork
Cover image by Ray Kennedy/Fairfax Syndication; back cover image by istock.com
Photographs are from the collection of Ashley Mallett, except as noted:
Photography credits: page 19 Wikipedia, photographer unknown (top), Aboriginal Australian cricketers in England 1868 with C. Lawrence & W. Shepherd as Manager and Captain, National Library of Australia, nla.obj-136410831 (bottom); page 69 source National Museum of Australia; page 103 Paul Rigby, reprinted with permission; page 153 State Library of New South Wales (IE1439598); page 169 Max Dupain, State Library of New South Wales (IE1712510); page 278 from Bill Ferguson's book *Mr Cricket* (Nicholas Kaye, London, 1957).
Typeset in ITC Bookman by Kirby Jones
Printed and bound in Australia by McPhersons Printing Group
The papers used by HarperCollins in the manufacture of this book are a natural, recyclable product made from wood grown in sustainable plantation forests. The fibre source and manufacturing processes meet recognised international environmental standards, and carry certification.

This book is dedicated to my grandfather, Alec West, who brought cricket into my life; to my mum and dad, Clare and Ray, who gave me belief; to my brother, Nick, for the mix of fun and fierce combat in our backyard 'Tests'; to all the players I played with and against; to all who watch, listen and read the game; and to my fiancée, Patsy Gardner, the love of my life.

Contents

Introduction
A bat, a ball and a pen ...

Two things fascinated me as a boy: the game of cricket and the art of writing.

From early in my life, I read avidly about the great cricketers of yesteryear, going way back to the Golden Age (1890–1914). I read the good writers, including the doyen Neville Cardus, who was the veritable Shakespeare among cricket writers. Cardus created a word picture so vivid that it lavishly massaged the imaginative senses. He might have been thinking about the comparative merits of Victor Trumper and Don Bradman, where Trumper's Test average of 39 paled into insignificance when put up against Bradman's 99, when he wrote: 'There ought to be some other means of reckoning quality in this the best and loveliest of games: the scoreboard is an ass ...'

Often I would stroll into a shop, pick a book up at random and read the opening paragraph. Throughout my early writing days I continued this practice. Still do. Noted novelist Ken Follett's first line in *The Pillars of the Earth* really sets the scene: 'The small boys came early to the hanging.' There is a powerful brevity here; you are compelled to read on. Similarly in Frank McCourt's *'Tis*: 'That's your dream out now.'

From the age of six, I wanted to become a Test cricketer and, from the age of 15, I maintained that ambition to play international cricket and added another goal: I wanted to become a really good writer. In 1960, the year I finished my secondary schooling, there was a sense of conflict in me. A cricket book – *A Century of Cricketers*, by Johnny Moyes – was my constant companion, however Charles Dickens's *Oliver Twist* was very much a must-read, because it was the book I had picked for my English examination.

Moyes wasn't a gifted writer like Cardus, but he had the ability to bring the cricketers of his time, even those he had only read about, to life. I felt as though I knew them. So Trumper, Clem Hill, FS Jackson, Fred Spofforth, Hugh Trumble, Clarrie Grimmett, Bill O'Reilly, Neil Harvey, Don Bradman ... all vicariously joined my cricket family. Even at the tender age of 15, to me Dickens's prose was too detailed; wordy description tended to lose the reader. I wanted to read writing which made the reader use his imagination. Ernest Hemingway certainly had that gift and so had Morris West. When the time came for me to leave school, my dear old dad had already told me, 'Aim for the stars, son, and you just might hit the treetops.' It was a hot Perth day in December 1960 when my form teacher at Mount Lawley High School, Don Melrose, took me aside and asked me what I was going to do.

'You are just 15 and about to start work in a bank. Is that the sum of your life's ambition?' he asked, with a curious pursing of the lips.

'Well, Don, I am going to play Test cricket and I aim to become a good writer.'

'Ah ...' His eyes narrowed and those normally thick lips instantly became thin, brown lines. 'There's no money in cricket and writing is completely out of the question, because you are hopeless at English.'

At that time, Melrose was right on both counts. Long before Kerry Packer rescued Test players and lined their pockets by bringing television to the game in an unprecedented, corporate manner, there *was* no money in cricket. And my English wasn't exactly tickety-boo. I couldn't fathom either the depth or the value of grammar in all its various pedantic forms.

Lunchtime at the bank was an eye-opener. In summer, the round-table conversation always embraced three main topics:

sex, cricket and how to rob the bank. Winter was slightly different: sex, football and how to rob the bank.

After a few weeks in the bank, I knew I didn't want to pursue a career in the stuffy atmosphere of that august establishment. Yet the banking experience had one advantage: there was the chance to contribute regularly to the suggestion box. None of my suggestions, I might add, was ever taken up, but the exercise got me writing. Eventually I hit on the idea that if you could articulate in speech, then you should be able to write clearly and succinctly. Channel Nine and England's Channel 5 cricket host Mark Nicholas is a fine example of someone who speaks eloquently and writes fluently.

As far back as the summer of 1954–55, my interest in cricket was sharpened by a trip to the Sydney Cricket Ground (SCG) with my grandfather to watch the last day's play of the Test match. My grandfather, Alec West, a man who idolised Victor Trumper and was a one-time vice-president of the Balmain Cricket Club, thought it a good idea to introduce his grandson to big cricket when Australia help the whip hand. Sadly for the home team, Frank Tyson had other ideas. He ran through the Australians with a devastating display of fast bowling.

Perhaps the writing was on the wall the night before. On the penultimate ball before tea, stand-in Test captain Arthur Morris fell to a stroke that the *Sydney Morning Herald*'s columnist Bill O'Reilly described as 'suicidally wild ... a shot borrowed from kerosene-tin cricket'.

While the gifted left-hander Neil Harvey batted bravely, standing up to the barrage of short-pitched deliveries arriving at typhoon velocity, Pop and I sat at the fence in front of the MA Noble Stand. On the ground at fine leg was no less a personage than Colin Cowdrey, then a man who resembled a plump, ruddy-faced schoolboy. Fourteen years later, at Kennington Oval in August 1968, he became my first wicket with the fifth ball of my opening over in Test match cricket.

In 1967, I found work as the professional-cum-groundsman at the Ayr Cricket Club in Scotland. During my stint there, I negotiated a weekly sports column with the *Ayr Advertiser,* the editor promising me £5. I thought that my summer's 22 1500-word articles educating the Scots about the game of Australian Rules Football would net me the grand total of £110. Maybe I should have stayed in the bank after all, because the editor at season's end presented me with a crisp £5 note for my summer's writing.

Within 18 months I was playing cricket for Australia and, after tours of India and South Africa in 1969–70, I sought to follow a journalistic career. Greg Chappell knew the Messenger Newspapers boss, Roger Baynes, a self-made, big-hearted rough diamond, who answered the phone when I called.

'So ya wanna be a journalist. Can yer type?'

I answered in the affirmative.

'Can yer do shorthand?'

'No.'

'Okay, come down to Port Adelaide and I'll give yer a job as an advertising salesman.'

I accepted a job as an advertising salesman. A salesman I was not, but I got to sell the odd ad after convincing the shop owner that my writing an editorial to complement his advertisement was a bonus. It worked and I loved the writing part. An opportunity in the editorial team soon eventuated.

I opted out of the 1972–73 Australian Test tour of the West Indies purely because I wanted to get into journalism. It was a terrific experience: I covered council, parliament, police rounds, wrote colour and hard-news pieces and did all-round general reporting. The day I retired from cricket in 1981, Geoff Jones, chief of staff at *The News* in Adelaide, offered me a job as a general reporter.

In the 1980s, there was a dearth of spin bowling in Australia. Then emerged the magical talent of Shane Warne. His brilliance was out of this world, inspirational to me. In the 1997 edition of *Wisden*, I wrote a piece on Warne that included the line: 'Until he came along, many feared wrist-spin was a lost art, gone the way of the dinosaurs, who vanished years ago when Planet Earth failed to duck a cosmic bumper.'

We all remember Warne clean-bowling Mike Gatting at Old Trafford with his first ball in a Test match in England.

Richie Benaud said simply: 'He's done it.' Ah, the power of brevity. Less is more.

Like Mark Nicholas after him, the great broadcaster John Arlott wrote as he spoke. I love Arlott's 'he played that cut so late it's positively posthumous'.

Over more than two centuries, cricket has been synonymous with good writing. And a writer needs to read good writing. The names of the good ones roll easily off the tongue: Neville Cardus, AA Thomson, John Arlott, RC Robertson-Glasgow, John Woodcock, Johnny Moyes and Bill O'Reilly among them.

Among the moderns, Mark Nicholas stands out, so too Michael Atherton, Malcolm Knox and Gideon Haigh, whose rather scholarly approach to describing cricket is highly sought by academics and laymen alike.

Nathan Lyon's rise and rise

Literally dragged from a roller and thrust onto the Test stage: that is the fairytale story of Nathan Lyon. What a remarkable rise to Test cricket. Lyon came through the junior ranks in Canberra, where he soon forged a reputation as an off-spinner who really gave the ball a rip. He found work as an apprentice curator and that job brought him to Adelaide from Canberra in 2010.

When 'resting' from his oval duties, Lyon would have a bowl to the South Australia batsmen. He also bowled to the Australians in the Adelaide Oval nets and his bowling impressed Test batsman Mike Hussey, who was destined to have a big influence on Lyon's career in terms of providing help and advice and extending the hand of friendship.

Lyon was spotted by Redbacks' Big Bash coach Darren Berry, who had kept wicket to Shane Warne when he was playing for Victoria. Berry knew talent when he saw it and within weeks Lyon was given a try-out for South Australia's T20 squad, then he made his first-class debut. Within seven months, Lyon was playing Test cricket.

On 31 August 2011, Lyon played his first Test at Galle, a picturesque harbour city in Sri Lanka. Skipper Michael Clarke said to Lyon at a drinks break: 'Ready to go?' Lyon was fortunate to have Clarke as his first Test captain, for Clarke knows spin and spinners and – like outstanding leaders such as Ian Chappell and Mark Taylor before him – he set good, sensible and attacking fields for his bowlers.

Lyon's first ball fairly buzzed from his hand, the amount of purchase he achieved had the ball dropping and curving in to left-hander Kumar Sangakkara, one of the world's best batsmen. Sangakkara came forward to defend; the ball dropped and spun, taking the outside edge and Clarke, at first slip, dived to take a brilliant left-handed catch. As Doug Walters would say, 'Bloody beauty ... one for none!' After 15 overs, Lyon had routed Sri Lanka – all out for 105. Lyon took 5/34. Some debut! In the second innings, he took 1/73 off 19.5 overs, and Australia won the match by 125 runs.

Before he was picked for the Test tour of Sri Lanka, Lyon toured Zimbabwe with Australia A. Then aged 22, the off-spinner topped the wickets tally in the 50-overs format, but wasn't selected for the three-day matches. That made it all the more surprising that he was picked for Sri Lanka. After searching for a quality spin bowler in the post-Warne era, Lyon was a godsend.

There have been a few bumps along the road for Lyon. From his early days in Canberra, one coach has had his eye on the off-spinner. Canadian-born John Davison was an off-spinner with a classical high arm. He played first-class cricket for Canada, Victoria and South Australia, taking 111 wickets at an average of 45.61. A modest return for having twirled down in excess of 10,000 deliveries, but his figures in no way reflect his real ability. As a spin-bowling coach working with all the best and emerging spinners in the land, I worked a lot with Davison. In the nets, he looked sensational. He could bowl big, top-spinning off-breaks, side-spinners and a square-spinner, all deliveries that Lyon bowls today.

I showed Davison the square-spinner, the same delivery I helped Graeme Swann and Daniel Vettori with all those summers ago. In 2003, Davison stunned the West Indies by scoring the fastest century in World Cup history, but it is as a spin coach that he has made his mark, especially his relationship with Lyon.

In 2013, during a Sheffield Shield match, I sat with Rod Marsh and John Inverarity at Adelaide Oval. All eyes were on Nathan Lyon. After he had bowled five balls, I turned to Inverarity and said, 'He's locking his left arm. Not completing his action. Obvious problem that he must put right if he's to survive.'

In the wake of Australia's disastrous tour of India in 2013, I was asked by two Australian selectors – Marsh and Inverarity – to run my coaching eye over Australian off-spinner Lyon at Cricket Australia's fabulous National Cricket Centre in Brisbane. There were huge concerns about Lyon's bowling. India won the series 4–nil, but the most worrying thing for selectors was the fact that India scored heavily on big-turning wickets.

So, long after that Shield season had finished and in the wake of Australia's disastrous Indian campaign, I found myself at the NCC in Brisbane. There were a few spinners of potential about, including left-arm orthodox bowler Ashton Agar, from Western Australia, and Victoria's Pakistani-born leg-spinner Fawad Ahmed. Selector Marsh rang often to check the spinners' progress. Agar was steady, so too Ahmed, and both spinners were more consistent than Lyon. However, instinct told me that the off-spinner was far and away the best prospect of that spin trio.

He was simply a small technical hitch away from being a top-flight Test bowler. To the trained eye of a good coach, Lyon was locking his lead arm and not following through properly, thus inhibiting his rhythm and putting his timing way out. The remedy was simple: the lead arm swings back in unison with the bowling arm as it swings down past his left knee.

A lack of consistency was all too apparent. At training, he was bowling three good balls out of 10. The other seven were dreadful. It was of great concern to all, because Australia did not have an obvious quality back-up spinner to Lyon and the 2013 Ashes series in England loomed.

I attempted to speak with Nathan at training. It was important that I got the message across to him. There was need for some repeat drills to work through to get the good feeling and comfort a bowler needs to build renewed confidence. When I approached Nathan to help, he shrugged his shoulders and refused to listen. 'No, I don't need to talk about anything. I'm okay.'

I was buoyed by his self-belief, but I wondered whether Nathan's seeming brashness was more about someone seemingly in denial, masking self-doubt. Over a beer that night, I spoke with Greg Shipperd, then Victoria's coach. He advised me to 'Write up a report and submit it at the end of the week.'

Certainly, I knew Shipperd's advice was way off-beam. I knew that I couldn't leave it there. That was a cop-out. If help was needed and it *was* required, I had to find a way. And the way forward materialised the very next day.

There was Lyon bowling away in the nets on Ray Lindwall Oval. And there was the NCC spin coach, John Davison, chatting with the young spinner. They enjoyed one another's company and I noted how Nathan listened closely to Davo's words. A voice within kept saying, 'Find a way. You must find a way, Rowdy. Get someone he knows well and trusts to tell Nathan what needs to be said to him.'

No doubt Davison was the perfect mentor for Lyon. I instinctively knew that if Lyon would not listen to the person who identified the problem in the first place and could offer a simple way forward, then I had to urge Davo to tell him. Davo and I spoke for a few minutes.

'Mate, Nathan's locking his left arm. If he doesn't free his lead arm at delivery, not only will he fail to take wickets and lose his Test spot, but he won't get enough batsmen out in Shield cricket to survive. He simply has to free the arm and complete his follow-through,' I said with conviction.

A few minutes later, Davo took Nathan aside. Then he showed him a replay on a video screen set up next to the net. The locking of his lead arm was obvious and Nathan must have seen it all too clearly and realised what must be done for him to return to consistency.

Happily, a few months later Nathan Lyon was clearing his left arm and completing his follow-through with energy.

Lyon toured England in 2013 and, after an early hiccup when he was axed in favour of Agar, Lyon returned. He bowled so well that he was favourably compared with Graeme Swann, who bowled well all that summer. Lyon probably didn't know that I had worked with Graeme Swann, then the best off-spinner in the world, for more than 10 years.

Now Lyon is a top-notch Test match off-spinner. He no longer locks his non-bowling arm, allowing him to bowl with freedom and rhythm. He also spends more time on his front foot at delivery, a hallmark of the best spinners. His best is world-class. He still tends to bowl better on the bouncy Australian pitches; certainly better and more consistently than in India, where he has struggled to build pressure and get among the wickets at a reasonable cost.

There are certainly no 'miracles' about Nathan Lyon's Test career resurrection, but Lyon became better because commonsense prevailed and I found a way to get a vital coaching message across. Most players, when they reach international level, have actions which work for them, are repeatable and allow them to bowl with good rhythm. However, when a coach sees something in a bowler's action which is inhibiting his progress, it is time to speak up. He must find a way. To my mind, any coach of top-flight sportsmen must learn to find a way to help his charges become the best they can become.

At the end of the 2016–17 series against Pakistan in Australia, Lyon had taken more Test wickets than any other Australian off-spinner and will perhaps soon surpass Richie Benaud's wicket tally of 248 wickets in 63 Tests. After the same number of

Tests, Lyon had reached 228 wickets. This equals the legendary fast bowler Ray Lindwall, and is 12 more wickets than Clarrie Grimmett, who captured 216 wickets in 37 Tests. With the number of Test matches played each calendar year, a fit Lyon may well play more than 150 Tests. What a wicket tally he will have by then!

His figures, with the other off-spinners who have taken 100 or more wickets in Tests for Australia are listed below:

BOWLER	TESTS	WICKETS	AVERAGE
Nathan Lyon	67	247	33.39
Hugh Trumble	32	141	21.28
Ashley Mallett	38	132	29.84
Bruce Yardley	33	126	31.63
Ian Johnson	45	109	29.19

Before the age of professional sport, Australia's Test cricketers had to eke out a living away from the game. Some, such as Doug Walters, Keith Stackpole and Ian Chappell, worked for cigarette companies; some, such as Bob Massie and Dennis Lillee, had bank jobs. I had various jobs during my cricket career. For a period, I was a clerk in the Hospitals Department and for a short time the complaints officer at the South Australian Gas Company. Those jobs sure had an impact on my life: I found out there were some jobs I definitely did not want to pursue.

I wanted to get into journalism and the day the chance came my way was the day I told the Test selectors I was not available for the tour to the West Indies in the summer of 1972–73. The struggle of juggling work with cricket cost me dearly in terms of playing a lot of Tests. I missed tours to Pakistan, the West Indies and England due to my unavailability. I played 38 Tests, stretched over 12 years. That was partly due to Australia not playing anywhere near the number of Tests they do today and partly because of my unavailability for a few tours. Lyon took less than five years to play his first 63 Tests.

Some players with jobs were lucky enough to be paid while they were on tour, others were not so lucky. There is no doubt the players of the 1960s and 1970s were professional about the way they trained; however, the need to have full-time employment shortened many cricket careers. Simply put, players of yesteryear played fewer Test matches and they generally retired long before their ability waned.

The world is a vastly different place now than it was in the 1970s. Television – thanks mainly to the vision of Kerry Packer – brought big money into the game. The players are now paid the sort of money they deserve. Not having to worry about making ends meet must be a fabulous luxury for the modern player.

David Warner: cricket's new master blaster

With a heart as big as Phar Lap and a bat as wide as the Sydney Harbour Bridge, David Warner sets every summer of cricket alight. His energy creates a collective mood of enthusiasm wherever he might be playing. A rare Warner failure and the people fall silent but for a hushed, yet audible, groan of disappointment echoing throughout the stands.

In a season of Warner highlights, the little Aussie dynamo's most sensational knock was his century before lunch in the Third Test against Pakistan at the SCG on 3 January 2017. It was an Australian first on home soil. Only three other Australians have achieved a century before lunch on the first day of a Test match and they were all against England in England. And an impressive three they were: Victor Trumper (Old Trafford, 1902), Charlie Macartney (Headingley, 1926) and Don Bradman (Headingley, 1930).

Fans love Warner's celebratory 'Toyota' leap after every century and he celebrates in this way regularly. Warner proved to those of the old school, who were sceptical, that he could indeed make a smooth transition from the hectic T20 format to the Test stage.

Born in Paddington, Sydney, on 27 October 1986, Warner was always a sports enthusiast. When he was 13, his cricket coach advised him to change from being a left-hander to batting right-handed. The reason: 'You're hitting too many balls in the air.' Wise counsel from his mother, Sheila. That very season, when David returned to batting left-handed, he broke the under-16s batting record for his team, the Sydney Coastal Cricket Club.

Word soon got around that the explosive Warner was destined for greater things and he made his first-grade debut for Eastern Suburbs at the age of 15. Within two years, he was a member of the Australian Under-19 team touring Sri Lanka.

He first played for Australia in 2008–09 in a T20 international match, when he nearly brought the house down at the MCG by smashing the strong South African attack to the tune of 89 runs in 43 deliveries. Even Dale Steyn was dispatched over midwicket for a massive six. That day also confirmed that David Warner was the first player since 1877 to represent Australia before first playing a first-class match.

Because of the way he played, there were those who had their doubts that he would ever succeed in the longer form of the game. His style was all-out attack and he usually threw caution to the wind and hit out at any ball within reach of his bat. He continued to hit out with gay abandon, but he did so while compiling a glut of runs and keeping the score ticking over at a rapid rate.

Warner's One Day International (ODI) debut came a week after his sensational batting against South Africa at the MCG. He hit 6 sixes and 7 fours in a blistering performance which captured the imagination of all who witnessed that innings, delighting the young with its boldness and range of strokes and tickling the memories of the old. His strike rate that day was an 'impossible' 206.97.

A few weeks later, on 5 March 2009, the New South Wales selectors belatedly named Warner in the state's Sheffield Shield side. He batted once in that match, trusting his attacking style with 42 in 48 balls against Western Australia at the SCG.

Nowadays, Warner opens the batting for Australia in all three forms of the game. Wearing his heart on his sleeve, Warner's intent is all too clear. He can't wait to get to the middle and belt hell out of every ball.

Early in his international career, many thought David would not cut it in the longer form of the game because of trying to smash any ball within reach. He proved all the dissenters wrong by tightening his technique and becoming patient. These days, he easily adapts to any form of cricket.

Boy, does he love the contest; especially the red-blooded battle between bat and ball on the Test stage. Warner is a solid little bloke, akin to the old village blacksmith, possessing powerful forearms and a will to strike fear into the hearts of his opponents. Mind you, Warner needs power, for the bat he wields is very much a 'Big Bertha', heavy for others, perfect for him. He merely leans on a ball, which meets the full face of the bat and fairly races across the turf.

There is something very intimidating about Warner. Test bowlers eye with trepidation the pocket dynamo rushing towards them: Warner the batsman on the hunt. Deliver a wide half-volley and it will career to the cover fence; anything short is whipped over midwicket. From ball one, the fast bowler has to be on the money.

It's been an interesting international ride for Warner. To his credit, he has turned his world around since an altercation he had with England's Joe Root in a Birmingham bar and was suspended by Cricket Australia. That was back in 2013. Meeting Candice Falzon, a Maltese-born ironwoman and model, was a godsend for him, for his cricket and life in general. The couple married in April 2015, and are now the proud parents of two girls, Ivy Mae and Indi Rae.

Warner's brilliance as a cricketer has earned him more money than he could possibly have dreamt of during those early days when the family lived on a housing commission estate in Matraville. He believes that 'making a good living out of playing cricket is all about providing opportunities for my family that I never had'.

Some pundits predict that Warner will earn up to $50 million over the next five years. Of course, that is very possible given his world-wide profile and the sponsorship opportunities available to the most explosive batsman playing all three forms of the game on the international stage.

In January 2017, Warner claimed top spot in the International Cricket Council (ICC) one-day rankings, in the wake of a sensational run of big scores from the beginning of 2016. Since that time and leading up to the Indian Test tour in February 2017, in 28 ODIs Warner amassed 1755 runs at an average of 65, with 9 hundreds and 4 fifties. His strike rate was an amazing 106.94, overtaking South Africa's AB de Villiers and India's Virat Kohli.

Warner celebrated the last match of the 2016–17 ODI summer with a brilliant 179 off 128 balls against Pakistan in Adelaide, leading Australia to a 4–1 series win over the hapless visitors, who had already lost the Tests 3–nil.

As a fieldsman, Warner is pretty much a super-energised version of a Jack Russell scampering about the field on a mission, chasing down every ball like tennis player Lleyton Hewitt did all his career. Warner catches anything within reach and always dives desperately to prevent a ball reaching the rope for a boundary. His enthusiasm with the bat and in the field is infectious and he can also bowl a pretty decent leg-break. He has been Steve Smith's deputy in Tests and ODIs since 2015.

A batsman who fears no fast bowler throughout the world, Warner does struggle against top-class spinners on spin-friendly tracks, especially in the Indian subcontinent.

The Sri Lankan left-arm spinner Rangana Herath tied the Australians in knots when they played Sri Lanka on their home decks in 2016. It was a 3–nil whitewash. And not only the batsmen struggled, so too did the bowlers. Mitchell Starc toiled manfully, but he received little help from the other members of the Test attack.

In 2013, India thrashed Australia 4–nil. It was disastrous for Australia, including Warner, who averaged just 24 and really had to fight to survive for these meagre scores. Three years later in Sri Lanka, he averaged just 27 in the three-Test series.

Quality spin is David Warner's Achilles heel. Good spin bowling on turning wickets worries him. He has to make the pace and the top-class spinner has his measure. In March 2017 Warner struggled against the spinners, Ravi Ashwin and Ravi Jadeja, again averaging in the 20s.

His modest returns in the subcontinent are a contradiction to his overall splendid batting statistics. After 64 Tests, Warner had amassed 5454 runs at an average of 47.42 with 18 centuries and a career high of 253.

The great West Indian Viv Richards was the original 'master blaster'.

David Warner is cricket's latest.

That first Boxing Day classic

The first great cricket match at the Melbourne Cricket Ground (MCG) was the clash between Tom Wills's Aboriginal cricketers and the Melbourne Cricket Club, before a first-day crowd of 8000 on Boxing Day, 1866. This game was the genesis of the nation's most loved summer fixture, the Boxing Day Test. The Aboriginal team (185) led the Melbourne Cricket Club (MCC) (164) in the first innings, but having bowled MCC out for 120 in their second innings, they collapsed when batting a second time for a paltry 45 and lost the match by 54 runs. But while the outcome of the match was not important, it was the catalyst for Australian sport's first major overseas tour – the 1868 Aboriginal cricket tour of England.

Melbourne businessman William Hayman, later a key figure in the 1868 tour, had sent photographs of the Aboriginal cricketers to MCC in the hope of a big match being staged at the MCG. Wills had initially wanted the match staged in November. However, most of the Aboriginal players were top-flight shearers and there was a strong demand from the stations for their labour at shearing time. It was decided to stage the match after the shearing on Boxing Day.

The big day finally arrived and some 8000 people turned up to watch the game. MCC batted first. Johnny Cuzens (Zellanach) bowled like the wind, taking six wickets and helping Tom Wills and Johnny Mullagh (Unaarrimin) to bowl them out for 101. The crowd roared their approval at the Aboriginal team's fielding performance, their athleticism

The Aboriginal Australian cricket team of 1866.
Front row, left to right: King Cole (with leg on chair), Dick-a-Dick, Jellico, Peter,
Redcap, Harry Rose, Bullocky, Johnny Cuzens.
Back row, left to right: Tarpot, Tom Wills, Johnny Mullagh.
(Note: Jellico, Harry Rose, Tarpot and Tom Wills did not tour England with the
Australian team in 1868.)

Photograph taken in England during the 1868 tour, including team captain
Charles Lawrence (standing, centre) and umpire William Shepherd (sitting, centre).

delighting all and sundry. Like top fielders of the modern era, all the Aboriginal fieldsmen walked in briskly, always on the balls of their feet to move swiftly in any direction.

Cuzens starred at point, Tarpot was at long stop, Billy Officer fielded either long leg or cover, Peter (Arruhmunyjarrimin) was at short leg, Dick-a-Dick (Jungunjinanuke) mid-on, Jellico was cover or long leg, Sundown was long slip, Paddy was at third man, and the skipper Wills fielded either short slip or point.

The Aboriginal players wore different-coloured hatbands so that spectators could easily identify them. Cards with the players' names and 'colours' were sold around the ground. Today players have numbers on their backs, but the Aboriginals' coloured clothing beat Kerry Packer's World Series Cricket in that area by 109 years.

When Ben Wardill came to the crease, the Aboriginal players became very excited and, according to a contemporary newspaper report, 'The darkies took off their hats and gave the hurrah in fine British style!' Wardill was an Englishman who had emigrated to Australia in 1861. He kept wicket for MCC and Victoria, became secretary of the club in 1879, and later managed three Australian Test tours of England in 1886, 1899 and 1902.

When Tom Horan – who was the colony's leading batsman and later one of Australia's first Test players – was brilliantly caught at long leg, the crowd went wild, inspiring Tarpot to further entertain them with a double somersault, which nearly brought the house down.

In the Aboriginal team's innings, Jellico fell for a duck, but Mullagh revealed his artistry with a compact 16 while wickets tumbled about him. It was a very courageous knock, given that his middle finger was split, the flesh laid bare to the bone. Despite Mullagh's courage in the first innings and his classy 33 batting a second time, the MCC won the day easily.

While the outcome of the match was of no real moment, the statistically minded need only know that MCC hit 101 and the Aboriginals 39 and 87. So MCC required just a few overs batting to complete the rout. To entertain the spectators, some sport displays were then organised and Tarpot stole the show with his feat of running 100 yards in 14 seconds ... backwards!

Jellico was the crowd favourite. A youthful humourist, he won them with his antics. Newspaper reporters loved speaking with Jellico. Little wonder, when he came up with this gem in the wake of all the general conversation about Melbourne's scorching weather: 'I spoil my complexion. When I go back my mother won't know me.'

A newspaper article quoted him answering a question put to him by a white fan: 'What for you no talk to me good Inglis? I speak him as good Inglis belonging you.' Having settled with the European cricket fan, Jellico turned to his teammate, Tarpot, saying, 'Big one fool that fellow. He not know him Inglis one damn.' When someone suggested that Jellico ask Tom Wills to teach him to read and write, Jellico replied: 'What usy Wills? He too much along of us. He speak nothing now but blackfellow talk.'

While the Aboriginals were outclassed in this match, their appearance had impressed members of the Melbourne Cricket Club. Members and cricket writers praised some of the players such as Johnny Mullagh, Bullocky (Bullchanach) the hard-hitting wicketkeeper–batsman, and Johnny Cuzens, who was called a 'capital' bowler.

Team captain Tom Wills was a legendary footballer and cricketer for Geelong and Victoria. But he lived at a time when racism was rife throughout the colony and those who suffered most were Indigenous Australians. In 1883, the British High Commissioner, Arthur Hamilton Gordon, wrote privately to his friend, William Gladstone, the British Prime Minister:

The habit of regarding the natives as vermin, to be cleared off the face of the earth, has given the average Queenslander a tone of brutality and cruelty in dealing with the blacks which is very difficult to anyone who does not know it, as I do, to realize.

I have heard men of culture and refinement, of the greatest humanity and kindness to their fellow whites and who when you meet them here at home you would pronounce to be incapable of such deeds, talk, not only of wholesale butchery (for the iniquity of that may sometimes be disguised from themselves) but of the individual murder of natives exactly as they would talk of a day's sport or having to kill a troublesome animal.

– from Colin Tatz, *Genocide in Australia*

However, Tom Wills was one white man who formed a strong relationship with the Aboriginal people. After a stint in Queensland, where his father and other family members died in a massacre at the hands of Aboriginals, Wills returned to Victoria and renewed friendships with the Aboriginal people he had known as a teenager.

Wills was an excellent footballer whose introduction to the Indigenous game of 'kick and catch' football was when his family had a squatting run near Ararat, in southwest Victoria. His earliest playmates were Djab Wurrung children. He loved the excitement of the kick and the mark and later revisited the possum-skin football of his youth and took the embryo of Australia's most exciting football code into the white man's world.

He was also a brilliant all-round cricketer, who played intercolonial cricket for Victoria, and he set about putting an Aboriginal cricket team together. First there was the 1866 Boxing Day match, then he took a team to Sydney, where he was keen to drum some tough cricket into his charges, with a view to taking them to England.

However, the finances and organisation of the tour were a shambles and it had to be called off early. Watty, a replacement for Sugar (who had died suddenly before the Boxing Day match), died just 25 kilometres from Edenhope on the return journey to Victoria by bullock cart.

Soon after the side returned home, Jellico – the MCG crowd favourite on Boxing Day – and Paddy died from the ravages of pneumonia. Although an inquest failed to find the true cause of death of these men, Wills came under a cloud over allegedly having plied his men with 'the demon drink'.

Wills missed the 1868 tour. He was shoved aside by Charles Lawrence, who had come to Australia with HH Stephenson's first England touring team and became captain–coach of the Aboriginal team to England.

Boxing Day wasn't always the time for Test matches. Over the Christmas period in the 1950s some classic hard-fought contests were played by Sheffield Shield heavies New South Wales and Victoria at the MCG. With all the Test men available, these games were often of a better quality than the actual Tests of the era. However, these days the Boxing Day Test is the showpiece cricket match of the Australian summer.

Spare a thought for those who played that first big match on Boxing Day 1866: what a legacy those players left Australian cricket.

Note: The Aboriginal players were given sobriquets because their pastoral landlords could not pronounce their tribal names. This is the popular theory, although there is a condescending tone in some of the nicknames. Apparently, cricket scorers were relieved. Instead of Murrumgunarrin or Jarrawuk the player was called Twopenny; Brimbunyah was Redcap; Unaarrimin was Johnny Mullagh.

Michael Clarke walks with the best of them

Even Australian prime ministers envy those chosen to captain the Test team. Apart from Paul Keating, who was more in touch with antique French clocks, famous PMs such as Billy Hughes, Bob Menzies, Bob Hawke and John Howard loved cricket. Every now and then, a Test captain comes along and presents not just as a wonderful leader on the Test cricket stage, but as a true statesman in the public eye. Michael Clarke is such a man.

His stirring speech at Phillip Hughes's funeral in December 2014 inspired all Australians. Playing for South Australia at the SCG, Hughes was struck in the back of the neck while attempting to hook a short ball. The stricken batsman was taken to hospital, where he was placed in an induced coma but never regained consciousness and died two days later. The Hughes tragedy stopped the nation. Hughes was a diminutive figure with a big heart and he was brought undone by a cruel quirk of fate. Clarke, the Australian Test captain at the time, was there for him and the Hughes family throughout this terrible ordeal. Clarke was, of course, Hughes's friend, Test teammate and then his captain. He led the Australian cricket family in tribute to his fallen mate. Clarke was a constant at Phillip's side as other prominent players past and present came to say their last goodbyes at Sydney's St Vincent's Hospital and what was clearly evident was the leadership shown by Michael Clarke – leadership far beyond the game of cricket. There was a statesman-like quality to the words he articulated so vividly at Phillip's funeral held in a crowded school hall.

His spirit has brought us closer together. Something I know must be him at work because it is so consistent with how he played and lived. The bonds that led to cricketers from around the world putting their bats out, that saw people who didn't even know Phillip lay flowers and that brought every cricketing nation on Earth to make its own heartfelt tribute. The bonds that saw players old and new rush to his bedside, from wherever they heard the news, to say their prayers and farewells. This is what makes our game the greatest in the world.

Phillip's spirit, which is now part of our game forever, will act as a custodian of the sport we all love. We must listen to it. We must cherish it. We must learn from it. We must dig in and get through to tea. And we must play on. Rest in peace, my little brother, I'll see you out in the middle.

There seems to be a common thread linking the great Australian Test captains. Since Don Bradman we've had a few outstanding leaders who don't merely shine as great leaders of cricket teams but excel as human beings in a range of different ways. They include Richie Benaud, Ian Chappell and Mark Taylor.

Clarke played 115 Tests, scoring 8643 runs at an average of 49.10, with 28 centuries and a top score of 329 not out. He also took 31 wickets at 38.19 with his left-hand spinners, with a best Test haul of 6/9.

He scored 151 on debut against India at Bangalore in October 2004, helping Australia to win the Test by 217 runs. When Ricky Ponting stood down from the Test captaincy after the 2011 World Cup, Clarke was appointed as his replacement. Against India at the SCG in January 2012 Clarke became the first Australian batsman since Matthew Hayden (380 versus Zimbabwe in Perth in 2003) to score a triple hundred. Clarke's classic knock of 329 not out beat the previous highest Test score at the ground of 287, set in the 1903–04 season by England's Reg Foster. The triple century was followed by a brilliant 210 in the first innings of the Fourth Test in Adelaide, and his 386-run partnership with Ponting (221) was the fourth-highest in Australian Test history.

Later that year, he scored double centuries in each of the first two Tests against South Africa. His brilliant double century in Adelaide wreaked maximum damage upon a South African attack of Morne Morkel, Dale Steyn and leg-spinner Imran Tahir, whose ill-directed and scattered-seam leg-breaks were simply not up to first-class standard. At 130, Clarke looked about the field and found it in total disarray, and not one bowler was worth his wicket. So he batted on and thrashed Morkel for 5 fours in one over to race to 150. When he hit Morkel over mid-off off the front foot, there was the style of Greg Chappell and the power of Viv Richards. As a cricket stroke, it provided sheer ecstasy.

In style and grit, Michael Clarke could well be an amalgam of Trumper and Bradman. There is no suggestion here that Clarke was as good at his peak as either Trumper or Bradman. Clarke had style and was very efficient at the crease. His batting possessed the majesty of Trumper, whose batting in full flight was that of an eagle, and much of the efficiency of Bradman, who collected runs like a frequent flyer clocks up the miles.

His amazing run of big scores in 2012 saw Clarke at his most adventurous, his best. Short of playing the dog shot – a unique Trumper stroke – Clarke exhibited every stroke in the book with a style and power that would have had the greatest batsmen to walk the Earth stand and applaud. Yes, Clarke walks with the greats.

While some didn't always warm to his on-field leadership, Ian Chappell said quite early in Clarke's captaincy:

Clarke is quickly establishing a well-deserved reputation for brave and aggressive captaincy. His entertaining approach is based on one premise: trying to win the match from the opening delivery. This should be the aim of all international captains, but sadly it isn't.

Interestingly, Clarke's captaincy has been greatly influenced by Shane Warne. Not only Test and ODI teammates, Clarke and Warne played together for Hampshire in the England county championship. Clarke was like a sponge, soaking up all the experience of the great leg-spinner, just as Benaud learnt from the brilliant Australian all-rounder Keith Miller. Both Miller and Warne would have made outstanding Test captains, but neither did so, perhaps because they were a little headstrong and too 'out there' for the Establishment's liking. As Mark Nicholas says, 'Shane ploughs his own field.' I suspect Miller used that plough first up. Before Michael Clarke came Mark Taylor, who led Australia with similar zest and authority as his famous predecessors, Benaud and Chappell. It is perhaps testimony to Taylor's mark as a human being that he didn't play cricket at the highest level for personal glory. Either directly or indirectly, Benaud, Chappell and Taylor all influenced Michael Clarke's cricket. Their Test records as captain are:

CAPTAIN	TESTS	WINS	LOSSES	DRAWS	TIES
Richie Benaud	28	12	4	11	1
Ian Chappell	30	15	5	10	–
Mark Taylor	50	26	13	11	–
Michael Clarke	47	24	16	7	–

The nation will long remember the caring and sensitive manner in which Clarke handled the days after Phillip Hughes's tragic death. Clarke spoke not only for the Australian cricket family, but for all Australians. Undoubtedly he stands shoulder to shoulder with the greatest of Australian Test cricket captains.

Backyard Test matches

Some of the most enjoyable cricket you will ever play is in what we call Down Under the time-honoured 'backyard Test'. Most celebrated Australian cricketers experienced these games in the backyard, where a bunch of mates or family members gathered daily in summer to imitate their cricketing heroes. The games are highly competitive affairs and sometimes end in bruises and tears and parents having to adjudicate dodgy decisions or break up the odd bit of fisticuffs.

Those who didn't have siblings or mates nearby had to find other ways to improve their game. Two of these individuals – Victor Trumper and Don Bradman – did it their way and they excelled.

At Crown Street Superior School, Sydney, in the 1890s Victor Trumper became champion of the schoolyard. There was an unwritten law at Crown Street. If you dismissed someone, you could bat until someone got you out. Trumper was aged 10 when he clean-bowled the school captain with a change-up off-break. Then he batted in the before-school period, during play-time, lunch breaks and after school every day for a monumental and school-record six weeks. His father, Charles, decided to give him more training. So, every morning for four years – daily from 6 am to 8 am – Charles Trumper bowled to young Vic at Moore Park, a Trumper drive from the famous Sydney Cricket Ground.

Similarly, the young Don Bradman needed a family member to help him along with his batting. He usually practised his cricket at home alone, hitting a golf ball with a cricket stump after it rebounded from the concrete base of a water tank. But each school day he would rush home to Shepherd Street in Bowral, cast his school bag over the front fence, rush through the wicker gate and call out: 'C'mon, Mum, how about bowling me down a few?' Emily Bradman bowled slow left-arm and she often agreed to accommodate her son who was, at the age of 12, starting to show some promise with the bat.

The nearest thing for him to a backyard Test was in the 15-minute morning recess and 45-minute lunch break at Bowral Primary School. The boys played a crude form of cricket. Stumps were drawn on the bell post, the bat was hewn from the branch of a gum tree and the 'compo' ball was a hard composition of cork and rubber. At the age of 13, Don scored the first of the 211 centuries he hit in all games during his extraordinary career.

In 1921, representing Bowral Intermediate High School, he thrashed Mittagong's attack to the tune of 115 not out in a team total of 156. Next day, the headmaster called the school to assembly: 'I understand there is a certain boy who yesterday scored a hundred in a match. This is all very well, but it is no excuse for his having left the bat behind.'

When Doug Walters was a boy, he and his brothers, Terry and Warren, made their own backyard pitch on their dairy-farming property in the New South Wales country town of Dungog. One day during the Christmas holidays, Doug and his younger brother Terry noticed how the car and tractor wheels had flattened the anthills along the track. The boys made a close inspection of the flattened ant beds and were amazed that the surface was rock-hard. 'Bet that soil would make a good cricket pitch,' Doug laughed. After lots of hard work carting the ant bed soil home, they laid the new pitch in a specially prepared hole

6 metres long, 2 metres wide and 380 millimetres deep. Directly behind the ant-bed pitch was the backyard dunny.

It was on that pitch of uneven bounce and exaggerated turn that Doug learnt to read length and play the ball turning in from the off with such power and confidence. Doug recalled:

Our pitch had to last for about three years, so you can imagine that soon enough huge cracks appeared and the ball did some weird and wonderful things. We used to bowl from about 15 metres and bowling on this track may have given me the idea that I was a better bowler than a batsman. Looking back, I reckon I might well have learnt how to defend, for you had to defend soundly to survive the sideways movement on that wicket. Any ball of full length could be easily played. Very short balls hit the rough grass short of the anthill surface and lost most of their sting. We used old palings dragged from the wood pile or an old kero tin to double for a set of stumps and bails at the batsman's end.

The Walters boys' 'teams' always included the champs of the day, such as Australia's Alan Davidson, Ray Lindwall, Richie Benaud and England's Ken Barrington, Len Hutton, Jim Laker and John Edrich. The boys emulated their heroes: when Lindwall bowled, they took a long run and bowled as fast as they could and, when Benaud was operating, it had to be right-arm leg-breaks.

Doug's enthusiasm for the game was fired by listening to the dulcet tones of Alan McGilvray broadcasting the Tests from faraway England. When Doug faced his first ball in Test cricket, at Brisbane on 10 December 1965, he wore a broad grin, for this was the ecstasy of life.

'I knew every mannerism, every aspect of Fred Titmus and the other England bowlers' technique and mannerisms, because I had "seen" them on the radio. They were in my mind's eye and as Titmus came in to bowl that first ball, I appreciated the funny side of it.'

In Australia's first innings, Doug hit a debut 155.

The Chappell brothers – Ian, Greg and Trevor – played in the backyard with a ferocity that almost beggared belief. One hot December day, six-year-old Trevor winced and trudged off the wicket in the North Glenelg backyard after copping a nasty blow to the left elbow, legacy of Ian's quicker ball. Fighting back tears and after his mum, Jeanne Chappell, attended to the wound, Trevor returned to the fray. His older brothers greeted Trevor's return to the wicket with a barrage of bouncers.

Champ, the family Labrador, was a brilliant fieldsman and often caught the unwary player who dared hit the ball in the air. One day Greg smashed an on-drive and Champ latched on to it, but for days he trotted about shaking his head, no doubt hearing the rattle of loose teeth. During the 'Tests', Jeanne often had to adjudicate. She became a mediator between two warring factions – a heated bowler and a stubborn batsman. Most youngsters use a soft ball in the backyard games, not so the Chappells. It was always a regular hard cricket ball. The likelihood of getting a blow to the unguarded legs made them watch the ball closely.

Their father, Martin, had to somehow appease the insurance company for all the window breakages There were, however, times when you just had to laugh. One early morning Greg clobbered an Ian Chappell full toss over the protective wire netting and shattered the neighbours' kitchen window. There was pandemonium. Jeanne and Martin were sitting at the kitchen table when 14-year-old Greg burst into the room. 'You'd better come quick, Dad!' Martin saw the damage to the window and heard the angry shouts of their Italian neighbour. When they ran next door, they tried not to laugh. Before them was the forlorn sight of their irate neighbour, with a conglomeration of bacon, eggs and tomatoes meandering down his pyjama pants.

Down the years, hundreds of thousands of cricketers played cricket in the backyard. They included the likes of Kim and Glenn Hughes, Steve and Mark Waugh, Mike and David Hussey, and I am sure many emerging stars of today.

Before the turn of the twentieth century, Clarrie Grimmett played cricket with his neighbours, the Harris brothers – all of whom bowled leg-breaks – in Roxburgh Street, Wellington, New Zealand, until the gas lamps came on to brighten the gloom and Constable Thirsk arrived to clear the urchins out. They also used to venture down to the 'bumpy' end of Basin Reserve to bat and bowl in earnest on corrugated turf.

Ray Lindwall bowled in the street with his mates when the great Bill O'Reilly was on his way home after a day at the office, to illustrate that the St George Club would do well to sign him up.

Neil Harvey was one of six brothers. His father, Horace, taught them all to play the game and they trained on the cobbled laneway next to the family home in Fitzroy. His elder brother Merv played one Test for Australia, while Mick and Ray both played for Victoria, and all six Harvey brothers (including Brian and Harold) played for Fitzroy in Victorian district cricket.

Tony Mann, the leg-spinning Western Australian all-rounder, hailed from the Swan Valley, a famous wine-growing area north of Perth, where his father, Jack Mann, was at the helm of Houghton's Winery. As a young man, Jack had been injured in a shooting accident and could not bowl overarm, so he propelled his hard-spun leg-breaks underhand. He also developed a ball called the 'Midland Hanger', a highly tossed ball designed to drop from a steep angle on top of the batsman's bails. Clarrie

Grimmett would have approved, for he always advocated a spinner bowling a trajectory which was hard-spun and dipping from above the eyeline.

Across the road from the Mann family lived Dennis Yagmich. Most days in summer, whether on the weekend or after school, Dennis and the Mann brothers, Tony, Bill and Dorham, played a form of backyard cricket on the brick-paved veranda which encircled the Mann homestead. Dennis was destined to become a wicketkeeper, for it was his job to take up position behind the little wall to the rear of the batsman which always protected Mrs Mann's prized geraniums. Dennis later kept wicket for Midland–Guildford, Western Australia and South Australia, with a short stint with World Series Cricket.

'Tony was forever bowling his fizzing leg-breaks and Dorham or Bill seemed always at bat,' he recalls. 'When Dorham batted, the bowler delivered, then slipped behind the house wall to ensure being safe from his powerful drives. Bill Mann, a left-hander, was adept at working Tony's leg-break through the Cape Suckle hedges at midwicket ... that is, until Tony developed his wrong'un, then I got into the play via an outside edge.'

I was introduced to backyard Tests in the 1950s, a time when my heroes Neil Harvey, Alan Davidson and Richie Benaud prevailed Down Under. My brother, Nick, drew up the team lists. He was always Australia and I had to contend with being England. Whenever Harvey batted in the backyard, you had to assume a left-hander's stance, when Davo bowled, it had to be left-handed, and you had to bowl right-arm leg-spin when Benaud came on.

These games came round about the time Jim Laker took 19/90 on an Old Trafford dustbowl which might well have looked like the lunar surface. But Laker's performance inspired me in those backyard Tests because I was bowling offies with a bald tennis ball and became something of a local bowling wizard to my opponents, David Cowlishaw, Evan Jones, Gavin McCoy and Don Moran.

All but Moran turned up to the backyard Tests barefoot, wearing shorts and T-shirts. He always arrived immaculately dressed – creams, proper cricket boots – and he was always padded up ready to bat. We always allowed Moran to bat first and no amount of padding could prevent the swinging bald tennis ball from evading the bat. As soon as he was hit on the pad, a raucous appeal went up and five or six index fingers were immediately thrust skywards. Don Moran never did score many runs in our backyard Test matches.

Warne's six best deliveries

Shane Warne emerged on the Test stage in the nick of time. Spin bowling the world over was struggling. Few of the cricketing nations throughout the world could claim to have a spinner of genuine Test match class.

If David Boon square-cut a short ball from Devon Malcolm to the point boundary, it was described as a brilliant stroke. However, if Boon advanced down the track to drop-kick England off-spinner John Emburey to clear mid-on, one bounce over the fence, it was a 'bad ball'. The bowling of any type of spin was misunderstood, batting against quality spin disappeared and the understanding of the art was nearly lost to the ages.

Then out of the spin wilderness emerged Shane Warne. He had a simple philosophy: spin the ball hard and have it drop from above the batsman's eyes. Because of how it arrived to the batsman, his area of danger was the size of a dining-room table. A spinner who doesn't give the ball a big tweak has to be super-accurate, for his area of danger is only the size of a dinner plate, in comparison to Warne and Murali's dining-room table.

Warne's arm speed was as fast as Glenn McGrath's, so his energy went up and over his braced front leg rather than direct to an area as does the fast bowler's. Warne spent a lot of time on his front leg and that, allied to his wrist and great shoulder rotation, provided the big revolutions which excited thousands of fans for more than 15 years on the Test stage. He had six deliveries: the leg-break, top-spinner, wrong'un, flipper, slider and zooter. And each figured more than once in getting a famous wicket.

But Warne's great attribute was his ability to break the rhythm of the batsman. He would bowl his stock ball for hours on end, each ball of slightly different pace. It was his subtle changes of pace, allied to his big spin and his patience, which consistently broke the rhythm of the batsman. Each delivery landed in a different spot. As you watched Warne weave his mastery over the batsman, you figured that he was operating with pinpoint accuracy, but in reality his great spin and changes of pace had him working to a huge area of danger. Players lost their way against him, because his great spin got the ball to curve and they often found themselves with their bat a long way from their pads.

Leg-break

They called it the 'ball of the century' when Shane bowled that magnificent leg-break to dismiss Mike Gatting at Old Trafford, Manchester, in 1993. It was his first Test match delivery on the tour. The ball hummed as it left Shane's hand. Gatting seemed to have it covered, but the great side-spin made the ball curve dramatically and late and Gatting found himself playing across his front pad.

The ball pitched well outside the line of leg stump and spun prodigiously, slipping past the nonplussed England batsman to hit the top of the off stump. It was a freakish ball which would have defeated anyone – a Don Bradman or a Victor Trumper – just as it beat Gatting. The Englishman did everything right; he had the ball covered in his forward defence, but it was the late curve towards the leg side which confounded him. Only a batsman of no ability, like a Phil Tufnel, might have survived to hit it in the middle, for Tufnel would have been playing down the wrong line.

A leg-break is spun over the wrist, the ball spinning from leg to off. When executed correctly, the palm of the hand points directly at the batsman just after release. Warne had a couple of versions of leg-break. The one that got Gatting was a ball with lots of side-spin, the seam angled towards the gully region. He also bowled a leg-break with more top-spin, and the seam for this ball – Shane's stock ball – angled towards first slip. The side-spinning leg-break tends to bounce less than the top-spinning leggie, but will achieve a greater width of turn.

Warne usually bowled his leg-break on the line of leg stump, so that if the batsman missed it, the ball would hit the stumps. Often he bowled to a line outside the leg stump to take advantage of rough spots; however, he was always attacking and searching for a batsman's weakness. Had Warne only had variations of the one ball – a leg-break – and no other type of delivery, he still would have been a champion of the Test stage.

The wrong'un

Shane Warne had just finished an enthralling battle with Sachin Tendulkar, getting him caught bat-pad when his bat was clearly a long way from the ball. It was a poor umpiring decision in that Test against India at the Adelaide Oval in December 1999. Warne rarely bowled a wrong'un to Tendulkar, for the batsman could pick the change. Unlike Stuart MacGill, Warne didn't get a lot of work on his wrong'un, thus it didn't have too many revolutions, it did not drop dramatically, and batsmen such as India's Tendulkar and VVS Laxman were down the track to hit the ball on the full or the half-volley.

The left-hander Sourav Ganguly was different. He would work Warne's leg-breaks to the leg side, hitting with the spin from outside off stump. In that same innings, Ganguly got to 60 before Warne tossed up his wrong'un. The ball dipped a bit, but Ganguly's mistake was to completely misread it. He came down the track to drive what he thought to be a regulation leg-break, but the ball dropped and turned away a fraction. Ganguly missed it by a mile and Adam Gilchrist had the bails off in a flash.

The wrong'un was not Warne's favourite ball. In fact, he rarely bowled it. Unlike the leg-break, which is bowled over the wrist, the wrong'un is bowled out of the back of the hand and when released properly the back of the hand faces the batsman. When Warne bowled the wrong'un, he found that it hurt his third finger and would take skin off if he bowled it too much. He had enormous power in his wrist and his right shoulder and found that he could impart extraordinary spin to a leg-break or a top-spinner; not so to the wrong'un because his own method required use of wrist, shoulder and fingers.

Richie Benaud used to suffer from a sore and skinned spinning finger during his career and he did not get anywhere near the purchase on the ball Warne could achieve, yet Warne's fingers today are as soft and as sound as though he had never spun a ball. He was the ultimate in wrist-spin.

The top-spinner

Warne had a magnificent top-spinner. The ball is released with the seam pointing straight down the wicket. It is bowled completely over the wrist, no side-spin at all, and it will loop and drop and carry on straight. The top-spinner usually achieves a lot of bounce. Warne gave all of his over-the-wrist deliveries a big rip and his top-spinner dropped quickly and bounced. It hurried through on the batsman.

It was in the second innings of Australia's clash with South Africa, the Second Test match of January 1998. The South Africans had been completely outplayed, but they were trying to hold on for a draw. Warne had steadily spun his way through the South African line-up, but one stumbling block remained, the solid and seemingly impregnable defence of Jacques Kallis.

He repeatedly played forward and anything on off stump he let go, only playing deliveries pitched in line with his stumps. Balls outside the line of leg stump he padded away. Warne to Kallis that day was almost a stalemate.

Warne decided to go around the wicket, creating a huge angle across the batsman. Kallis played solidly, taking care to let the wider deliveries go by and pad away anything outside the line of leg stump. Then Warne served up a ripping top-spinner. The ball dipped sharply. Kallis shaped to pad it away, then changed his mind – this ball was different, a bit flatter, a bit quicker, a bit straighter. Too late. The ball skimmed through the little gap between bat and pad and hit the middle stump. Kallis's defence had been immaculate, seemingly nothing was ever going to get through, but this one did. It was Shane Warne's 300th Test wicket.

Warne's top-spinner was one of his favourite weapons. It fizzed and dropped and bounced. He rarely bowled the wrong'un. Instead of the wrong'un beating the bat of a left-hander by a long way, Warne preferred to use his top-spinner. That was more likely to catch the edge.

The flipper

The great leg-spinner between the wars, Clarrie Grimmett, invented the flipper. Grimmett, the first Test bowler to take 200 wickets (he finished with 216 in 37 matches), worked on his mystery ball, the flipper, for 12 years before he bowled it in a match. He passed on the flipper to South Australian leggie Bruce Dooland, who later taught Richie Benaud. Victorian batsman and part-time bowler Jack Potter showed Shane Warne how to bowl it when he was at the Australian Cricket Academy in Adelaide.

To bowl the flipper, you hold the ball between your second finger and your thumb. If you can flick your fingers, you can bowl the flipper – it is just like flicking your fingers while holding a cricket ball. You can hold it with the seam parallel to the ground, or upright, so the ball can land either on the smooth part of the leather, or on the seam. To bowl the flipper effectively requires strength of fingers, but also there is a need to bowl with greater arm speed than normal. Warne possessed such strength in his forearms, wrist and shoulders that he found this ball relatively easy to bowl and to control.

Warne's Test bunny, the South African Daryll Cullinan, always used to say, 'I pick Warnie's flipper every time.' Picking it and successfully playing it, however, were for Cullinan two entirely different things. He was usually bowled or lbw very quickly when Warne bowled to him.

Englishman Alec Stewart failed to pick the Warne flipper on a number of occasions. In Brisbane in 1994, Warne was hit through the covers off the back foot by Stewart. That boundary gave him great confidence and he planned to hit the next shortish ball in a similar way. Warne had set up Cullinan a number of times – a couple of boundaries off the back foot, then the flipper and it was all over. Stewart didn't detect the flipper, he moved away to give himself room to hit through the off side and the ball skidded on to smash into middle and off stumps.

The zooter
The zooter is really a back-spinner, the palm of the hand shown to the batsman as the ball is spun backwards. When the ball lands, it tends to skid on straight and stay low. This ball is particularly effective to a batsman who doesn't get well forward and there is always the chance of an lbw when such a player is struck on the front pad with the zooter, especially on a slow, low track.

Such was the wicket when Australia played England at Old Trafford in June 1993. In the England second innings, Alec

Stewart had comfortably reached 11, with one boundary, when Warne bowled him the zooter. Stewart must have read the ball to be a flatter leg-break, for he seemed to allow for turn. The ball was close to the off stump and Stewart expected to be able to cut the ball away with the turn. However, the zooter skipped off the pitch, straight and a little lower than he expected. He got a touch and Ian Healy took what looked easy from a distance, but because it kept low it proved a tough catch.

While the ball is spun backwards for a zooter, it is not held in the manner of a flipper. However, the ball doesn't come off the wicket anywhere near the pace of the flipper. Depending upon the surface of the wicket, the zooter can sometimes skip off quickly or tend to hold up or lose pace. Either way, it is a handy variation and another ball to help the bowler break the rhythm of the batsman.

The slider

Unlike the zooter, which is a slow back-spinner, the slider is pushed out of the front of the hand. It revolves slowly and tends to skid straight when it pitches. Sometimes it will fade slightly like a little inswinger. This ball is very effective against the stodgy type of player who plays continually forward but doesn't stretch far enough forward. Even a delivery hitting the front pad is a potential lbw wicket ball.

In an ICC Trophy match at Colombo in 2002, Sanath Jayasuriya had hit 42 in 52 minutes with six boundaries when Warne bowled him the slider. Jayasuriya thought the ball would come on a lot more quickly, with more bounce, and turn in towards his stumps, but the left-hander was fooled by the pace, the lack of bounce and the fact that it didn't turn at all. He got a faint touch and the ball crashed into his stumps.

Late in his fabulous career Warne bowled more and more sliders and fewer flippers. England's Ian Bell was a veritable sitting duck for Warne's slider. Bell played forward in nonchalant style. He didn't get far forward or have very good judgment of length. When in doubt against a bowler like Warne, Bell leant forward. He also failed to adjust swiftly enough to changes of pace. Warne found it as easy as pie to fool Bell with changes of pace.

The slider is just another little change, something for batsmen to contemplate when they battle to combat the big-turning leg-breaks and the fizzing top-spinner.

Bradman versus Warne

Having lived through the epic Shane Warne versus Sachin Tendulkar contests – the master bowler of the age versus the champion batsman – I have always wondered how Bradman would have dealt with the sublime spin of Warne. However, in the absence of a time machine, we can use our imagination. We can look at old footage of Bradman and film of Warne; we can research and analyse and use part of the 95 per cent of the human mind we usually don't utilise and come up with the unimaginable – a contest between Bradman and Warne. Sometimes the unreal melds with the real, but fantasy is fantasy; or is it? Imagine such a contest:

As the hand on the clock struck the hour, fans in their thousands poured into the Melbourne Cricket Ground to witness first-hand the greatest cricket battle of them all – Bradman versus Warne. Sid Barnes, stalwart of the 1948 Invincibles and Arthur Morris's opening partner, fell to Shane Warne's second ball, a hard-spun leg-break which left his hand and curved down the pitch in a lovely arc to send Banjo Paterson into his own poetic 'Song of Spin'.

As Barnes probed forward, the hissing Warne leg-break ducked swiftly, like a diving Spitfire, and the batsman's failure to cover either the length or the breadth of spin presented Mark Taylor with a dolly at first slip. Already 100,000 people had packed the MCG and they rose as one to give the greatest batsman of all time the most magnificent reception. Taylor sidled up to Warne. They had a brief chat as they watched Bradman walk briskly to centre stage.

'Well, Tubs, this could be quite something if I can get him to take the bait.'

Taylor's smile said it all. He patted his champion leggie on the shoulder and headed back to slip, making sure Jason Gillespie was in nice and close at mid-on. Bradman's trademark single to get off the mark was invariably a run just wide of mid-on.

Barnes tried in vain to mention to Bradman that the ball was dipping wickedly and that the leg-spin magician had the ball on a string. The Don was in no mood to talk to anyone about the merits of a bowler for whom he had great respect, but a man he dearly wanted to thrash unmercifully.

On the 1930 Australian tour of England, the brash 20-year-old batting phenomenon told his teammates, 'Plenty of batsmen watch the bowler's fingers hoping to detect what sort of ball he's going to deliver, but that's no good to me. Let me see the ball coming and then I'll decide the best place to hit it.' He would never stop on his way to the wicket to hear the outgoing batsman describe the amazing swing, cut or spin the bowler had achieved to cause his downfall.

Maybe Clarrie Grimmett had told him of the Test trial at the SCG in 1925 when Grimmett had spun one a good deal to trap Tommy Andrews. Grimmett watched the departing batsman and saw how he stopped to chat to the man next in, Alan Kippax, demonstrating with outstretched arms how the ball that got him 'spun a mile'. Kippax lasted one ball – a fizzing Grimmett top-spinner ripped between bat and pad to hit middle stump as Kippax played with his bat away from the pad to counter the 'excessive turn' he expected.

So the stage was set. Taylor remembered how Sachin Tendulkar attacked Warne in India and succeeded with big hundreds in three innings. Would Bradman go at Warne in similar vein? Bradman took guard, looked about the field, and took up his stance. Warne had a slip, backward point, short cover, extra cover and mid-off. To the on side was a man behind square leg, a very straight midwicket, mid-on and a man in the deep just in front of square. The crowd fell silent. They knew that this contest would provide something very special, for both players were at the pinnacle of their powers.

When the world thought that the art of leg-spin had disappeared forever like the dinosaurs, who failed to duck a barrage of cosmic bouncers, Warne turned up to charm the cricket world with his magnificent slow bowling. He never got the chance to bowl to Victor Trumper, the one regarded as the greatest batsman of the Golden Age of Cricket, and that would have been fascination enough, for Trumper batted to entertain.

But today it is all about Bradman and Warne. While Trumper came from an era when a batsman, after hitting a century, looked for a worthy opponent to 'present' his wicket to, Bradman simply re-marked his guard and went for the next hundred. He was totally ruthless and was said to have targeted bowlers, setting out to destroy them on the field.

Once, in a grade match in Adelaide, he went to the wicket late on a Saturday afternoon. The light was fading and the big fast bowler standing at mid-on might ruffle the champion's feathers if he bowled fast next over on the green track in bad light. So the Don hit all eight deliveries of the bowler's over just out of reach of the big quick at mid-on. By the time the over ended and he was expected to bowl to Bradman, the poor man was so exhausted he couldn't scratch himself.

Today Bradman was up against Warne, the man he said, in the late 1990s, was 'the best thing to happen to Australian cricket in 30 years'. Round about that time, Sir Donald invited Sachin Tendulkar and Shane Warne to his Kensington Park home in Adelaide. It was a pleasant change from having busloads of people – even Japanese tourists – turn up unannounced to snap their cameras in a frenzy of celebrity worship of this perky little champion who, because of his extraordinary skill with a cricket bat, was given a life sentence as a prisoner of fame.

At the age of 16, Len Hutton faced 62-year-old SF Barnes in the nets and years later he declared that Barnes was 'the best bowler I've faced'. Bradman considered Bill O'Reilly to be the greatest bowler he had played with or against. As far as I know, Sir Donald never aired in public any comparison of Grimmett with Warne. Perhaps Warne's emergence was too late in Bradman's life to make such comparisons, for invariably it would have led to his being hounded by the press. Who'd want that as you enter your nineties?

So today Bradman will learn about Warne's greatness.

He again looks about the field. Warne has Taylor at slip, Matthew Hayden at backward point, Ricky Ponting at short cover, Mark Waugh at extra cover and Steve Waugh at mid-off. As the wicketkeeper Ian Healy settles down with a 'Carn Shane', Merv Hughes moves in at backward square leg; so too does David Boon at short, straight midwicket and Jason Gillespie at mid-on. At deep square leg, Glenn McGrath ambles in a few metres. There is a hush in the crowd. Mark Nicholas says in his quiet, authoritative tone: 'Well, now the stage is set ... The greatest batsman of all time is about to meet the greatest bowler of the ages.'

Warne stands at the top of his mark. His spinning fingers move a little up and down as he caresses the ball, ensuring the grip is neither too loose nor too tight, but firm. Bradman's eyes are set on the blond leg-spinner. When the camera zooms in for a close-up, TV viewers are looking at a man totally focused, a man on a mission.

All eyes turn to Warne as he starts his methodical way to the wicket. When he gets within a yard of the crease, his wrist cocks and he drives up and over his front leg with amazing energy and strength. The ball spins so hard it hums, dipping away in a lovely curve with the trajectory of an archer's arrow. Bradman can't hit this one for six, four, three, two, or one, so he goes well forward and meets the ball with a dead bat. No run.

Warne stands at the end of his follow-through and rubs his chin. Bradman avoids his stare, looking about the field. He sees gaps on the on side, but knows all too well that hitting those gaps will be risky against hard-spun leg-breaks, which – if Warne is on song – will arrive in a fizzing, dipping arc.

Warne again. A leg-break. It curves in towards leg stump and upon pitching it fairly buzzes, spinning past Bradman's forward defensive stroke. The ball misses off by a whisker and as the crowd roars in appreciation of the bowler's skill, Healy takes it, throwing his head back.

Almost.

Ball three arrives, again dipping menacingly in a lovely curve. Don Bradman pounces with feline reflexes, his feet moving swiftly yet with silky smoothness, to reach the ball the instant it strikes the turf. There can be no error, for to misjudge the length would be fatal. Bradman pounces like a cat nailing a mouse and his cover drive scorches past Ponting at short cover, beats Mark Waugh at extra and scuttles like a startled rabbit to the boundary.

The enthralling battle goes for an hour. Bradman has scored freely up the other end and has taken about a dozen runs off Warne. Two boundaries and four singles. In the meantime, Arthur Morris, who was Clarrie Grimmett's last first-class wicket, falls to Glenn McGrath, but Lindsay Hassett, one of the few batsmen to repeatedly play well against O'Reilly, proves a good ally for Bradman and a big partnership looms.

But Warne has other ideas. He has used his full repertoire: the leg-break, fizzing top-spinner, back-spinner, zooter, wrong'un and flipper. Just one wrong'un to Bradman, which he latched on to as he so often did when Grimmett bowled that ball. Bradman always said Grimmett's wrong'un was easy to pick and he found that with Warne.

His flipper, too, made little impact. Bradman was alert to that ball, which Grimmett invented and Warne bowled so well to so many, especially the South African Daryll Cullinan, who once told me he always 'picked' Warne's flipper, but he kept getting bowled by it.

Some 75 minutes into the match, the Invincibles' score stands at 2/94: Bradman 49 and Hassett 17. Warne decides to go back to total reliance on his stock ball. He concentrates, as he always did early in a spell, on bowling hard-spun leg-breaks and vary, ever so slightly, the pace of those deliveries.

Bradman has batted with assurance and skill, but he has found Warne's bowling to be an extraordinary mix of O'Reilly and Grimmett wrapped up in one amazing bowler. Warne has the spin and the guile of Grimmett – in fact, he spins harder and the ball drops more dramatically than the man they called Scarlet – and he also possesses O'Reilly's 'unrelenting hostility'.

Warne moves in again. He bowls a hard-spun leg-break, but this time with a slight, almost imperceptible change of pace. The 100,000 people watching at the ground, plus millions on television, are fooled. So too is Bradman. Although Bradman's footwork is swift and sure, the ball dips suddenly and wickedly and lands well short of where the Don expects. Too far into his stroke to check it, his lofted drive goes straight into the sure hands of Ponting at short cover.

Bradman c Ponting b Warne 49.

Mandela breathed life into Test cricket

As the January sun set low over Robben Island, just off the coast of Cape Town, South Africa, Nelson Mandela's incarceration had entered its seventh year (out of 27 years). The 1970 Australian cricket team, captained by Bill Lawry, were being feted at a garden party hosted by the South African Prime Minister, John Vorster, at his Cape Town residence. I noted with discomfort the attitude of Vorster and his ministers towards the black waiting staff. While this was a far cry from Hitler's retreat at Berchtesgaden, I imagined this was the closest thing to a Nazi garden party I would ever experience.

By some obscure take on a religious text, blacks were perceived by the South African whites, especially the Afrikaners, as 'hewers of wood and drawers of water'. Once, I set eyes on a scene that would have seemed perfectly realistic if I'd been riding a buggy down a street in 1840s New Orleans. There I was, in 1970, driving through an opulent, leafy suburb close to the Wanderers Cricket Ground in Johannesburg, where 10 black men chained together dug the road with picks. There was a surreal rhythm as the boss man blew a whistle and the men raised their picks and swung them in unison, all to the sound of a low, murmuring lament.

The gloom of Apartheid made South Africa a living hell for non-whites, although I gathered that the Indian population fared better than the other non-whites. An Indian businessman told me, 'I'd rather be a second-class millionaire than a first-class pauper.' A pall of hopelessness had enveloped the non-whites of South Africa – their collective spirit cowed by the inhumane whip of Apartheid. Separate toilets, buses, beaches, the Group Areas Act, carrying the pass which designated a black person as 'second class', were all huge burdens – psychologically and practically, too heavy a cross to bear.

When Bill Lawry's men played at Berea Park in Pretoria, as *Wisden* recorded matter-of-factly, 'No coloured-skin people were permitted to attend.'

When Lawry's team left on a seventh-month tour of Ceylon (present-day Sri Lanka), India and South Africa in October 1969, each of us received a letter from Peter Hain, an anti-Apartheid activist, who pleaded with us to abandon the South African leg of our tour. No-one quit the tour, but Hain's movement helped stop the South African tour of England in 1970 and Australia's four-Test series proved to be the last Test cricket series that a South African cricket team played during the Apartheid era.

The South Africans had a host of fabulous players, including Graeme and Peter Pollock, Barry Richards, Mike Procter and Eddie Barlow. They were led by a medical doctor, Ali Bacher, the son of a Lithuanian Jew who had fled the Holocaust to settle in South Africa. Ali played impromptu games of cricket with his brothers in the garage of their father's home near Johannesburg. Their mother loved sport and she helped fire Ali's passion for the game of cricket by presenting him with Bradman's book, *The Art of Cricket*. There was one little gem of Bradman advice in that book which Ali always remembered: 'Never hit the ball in the air.'

Once, during a golden run with the bat, teenager Ali was described by one local newspaper as 'the Bradman-like Bacher'. The following week, he was dismissed first ball and his mother said with a smile, 'Donald Bradman, eh? Next they'll be calling you Donald Duck!' Bacher eventually got into first-class cricket and excelled for Transvaal.

In one Currie Cup match, he helped saved the life of an

opposing player, an epileptic, who suffered a seizure on the pitch. It was none other than Tony Greig, the man who later captained England and played such a vital role in the formation of World Series Cricket. Greig was on the ground thrashing about uncontrollably when Bacher quickly went to work, preventing the convulsing Greig from swallowing his tongue and choking to death. The incident happened at the Wanderers Ground, Transvaal's home ground, the place they now call the Bull Ring.

As well as being beaten by the South Africans, there were a couple of incidents in that series which made our blood boil.

When Lawry and Bacher tossed before the Durban Test, the wicket had a distinctly green tinge about it and we thought our fast men would do well on that Kingsmead surface. Bacher won the toss and decided to bat, but just as Lawry entered the Australian dressing-room some 40 blokes in blue tracksuits flooded the ground. Each had a lawnmower and they darted to the centre wicket and mowed down every blade of grass. Lawry was aghast. He looked out of the window and said: 'They can't do that ... we've just tossed.'

Doug Walters replied, 'No, Phanto, they can't do it ... but they *are* mowing the pitch!'

Lawry had been outwitted by the doctor. Bacher knew the laws of cricket backwards and in the small print it stated that the wicket could be mown up to 30 minutes before the start of play. That is why Bacher had wanted to have the toss early, so that if he won it he could do as he had just ordered – mow the pitch bare. It all worked for him. Thanks to two glorious innings – Graeme Pollock 274 and Barry Richards 140 – South Africa hit a first innings 622 and we were belted unmercifully.

In that match, Doug Walters scored 74 in our second innings. He had just hit off-spinner John Traicos into the stand for six when another long-hop came along. Umpire John Draper thrust out his right hand and called, 'No ...' There was a definite arm signal and call from the umpire. Walters tried to hit the ball into the stand again, but he got a top edge and Graeme Pollock ran 30 metres around the boundary edge and caught it.

Next, we saw umpire Draper with his index finger thrust skywards. The non-striker, Ian Redpath, was incensed. A very calm man, Redders remonstrated: 'You called a no-ball! How can you give Doug out?' The umpire explained, 'Well, I thought it was going to be a no-ball, but as it was not I didn't go on with the call, so the batsman was out fair and square.'

Next game, Ian Chappell sliced a ball from medium-pacer Trevor Goddard to Tiger Lance at backward point. From our side-on view from the players' area at the Wanderers we could plainly see the ball had bounced well before Lance got it.

Chappelli asked Lance, 'Did you catch it, Tiger?'

'Ja, Chappelli, I caught it.' All our players told Ian that the ball had clearly bounced and, on the eve of the last Test at Port Elizabeth, Chappelli approached Lance and asked, 'Did you really catch me at Jo'burg, Tiger?'

'Ja, Chappelli, I caught it all right ... but you didn't ask me how many times it bounced.'

In the wake of the Basil D'Oliveira affair, the 1970 South African tour of England was called off and the International Cricket Council (ICC) imposed a moratorium on tours to or from South Africa. The nation was ostracised from big sport for over 20 years.

The South Africans' initial reaction to the international ban was to follow in the steps of the Boer: they were angry that a Test recall was light years away, so they circled the wagons and retreated deep into the *laager*, where purely domestic cricket was played.

Ali Bacher realised that cricket in his homeland would die if the youngsters were denied a chance to play for their country. He fought for a form of international cricket in the guise of 'rebel' tours, where teams from England, Sri Lanka, Australia and the West Indies toured South Africa.

However, after years of international isolation, Bacher knew that the game had to be taken to the black man in his country. On 6 October 1986, Ali Bacher took cricket to Elkah Stadium in Soweto, a teeming black township of more than two million people. Nelson Mandela, who had been transferred to Pollsmoor Prison from Robben Island in 1982, knew of Bacher's planned visit to Soweto. The banned African National Congress party, which Mandela had helped found, held the whip hand in the townships and, if Mandela so ordained, the white 'crusaders' could have been in dire trouble. Mandela had himself formed the armed wing of the ANC, *Umkhonto we Sizwe*, or 'Spear of the Nation'.

At that time, few whites, unless they were secure inside an armoured personnel carrier with appropriate firepower, dared to venture into the black townships. Armed with Baker's Biscuits T-shirts and cricket bats made from wood palings and dozens of red balls, Bacher's team of cricket crusaders arrived to be greeted by 1000 cheering kids and a host of smiling mothers.

'Okay, Mr White Man. You want to show us how to play cricket. We want to learn. Show us, and one day we'll beat you at your own game.' Bacher felt like Daniel in the lion's den.

Mandela sent word that no harm would come to Bacher or his men when they took cricket to the townships. The man who would later become the South African President enlisted special ANC security men to ensure the safety of the Bacher expedition.

They later became good friends and, after his release from 27 years in jail and as South Africa's President, Mandela would ask Bacher, 'How's Donald Bradman?' I was standing near Dr Ali Bacher in a Johannesburg hotel in 1989 when I overheard a black porter utter in hushed tones to his colleague, 'That is the Godfather, Dr Bacher ... He has the ear of *Madiba* ...'

Mandela's influence helped get South African cricket back on the world stage, just as his appearance at the 1995 Rugby World Cup final, where he wore the iconic Springbok jersey, galvanised the spirit of the people.

Bradman: caught and bowled Bob Hawke

By September 1971, South African cricket was perilously close to falling into the abyss.

The incumbent chairman of the Australian Cricket Board, Sir Donald Bradman, was about to go head to head with union boss Bob Hawke. The fate of South Africa's proposed tour of Australia that summer hung in the balance.

On or off the field, few deliveries got past Don Bradman's guard. As a cricketer, Bob Hawke was a competent wicketkeeper–batsman and he didn't bowl, but a verbal delivery by him to Bradman in 1971 had the legendary batsman floundering.

In 1971, as head of the Australian Council of Trade Unions (ACTU), the nation's peak trade union body, Hawke had led opposition to the South African Springbok rugby tour, and Bradman had seen for himself how difficult it had been for officials, security staff and police to prevent protesters from damaging the grounds and disrupting play. However, the Australian Cricket Board wanted to host South Africa and months earlier had issued an invitation for the South African cricket team to tour Australia in the summer of 1971–72. To that end, Bradman invited the ACTU president to Adelaide for a secret meeting.

'The 1971 Springbok rugby team had just flown home and Bradman rang me,' Hawke told me when I interviewed him in 2014.

I went out to his home in Kensington Gardens, and he said, 'Bob, I don't think politics should come into sport.'

And I said, 'I couldn't agree with you more, Don. We haven't brought politics into sport; it is the government of South Africa which has brought politics into sport, because the government of South Africa has a policy that no person who isn't white is allowed to represent their country in sport. That's bringing politics into sport.'

He looked at me for about 30 seconds and then he said, 'I've got no answer to that, Bob.'

Hawke, in a sentence, had managed to get Bradman to see the light. On 9 September 1971, the board met and decided to withdraw the invitation for South Africa to tour. Bradman informed the press and that announcement was the start of more than 20 years in isolation for South Africa's cricketers. South Africa's isolation from international cricket ended in a celebratory 'goodwill' tour of India in 1992.

As with a couple of legendary politicians – Robert Menzies and HV 'Doc' Evatt – before him and John Howard after him, Hawke is what is known as a 'cricket tragic'. Born in Bordertown, South Australia, in December 1929, one of Hawke's earliest cricket memories was listening to the 1938 Ashes series in England.

'I'd go to sleep very early, so I could wake up and listen to the simulated wireless broadcast of the Test matches. Don Bradman was god. I can still feel the world falling apart when Len Hutton hit the world-record Test match score of 364, overtaking Bradman's 334.'

Hawke remembers the Australian 1948 team playing a game against Western Australia before sailing to England from Fremantle:

Keith Miller was bowling and Western Australian batsman Basil Rigg drove him majestically for four. Next ball was

*a vicious bouncer and down went Rigg and he was
stretchered off the ground. Western Australia lost three or
four more quick wickets and back came the injured Rigg,
and there was Don Bradman, after calling back Miller to
bowl, rushing to meet the incoming batsman and showing
him how to hook!*

Hawke's parents, Clem and Ellie, travelled from Bordertown to
Perth at the start of World War II, and the youngster was soon
revelling in his studies and sport at Perth Modern School. There
he was for two years the wicketkeeper–batsman for the school's
First XI.

*One game I particularly recall was in the annual Boys
versus Masters match. Traditionally any boy hitting a
hundred was given a brand-new cricket bat and this day
I had reached 93 when the physics teacher, a slow leg-
spinner called Cyril Calcutt, had his lbw appeal upheld for
a ball which pitched a mile outside leg stump and I was
given out. So I missed getting the new bat. I will never
forget the bastard.*

Young Hawke excelled in his studies and his great interest in
student affairs and in pursuing a political career inspired him
more than the prospect of becoming a top-flight cricketer did.

*I did have a lot of fun playing with University in the Western
Australia grade competition. I began in the A-grade team
the same day as John Rutherford, but I didn't have the
same almost-obsessive passion for the game which he had.
He was the hardest-working player of my experience.*

Rutherford toured England in 1956 and Keith Miller dubbed
him Pythagoras, because 'he was ever trying to work things out'.

'I caught up with Jack at the Perth Ashes Test [in December 2013] and he looked in good shape,' Hawke said. 'I cannot think of any cricketer who possessed such absolute dedication.'

As a wicketkeeper, Hawke was no mug behind the stumps. Once, when Ray Strauss, the star swing bowler for University of Western Australia, was operating, Hawke noticed the batsman, Bill Alderman (Test player Terry Alderman's father), tended to drag his back foot forward when attempting to glance a ball that strayed down leg side.

> *I approached Ray and said, 'Now, see if you can slide an inswinger down leg side on the second ball of this over.' Sometimes in a sporting life you just do something perfectly and that's what happened. Strauss bowled the perfect delivery; Alderman went forward and he got a faint nick which I caught, and in the same instant I whipped off the bails and yelled to the square-leg umpire, 'Howzat?'*
>
> *The square-leg umpire – who no doubt looked like an old-time version of David Shepherd – said in a booming voice: 'Bloody marvellous!'*

Cricket has been Hawke's greatest sporting love, and a Test cricketer once saved his life.

Early in the summer of 1952–53, the year the South African Test team was touring Australia, the 23-year-old Hawke was working as a gardener at the University of Western Australia.

> *I was filling in time getting some cash together before heading to Oxford. I had the noble task of spreading shit [manure] around the trees. Then came the time to refill the cart. The horse was reluctant to move, so I went to the front and pulled hard at his head, only for the shaft to somehow spring free.*

The point of the thing cut into my leg, causing a huge gaping gash from above the knee to below the groin. With blood streaming from the wound, I staggered out from the trees and collapsed on the outfield of James Oval, where the visiting South Africans were playing a match against the Governor's XI.

South Africa Test batsman Roy McLean dashed to Hawke's side. 'Roy held my leg together with his big strong hands and my leg remained in his vice-like grip until an ambulance arrived. No doubt, Roy McLean saved my life that day in 1952.'

Hawke was elected Australian Prime Minister in 1983. When South Africa were finally readmitted to the international cricket family, their board chief, Dr Ali Bacher, invited Hawke to be guest speaker at a function celebrating the first Test in South Africa in the post-Apartheid era. 'I told them the Roy McLean story and added, "I guess some of you people would have hoped Roy didn't do what he did," and a couple of blokes in the crowd yelled, "Yeah, yeah!"'

Round the time of the Centenary Test between Australia and England at the MCG in 1977, Hawke was invited to play in a charity match at Drummoyne Oval, in Sydney. I didn't know about the talks he was having with former Test players, including Ian Chappell and Bob Cowper, about helping them form a players' union, so I was surprised when Chappelli indicated that he would like me to go easy on Bob Hawke when he came in to bat.

He got 30-odd and batted well. And the players' union idea fell away pretty smartly when Kerry Packer took on the Establishment with World Series Cricket.

★

Hawke loves the cut and thrust of top-flight cricket, just as he revelled in jousting with the Opposition at question time in parliament. For him, the joy of cricket has long been the enduring humour in the game's characters and their stories.

I'll tell you a very interesting sociological fact. I can keep you entertained for a couple of hours telling cricket and golf stories, but I have not heard one funny story from any code of football. Cricket ... Now, that's a different story.

I suppose you've heard the one about Joel Garner ...? The West Indians were in Australia for a Test series and there were some girlies hanging about at the ground. One girl sidled up to Joel [6 feet 8 inches tall] and asked, 'Is it true what they say, that you are built in proportion to your height?'

'Young lady, if I was built in proportion I'd be 8 feet 10 inches.'

I had met Bob Hawke a number of times. Once, as Prime Minister, he came into the Australian dressing-room to join the players huddled round the radio listening to an important horse race. When I met up with him again at a Prime Minister's XI game in Canberra, we chatted about the possibility of my interviewing him when I was next in Sydney and that was in 2014.

Earlier that year – during the Sydney Ashes Test – Bob had stepped outside the confines of the viewing area in the Sydney Cricket Ground Trust suite to accept a Channel Nine challenge for him to stand with a sea of 'Richie Benauds' and skoll a beer on camera. The crowd erupted, and so too, I suspect, did those watching at home.

And to Australia's delight, he did it all again in January 2017. I was sitting in the Sydney Cricket Ground Trust suite only a few paces from where Bob downed his glass of beer before thousands of adoring fans.

Bob Hawke: a living treasure.

The Artful Dodger of the 1868 team

In June 1868, some of the gentlemen who presided over Lord's cricket ground were put to the test by a tall, black man from the Antipodes. Not since June 1844, when a tribe of Ioway Indians had encamped at Lord's, was there such excitement in London's St John's Wood. Eleven Marylebone Cricket Club (MCC) members shed their coats and ties and took off their hats. Lord's was about to witness a unique challenge. Each of the 11 MCC members was given a cricket ball. Their target was an Aboriginal man standing no more than 10 paces away from them, his back to the Members' Stand.

Dick-a-Dick (Jungunjinanuke) held a parrying shield, no wider than the blade of a cricket bat, in his left hand, and in his right, the L-shaped leangle or 'killer boomerang'. Each member had paid Dick-a-Dick one shilling for the right to hurl one ball at him. The members' challenge was to throw a cricket ball at Dick-a-Dick, get one past his defence and strike his body to pick up the 10-shilling prize. Dick-a-Dick was confident and said the men could all throw at once or one at a time.

He and the 1868 Aboriginal Australian Cricket team were elated, for it was late on 13 June 1868 and they had just defeated England by 22 runs at Lord's – which was to become a favourite hunting ground for successive Australian teams up to and including the twenty-first century. Johnny Mullagh (Unaarrimin) scored 75 in Australia's innings of 186, the batting backbone of the innings. His knock earned him a gold watch, presented to him by the MCC after the match and just before Dick-a-Dick challenged the members to try their skill.

They tried individual shots and in groups, but not one member got a ball past Dick-a-Dick's guard. High-flung balls he warded off with his parrying shield, and his skilful use of the killer boomerang easily deflected any ball coming at below knee level.

The eleven members each paid at least three shillings in their desperate attempts to defeat this black Australian warrior, but to no avail. They eventually gave up, put on their coats, straightened their ties, donned their bowler hats and adjourned to the Tavern Bar. Dick-A-Dick gleefully skipped away with the loot, a bag full of 33 shillings.

In purely cricketing terms, Dick-a-Dick was no great shakes. He scored only 356 runs at an average of 5.26 and took 5 wickets at 19.2. But he became the 1868 tour's Artful Dodger (the famous character in Charles Dickens's *Oliver Twist*, written almost 30 years before the Aboriginal tour of England). The team played a total of 47 two-day matches and he played in 45 of those games, but he was present at all venues, where before play, at lunch, tea and stumps, he challenged people to pay their shilling for the chance to get odds of 10/1 if they could get a ball past his defence.

There was only one occasion when a man got a ball past him. During the 31st game on tour, versus South Derbyshire, Samuel Richardson, who later captained the county, somehow got one past Dick-a-Dick's parrying shield and the ball struck him a glancing blow on his left shoulder. Richardson triumphantly claimed his 10-shilling prize.

Years later in 1890, he was Derbyshire County Cricket Club assistant secretary and was caught with his hand in the till by none other than Fred Spofforth, who was playing for Derby at the time. He got away with £1000 and fled to Spain, where he became court tailor to King Alfonso and lived to the age of 92.

I'm not sure of the moral of that story, but it is a good link to cricket history.

Dick-a-Dick was a tall, strong, bearded warrior, king of his tribe in the Wimmera district of Victoria. Four years before the 1868 tour, he and Redcap (Brimbunyah), who were both members of the 1868 Australian cricket team, had been unsung heroes in an outback drama.

In the late afternoon of 14 August 1864, the three Duff children – nine-year-old Isaac, Jane (seven) and Frank (three) – left Spring Hill Station, west of Natimuk in the Wimmera district of Victoria, to find brush for the making of brooms. The children quickly became lost and, as night fell, they became scared and disorientated. Mr Duff, friends and family scoured the bush, but it was not until after the children had been missing for six days that he decided to bring in the black trackers.

Within hours, the three black trackers – two of them Dick-a-Dick and Redcap – found the clearing where the Duff children had spent their first night in the cold. Within eight hours of being called in, the trackers walked into a clearing surrounded by kangaroo grass and found the children huddled together to keep warm – cold and hungry, but otherwise okay.

There were varying reports that the black trackers were given amounts ranging from a few shillings to £20, of which £5 was supposedly spent in the pub. Without their expertise, the Duff children would have most likely perished, but the trackers, apart from the cash handout, were given no official acknowledgement for having saved them. The story of the children's remarkable survival in the bush was told, but it centred on seven-year-old Jane Duff as heroine, protecting and 'saving' her brothers.

The Illustrated Australian News of 24 September 1864 told a thankful community: 'The painful account of the loss and subsequent discovery of the three children near Horsham is perhaps the most remarkable in the history of such cases in the colony.' In 1866, the story was dramatised in England in a rhyme narrative for the young, *The Australian Babes in the Wood*. A year later, the Victorian Education Department immortalised the saga for Australian schoolchildren as part of the Grade Four Reader. Sketches of the children depict them in the foreground with one of the white 'rescuers'.

The Aboriginal trackers were either omitted or relegated to the background. Even ST Gill, a prolific and skilled artist of the period, in his *Australian Sketchbook* (1864) drew the children's father on horseback, his hands raised, about to fall to the ground in prayer in relief at the children being found alive. The children are huddled in a clearing, the two boys asleep and Jane watching over them like a vigilant mother. The Aboriginal trackers are well in the background.

Noted artist and author William Strutt, who was born in Devon, England, in 1825 and came to Australia in 1850, wrote a fictional version of the Duff story, *Cooey, or, The Trackers of Glenferry*. Isaac, Jane and Frank became Roderick, Bella and David. His version ignores the Aboriginal connection in the saga – in keeping with colonial Australian community attitudes.

The 1868 Aboriginal Australian cricket team had a mob blessed with varied talents. The best cricketers were Johnny Mullagh (Unaarrimin), who hit 1698 runs at 23.65 and took 245 wickets at 10.00. The team's captain and coach was neither Australian nor Aboriginal – Charles Lawrence, who had toured Australia with HH Stephenson's 1861–62 England team, scored 1156 runs at 20.16 and took 250 wickets at 12.1.

Johnny Cuzens (Zellanach) was an amazing athlete, in the Jeff Thomson mould: high arm action, pace like fire. Cuzens scored 1358 runs at 19.9 and took 114 wickets at 11.3. He was also a very good runner, the team's champion sprinter. At The

Oval, in the team's 47th and last match of the tour, Surrey won despite a blistering 63 by Cuzens. A race was set up by the tourists' London host, William Holland, proprietor of the Old Canterbury Music Hall, who was full of admiration for Cuzens. A 'mysterious character from the north' challenged Cuzens to a running race and Holland placed £5 on Cuzens to win. Umpire William Shepherd suspected 'some jiggery-pokery', but before he could open his mouth in protest the race was started. Cuzens sent his supporters' hearts aflutter by being slow off the mark and then subjected them to something akin to heart failure by stopping dead in the middle of the race to kick off his running pumps. He then took off like a rocket and slipped past his rival at the death to breast the tape first. Holland, true to the open-handed tradition of the music hall, pressed both stake and winnings into the runner's hand.

Redcap (Brimbunyah), one of the black trackers to find the missing Duff children, hit 630 runs on tour at 8.46 and took 54 wickets at 10.7. He played in all 47 matches. 'Redcap' was the name adopted much later as a pseudonym by the respected *Sydney Morning Herald* and *The Australian* cricket writer Phil Wilkins.

Other players, such as Mosquito (Grongarrong) and Peter (Arrahmunyjarrimin), were experts at cracking the stockwhip, but Sundown (Ballrinjarrimin) only played a couple of games. He was a specialist batsman and did not bowl. He scored just one run on tour in three completed innings, but it was a personal best because no-one ever knew Sundown to score a single run in any match prior to the England tour and he never played after 1868. He must have been the original hero of the legend: 'In the first innings he made one and in the second he was not quite so successful.'

Lawrence's tour was a great success, although one man – King Cole (Bripumyarrimin, also known as Brippokei) – died after a short illness. King Cole had had a cold, but it wasn't considered sufficiently bad for him to miss the much-awaited game at Lord's, which ended on 13 June 1868. He died of pneumonia on 24 June at Guy's Hospital, London.

The Australian team management were fearful of more deaths on tour, so in September, a month before the expected departure of the team for Australia, two players – Sundown (Ballrinjarrimin) and Jim Crow (Jallachmurrimin, also known as Lytejerbillijun) – who had developed bad colds, were sent home on the same ship, the *Parramatta*, which had brought the team to England.

Off the field of play, the star turn of the 1868 team was undoubtedly Dick-a-Dick. His hand–eye coordination must have been exceptional and his dodging skills became legendary on the tour.

In 2001, I took an under-21 Aboriginal cricket team to England. It was a re-enactment of the 1868 tour. We played at Lord's and visited the Lord's Museum where, behind glass and only a couple of paces from the coveted Ashes urn, was Dick-a-Dick's leangle.

A couple of our team – captain Barry Firebrace and Adam Walker – were related to Johnny Cuzens, the fastest bowler and swiftest runner in the 1868 team. I had asked the then Lord's Museum curator, Stephen Green, over the phone before we left Australia whether one or more of my players could be photographed holding the killer boomerang. Like a Geoff Boycott forward dead bat, smothering the life out of my delivery, Stephen said defensively, 'I am afraid I cannot allow any of these precious objects, especially the boomerang, to be taken out from behind the protective glass.'

But the day we arrived at the museum, Stephen Green wasn't there, was he? What a moment for Firebrace and Walker! The joy on their faces was something to behold, for the significance of the moment was not lost on them. Almost certainly it was the first time since 1868 that an Indigenous Australian had touched Dick-a-Dick's killer boomerang.

During that tour, we even had a ceremony at King Cole's graveside at Meath Gardens in London. During the ceremony, ochre was sprinkled on the grave – the 'mother' (ochre, representing the land) was brought to the 'son'. As coach of the team, I was asked to read the same words uttered by Lawrence when King Cole was buried there in 1868.

In 2002, historians and cricketers, including former Test captain Ian Chappell, campaigned to bring national recognition (induction into the Australian Cricket Hall of Fame) to the 1868 Aboriginal Australian team. They were given special numbers (bearing the prefix AUS) so that Charles Bannerman – the man who opened the batting for Australia in the first official Test match at the MCG in March 1877, from the time the numbers system began – could retain number 1.

Chappell's great interest in the Aboriginal cricketers reflected that of his grandfather Victor Richardson, himself a famous Test cricketer and Australian captain, who in 1951 unveiled the monument dedicated to the 1868 team at Edenhope in Victoria, the area where the Aboriginals trained. In 2002, Ian Chappell was invited to travel to Edenhope and rededicate the monument. Chappell said: 'I took that to be a great honour.'

Victor Trumper and the Golden Age

Victor Trumper was the darling of cricket followers the world over. Arguably the most-loved cricketer who ever lived, Trumper appealed to the masses and connoisseurs alike. He carried his red-blooded attack to all bowlers with a boyish zest and a manly style which enthralled friend and foe in equal measure.

Trumper was born in Darlinghurst, Sydney, on 2 November 1877 and became the greatest batsman of cricket's Golden Age (1890–1914). His rise to fame didn't come without setbacks. While he became a hero of Crown Street Superior School in his home suburb of Darlinghurst (see 'Backyard Test matches' in this book), when the school champion bat was a tender 14 years of age he received a rebuff from the great William Gilbert Grace.

In December 1891, along with a bunch of other Sydney hopefuls, Victor bowled and fielded as the visiting England team had a hit-up in front of the old stand at the SCG. Trumper in the main bowled to WG and fielded as he hit the ball back. Victor so impressed Grace that he was invited to have a hit. Wearing knickerbockers and a brave face, young Trumper struggled to middle too many on the rough turf and Grace told him, 'You can surely bowl and field, m'boy, but I'm afraid batting is just not your forte! You'll never get anywhere as a batsman.'

He was undaunted. His father, Charles, had long heard talk of his son's batting – 'Have you heard of Crown Street School's Victor Trumper?' It was round this time that his father would daily take Victor to Moore Park, close to the SCG, where he would bowl his curious left-arm slows to his son for a minimum of two hours.

Soon enough, Victor Trumper would make his mark on the international stage. In 1894, aged 17, he was picked among 18 juniors to play against Andrew Stoddart's touring England XI. On the morning of the match, he was in bed with influenza. His mother pleaded with him not to go to the game, but this was his big chance to make an impression. He got himself organised and walked the 15 minutes from his Paddington home to the SCG.

The juniors won the toss and batted. Victor impressed all with his batting, hammering a stylish 67 out of the 97 runs scored while he was at the crease in 85 minutes. It was stirring stuff, especially as he was facing a top-flight attack which included tearaway fast bowler Bill Lockwood and the left-arm spinners Johnny Briggs and Bobby Peel, and he had played just a handful of A-grade matches for South Sydney. Trumper's 67 was greatly overshadowed by teammate Monty Noble's unconquered 152, but good judges could see the burgeoning genius in his batting.

Those who saw first-hand the Trumper batting genius never understood why Trumper believed he was doomed to failure if he spotted a man of the cloth wearing a 'dog collar' in the crowd. 'How can I get runs with all those clergymen standing about?' Trumper whispered to Clem Hill at Lord's in June 1899. The pair had just walked from the field, Australia having dismissed England for a modest 206. Despite the presence of many clergymen in the Lord's crowd that day and the next, Trumper scored his maiden Test century, 135 not out. Hill also made 135 in the Australian first innings of 421, which set the side up for an impressive 10-wicket victory.

Trumper's first Test match at Old Trafford was 50-year-old WG Grace's last. At Lord's, eight years after their exchange at the SCG, Grace had changed his mind about the young Australian. He knocked on the Australian dressing-room door and asked to

Victor Trumper: the greatest batsman of cricket's Golden Age (1890–1914).

see Trumper, who had just completed his maiden Test century. Grace handed him his bat, upon which he wrote the words: 'From the past champion to the future champion.'

At Manchester in 1902, Trumper scored 104 before lunch. He wrote in his diary that night: 'Wet wicket. Fourth Test. Won toss. Made 299. Self 104 ...' Only three Australians have scored a century before lunch on the first day of a Test match in England – Trumper at Manchester in 1902, Charlie Macartney at Leeds in 1926 and Don Bradman at Leeds in 1930. In all the Tests since the first at the MCG in March 1877, only one batsman – David Warner, opening for Australia on the first day of the match against Pakistan at the SCG on 2 January 2017 – has performed the feat in Australia.

Trumper played his last Test innings in March 1912, in the Fifth Test of the 1911–12 Ashes series at the SCG. Australia needed 362 runs to win the game. At the non-striker's end, little Syd Gregory contemplated the seriousness of the situation, as the great SF Barnes cruised past to deliver the first ball of the Australian second innings. England's finest bowler, Barnes operated a shade above medium pace, bowling a combination of swing and spin, the fast leg-break his most potent weapon.

Barnes had dismissed Trumper for 5 in the first innings, producing a near-perfect leg-break, which pitched leg and would have taken the top of the stump off had not Trumper's bat got in the way. The edge gave Frank Woolley, who stood tall and straight like a Grenadier Guard, a dolly at first slip. Trumper's fate didn't seem fair somehow, as Woolley himself had scored an unconquered 133 in England's first innings of 324.

Warwick Armstrong hit the top score of 33 in Australia's paltry 176, but today Trumper was setting out to make amends for a summer of discontent for Clem Hill's Australian team. Trumper's only century in the Test series had been in the first match at the SCG – 113 in the first dig – and it was the only match of the series that Australia had won.

By the Fifth Test, Australia trailed 1–3 and wanted to turn the tables on an England team which had some of the greats, including Jack Hobbs, George Gunn, Wilfred Rhodes, the captain JWHT (Johnny Won't Hit Today) Douglas, Woolley and the incomparable SF Barnes.

The first ball from Barnes was a searing yorker, but Trumper dismissed the ball in a flash, playing what he called the 'dog shot'. As the ball careered towards leg stump, having moved from off to leg in the manner of a late reverse swinger, Trumper merely lifted his front leg, swivelled neatly on his back leg, and meeting the ball on the half-volley, dismissed it from his presence like a shot out of a gun to the backward square fence.

Umpire Bob Crockett broke into a broad grin, unusual for such a stern soul, and the crowd rose to acclaim Trumper's mastery. This might yet prove to be Trumper's most glorious moment. The dog shot for four, then a two past gully and a single to mid-on, brought Gregory to face the music. Two balls in a row from Barnes just beat the Gregory outside edge by a whisker, but he survived. Trumper scored exactly 50 in that innings – again caught at slip by Woolley off SF Barnes – and Australia lost the game.

How could Trumper have known then that 1 March 1912 would be his last day in Test cricket? Nephritis, the kidney disease which took his life in 1915, was yet to show its ugly face.

As he watched Trumper at Lord's in 1902, using his feet to dance down the track and hoist a Wilfred Rhodes offering over the members' seats in front of the Long Room, Hill had wondered about his teammate's phobia. Bill Whitty, the left-arm medium-fast bowler from Mount Gambier in South Australia, once told me that during Trumper's brilliant summer of 1910–11,

He could do anything at any time. All the bowling came alike to him and he was just as likely to get a couple of

fours off the first two balls of the day as he was off the last two. But he could not relax at the batting crease if he saw a clergyman, either on the way to the wicket or in the crowd, while he was out in the middle.

Traditionally, cricketers are pretty superstitious. Well, most of them.

For Australia, the 'devil's number' has been 87 and it all came from a mistake. Twelve-year-old Keith Miller was watching Don Bradman play Victoria in 1931 when Bradman pulled a ball onto his stumps. Miller looked at the score on the board. 'Fancy getting out for 87, unlucky 13 from 100,' he mused. While 87 became the unlucky number for Australians, years later Miller looked up the scorecard. It read: 'Bradman bowled Alexander 89.' The scoreboard had been slow in registering the two Bradman had scored the ball before his dismissal.

The Victorian and Australian medium-fast bowler Alan Connolly always took the field for his country with a piece of Hugh Trumble's green and gold Test hatband. England keeper Alan Knott had a peculiar habit of having a handkerchief hanging precariously from his trouser pocket and, standing up to the wicket to Derek Underwood and company, he would always gently touch the top of the stumps for good luck.

Victor Trumper's legacy to the game of cricket was not the number of runs he scored, but the way he played the game. We don't rank Sachin Tendulkar above Don Bradman just because he scored a mountain more runs – albeit in 130 more matches. In 1980 Kim Hughes, the gifted yet wayward Australian batsman, hit a magnificent century at Lord's in the Centenary Test match in England. In batting terms, that innings was the epitome of Victor Trumper.

Hughes scored a first innings 117 (14 fours and 3 sixes) and 84 (11 fours and 2 sixes) in the second. One straight hit for six off speedster Chris Old landed in the top deck of the Lord's Pavilion. The stroke was like a choice offering from the cricket gods who delighted in similar majesty by Trumper. Former England captain Gubby Allen, who played against Don Bradman at his zenith, said he had never seen a more remarkable shot than Hughes's straight hit for six. Those two innings revealed a batsman whose red-blooded strokes delighted the young and tickled the memories of the old. There was a freedom of movement and a sort of boyish joy in his work that gave him ample time against the fast men and footwork to dominate the spinners. To me it was Trumper all over.

The great England player CB Fry summed it up: 'Victor Trumper is perhaps the most difficult batsman in the world to reduce to words. He has no style, yet he is all style.'

Trumper

Wrists of steel wrapped in velvet glove
No batsman in history has stood above
'neath hottest sun or dappled light
Victor, o Victor, our shining knight
When Trumper the boy became Trumper the man
The cricketing gods gave Vic a free hand
To drive and to hook; to soar to great height
Trumper back then, Australia's delight
Our 'Sticky-dog' hero, above Bradman's best
Trumper the batsman, fittingly blessed
The world's best bat in the Golden Age
Trumper the bold, no peer on Test stage
Long has he gone, like the flight of a dove
Eternally cloaked in a nation's love

© Ashley Mallett

Bradman or Trumper?

Who was the greatest Australian Test batsman, Don Bradman or Victor Trumper? Ever since Bradman stormed into Test stardom on the 1930 Ashes tour of England, old players and the press have pondered this question.

Bradman played his last Test in 1948, so few alive today saw him bat and certainly no-one remembers the artistry of Trumper's batting, given that his Test career spanned the years 1899 to 1912 and he died in 1915. On figures alone, Bradman is light years ahead of Trumper, but his teammates, men who played with and against Trumper and also saw Bradman at his peak, unfailingly said Trumper was the greatest batsman of them all.

For instance, Clarrie Grimmett as a boy in Wellington saw Trumper hit a big hundred, then in 1914 he bowled one over to Trumper. He also captured Bradman's wicket on 10 occasions, but Grimmett always maintained that Trumper was the best.

In 80 Test innings, Bradman amassed 6996 runs at an average of 99.94. Trumper in 89 Test innings hit 3163 runs at an average of 39.04. There is such a disparity in their batting records that we need an explanation for why the comparison is made.

Volume of runs or wickets and good averages dominate the game because we need a tangible measuring stick, but the old saying, 'lies, damned lies and statistics' has stood the test of time. Often in cricket statistics do lie. For instance, some of the best innings in big matches have been relatively small scores achieved on treacherous surfaces, such as many a knock by Trumper on uncovered wickets.

England's Wally Hammond thrashed the bowling of the great Australian leg-spinner Clarrie Grimmett in the 1928–29 series Down Under, but in 1930 Grimmett turned the tables on Hammond, who struggled to survive for Gloucestershire against the Australians at Bristol and recalled:

The match was a nightmare. I find it difficult to recall, except as an endless period of gripping my bat, wiping my hands and trying to score off balls which struck the pitch like a viper. Then my castle went down and I recall creeping into the pavilion exhausted as if I had been batting all day.

Hammond scored 89, but he thought that innings as good as the 336 not out he scored against New Zealand at Christchurch in April 1933.

Cricket is littered with similar occurrences.

In 1972 at Lord's, I saw Bob Massie take an incredible 16/137 in his debut Test. The other four England wickets were captured by Dennis Lillee. And yet the best and most sustained piece of bowling for Australia I saw in the match was the fiery spell by medium-fast exponent David 'The Fox' Colley. Operating with genuine pace and fire for seven consecutive overs from the Pavilion End in the England second innings, Colley beat the bat with blistering pace ball after ball, often shaving the off stump, while Massie was cashing in at the Nursery End, pocketing more than one scalp during Colley's brilliant little cameo. His spell went unrewarded, but his bowling that day was something to behold and remember.

In Bradman's case, do we judge him to be the greatest batsman purely on the runs he made? If this was the case, we would judge the worth of a building by the number of bricks in its walls or a book by the number of words.

I have seen all the best Australian batsmen since Bradman and to me Neil Harvey (79 Tests at an average of 48.41) was easily the best. There are many, including Greg Chappell, Justin Langer, Steve Waugh, Ricky Ponting and Michael Clarke, with superior averages, but statistics are merely figures and don't tell us the condition of the pitch, the quality of the bowling, the ability of the batsman to tough it out in the middle.

Today's batsmen have larger bats. A forward prod often sends the ball careering to the fence and a mishit often sees the ball clear the rope, which is well in from the boundary fence. Grounds are smaller, bats bigger and our Test men also have the opportunity to play against minnow teams such as Zimbabwe and Bangladesh with weak bowling attacks. Even the West Indians have fallen away, so much so that any decent Australia grade team would test them.

Neutral umpires have also made a significant difference. Years ago, the so-called 'hometown decision' was rife in Test cricket and in the domestic first-class game. One day when South Australian captain David Hookes stood next to the square-leg umpire in a Sheffield Shield match against Victoria on Adelaide Oval, the umpire – an Adelaide man – remarked, 'Gee, Hookesy, we need a wicket badly.' Neutral umpires in big cricket have helped level the playing field, and so too has the DRS third umpire system.

No doubt statistics play a part in any comparison between Bradman and Trumper, but they do not tell us the Don was a far superior player. Superb English cricket writer RC Robertson-Glasgow preferred watching a Wally Hammond cover drive or a Stan McCabe hook to observing Bradman's merciless attack. However, while he acknowledges other batsmen offer appealing style and grace, he cannot go past Bradman's extraordinary batting record:

*You go round the great ones and you come back – to Don
and his figures. You can't answer them. They don't speak.
They exist; and will exist; 'a monument more enduring
than bronze'. When I first saw Bradman, in England, he
was an exquisitely heartless murderer of bowlers. He
sliced them into smaller pieces; danced on them, neatly
and conclusively. There'll never be another innings like his
334 against England at Leeds in 1930; never. Maurice Tate
shaved Don's stumps with the first ball he bowled him, and
George Duckworth, that tough and expert keeper of stumps,
opened his mouth and let it go for four byes. From then on
Bradman batted as in dreams; or nightmares; and he never
raised the ball from the grass.*

In a letter to me dated 8 June 1984, Bradman was consistent
in his evaluation of style and efficiency; one did not necessarily
connect with the other. He wrote in part:

*I was interested in the view that you formed after reading
Fingleton's book [*The Immortal Victor Trumper*, Jack
Fingleton, 1978]. No unbiased person could form any other
opinion and it was really a continuance of the vendetta he
conducted against me throughout his life. Of course I did not
see Trumper play, but people [who did] like Arthur Mailey,
Charlie Macartney, HS Carter and Johnny Moyes spoke of
him in glowing terms. This adulation seemed to be largely
due to the style and elegance of his batting, very similar,
so they said, to Alan Kippax and Archie Jackson. Having
played with the last two named I must agree they were
beautiful to watch.*

*But style does not necessarily bring efficiency and
consistency ... Jackson toured England with me in 1930
and only managed one century on the trip, and that was
against a weak county, Somerset. His admirers after*

*Jackson's death excused his poor showing on ill-health, but
there was no evidence of this on that tour. It developed later.
Style is hard to define. Of the modern players, Gower is
probably the best example. Greg Chappell has an imperious
quality about his batting which his brother Ian lacked. But
which one would you have rather had in your team when
the going was tough? I seem to remember Cardus writing
on this aspect and the comparison he used was an eagle
looked much more beautiful in flight than an aeroplane but
could not possibly match it for speed.*

Kent batsman Fuller Pilch was the darling of English cricket in
the first half of the nineteenth century. He was described as 'the
greatest batsman ever known until the appearance of WG Grace'.
Pilch played 229 first-class matches between 1820 and 1854 for
a handful of counties including Kent, Hampshire, Surrey and
Sussex, as well as turning out for Norfolk and Cambridge Town.

He was an early exponent of what they call today 'the
forward press'. Arthur Haygarth wrote of Pilch in his 1862
edition of *Scores and Biographies*: 'His style of batting was very
commanding, extremely forward, and he seemed to rush to the
best bowling by his long forward play before it had time to shoot
or rise, or do mischief by catches.'

In his 229 first-class matches, Fuller Pilch scored 7147 runs,
with 3 centuries at an average of 18.61. These numbers seem
modest compared to those of players in Trumper's era and pale
into insignificance with those of Bradman's time and beyond.
However, the 10 centuries he scored throughout his entire club
and first-class career were considered 'remarkable' in the context
of playing conditions, round-arm bowling and the prevailing
attitude of players, administrators, spectators and the press.

As in Pilch's time, Trumper's averages were not the overriding
obsession they seemed to have become when Don Bradman
ran roughshod over all bowlers he confronted in the 1930s.

Victorian Bill Ponsford also had an insatiable appetite for runs. In 1922–23, in only his third first-class match, Ponsford scored 429 against Tasmania. In December 1927, he bettered that with 437 versus Queensland. Ponsford and West Indian Brian Lara are the only two batsmen to have scored over 400 in a first-class innings on two occasions. Bradman topped Ponsford's record in 1929–30, hitting 452 not out against Queensland at the SCG.

While Bradman's statistics remain a constant to bear in mind, in balance we need to consider the wickets at major grounds throughout Trumper's time. Long-term Adelaide Oval curator Charlie Checkett (1883–1919) used a horse-drawn heavy roller to flatten the pitch and his trusty razor-sharp scythe to give the face of the wicket a barber's close shave. Arguably the precision of motor mowers, which were well in vogue on cricket grounds by the time Bradman started, would have been superior to a man wielding a scythe and having to depend upon his skill to produce a pitch good for batting.

All things are relative. Wicket preparation in Trumper's era was vastly superior to that in Fuller Pilch's time. Before matches at Lord's throughout the 1820s and 1830s, the groundsman's first job was to shoo the sheep off the square and sweep up the droppings.

Weather played its part, too. Wickets were left open to the elements and a track which was ravaged by a combination of heavy rain, followed by a hot sun, produced a treacherous surface known as a 'sticky dog', where a ball would either skid or sit up like a spitting cobra. This was a wicket feared by all batsmen, and it proved a psychological barrier to all and sundry in all eras – to all, that is, except Victor Trumper.

Comparing averages across eras is fraught with danger, and there is no definitive answer as to who was a better player if we rely on the bare figures. We can get an idea of the quality of player by paying attention to the opinions of good judges, those who saw Trumper play: such as England's Frank Woolley and

SF Barnes; and Australia's Jack Ryder, Warren Bardsley and Clarrie Grimmett.

The case for Trumper

Trumper was the greatest batsman of the Golden Age of Cricket (1890–1914). On Australia's 1902 tour of England, he made a record 2570 runs, with 11 centuries. That English summer was decidedly wet, yet he handled the wickets with his usual mastery.

Included in his 3163 runs on the big stage was his highest Test score of 214 against South Africa on the Adelaide Oval in 1910–11. That summer was Trumper's best in a Test series on Australian soil: 661 runs, with the Bradman-like average of 94.42.

Apart from his brilliant 1902 England tour and his demolition of the South Africans in 1910–11, one statistic which kept, until now, under the radar is the fact that Trumper, among accomplished Test players, was the fastest-scoring batsman to play Test cricket.

BATSMAN	RUNS PER HOUR	TOTAL TEST RUNS
Victor Trumper (Australia)	40.1	3161
JH Sinclair (South Africa)	39.8	1064
Stan McCabe (Australia)	38.1	2748
Frank Woolley (England)	37.6	3264
Don Bradman (Australia)	37.6	6996
Charles Macartney (Australia)	36.7	2131
Reg Duff (Australia)	34.1	1311
Shahid Afridi (Pakistan)	34.0	1716
Clem Hill (Australia)	33.8	3411
Adam Gilchrist (Australia)	33.6	5570

Statistics for major top-order batsmen who scored a total of 1000 runs or more in Test cricket.

In Trumper's time, cricket was not yet very commercial. In the main, batsmen did not grind their way through a full day's play. Whenever a batsman got bogged down, it was either hit out and win or hit out and fall. Trumper loved the contest between bat and ball. If he had a day out with the bat and flayed all comers, when he reached a century he invariably looked about for the bowler who had performed the best against him that day and proceeded to throw his wicket away.

Trumper came into big cricket in 1896. There was a charming innocence to the Australian way of life: no aircraft, travel by rail or sea, and three-day Tests in England. Right up until the grim, dark days of World War I, batting was an ever adventurous, red-blooded attack, carefree.

Trumper's glorious England summer of 1902 included his becoming the first Australian batsman to score a century before lunch on the first day of a Test match. That day, Thursday 24 July, as Trumper walked to the wicket with fellow opener Reg Duff, the slender frame of a bespectacled 12-year-old boy pressed against the picket fence, and he said to himself: 'Please God, let Victor Trumper score a century – out of a total of 137 all out!'

Neville Cardus got his wish that day. The Old Trafford wicket was damp and deliveries from the fast bowlers, especially William Lockwood, would either skid low or rear menacingly at the batsman's throat, but Trumper hooked Lockwood to the fence twice to reach his hundred.

The boy who would establish himself as the greatest of all cricket correspondents wrote of the great Australian batsman:

> *Trumper's winged batsmanship was seen in the Golden Age of cricket; he was at his finest, master of some of the greatest bowlers the game has known. He will always remain for your true Australian the greatest batsman who ever lived. We make an artist's immortality by thinking*

upon and loving his work. Trumper was an artist-cricketer;
let him live again in the mouths of men whenever Test
matches are in action.

Throughout his long and celebrated career, as a wordsmith extraordinaire on cricket and music, Cardus listened to arguments for and against both Trumper and Bradman. He acknowledged, as logic must, that statistically Bradman was the superior exponent ... or was he? 'I am concerned with Trumper as an artist, not as a scorer of match-winning runs. You will no more get an idea of the quality of Trumper's batsmanship by adding up his runs than you will get an idea of the quality of Shelley's poetry by adding up the number of lines written by Shelley.'

Quality opposition is also a huge factor. Trumper batted against SF Barnes, arguably the greatest Test bowler after Fred Spofforth and before the likes of Harold Larwood, Frank Tyson, Ray Lindwall and Keith Miller. Trumper faced Barnes on treacherous surfaces, especially in Australia, many times.

Len Hutton, the great England opening batsman and first professional to captain England, told me during a trip to Adelaide in 1984 that when he was a boy of 16 he faced the bowling of 62-year-old SF Barnes.

SF must have been casting his eye over a few of the
emerging Yorkshire youngsters. After he bowled me half a
dozen balls I was convinced that here was a truly great
bowler. He bowled medium-paced inswingers which turned
from the leg. They swerved in to land round the line of
leg, then whipped away in the manner of a fiercely-spun
leg-break. That was easily the best bowling I had faced,
including the Australian attack when I hit 364 at The Oval
in 1938, until I met the pace and fire of Keith Miller in the
Victory Tests of 1945. Pity the batsmen such as the great
Trumper who had to face SF Barnes in his prime.

English cricket writer Harry Altham wrote:

> *Trumper's genius was essentially qualitative rather than quantitative, revealed in terms of spontaneous art rather than in any acquired technique. In other words, it was the manner in which this legend batted that separated him from the others. He did not believe that there was any ball, which could not be scored off. He was gifted with a great eye and a quick pair of feet. He was a true athlete. His strength lay in playing the ball late.*

Years after the England tour of Australia in 1907–08, the Marylebone Cricket Club (MCC) manager of the tour, Colonel Trevor, wrote of Trumper: 'He dealt with good-length balls in the way that ordinary first-class batsmen deal with half-volleys and long hops. He was totally selfless. He enjoyed cricket but not its attendant glories. He disliked the adulation of the crowds.'

The case for Bradman

No batsman in Test history has come close to Bradman's amazing record. Statistically he has no peer. Whereas Trumper glided poetically to the ball and dismissed it from his presence with an air of magic, Bradman, especially against slow bowling, was like a cat on the prowl for a mouse: a ball of fullish length was fair game and he pounced.

Bradman's amazing record began in the Australian summer of 1928–29 and ended with his final innings – a duck – at The Oval in 1948.

Neville Cardus once took Bradman to task when the Don announced that he needed to score 'at least two hundred tomorrow'. Bradman's tour of 1934 saw him with a run of low scores: 29 and 25 in the First Test at Nottingham; 36 and 13 at Lord's; 30 at Manchester. Cardus pointed out that Bradman's meagre scores in Test and county matches added weight to Cardus's contention that the law of averages was very much against Bradman getting a hundred at Leeds.

'I don't believe in the law of averages,' Bradman said, 'and I do not worry about the pitch or what the bowler is or is not doing. I merely concentrate on watching the ball, then I will determine where I am going to hit it – for one, two, three or four.'

From the outset in big cricket, Bradman was supremely confident in his own ability. In 1981, he wrote to me saying how disappointed he was in Kim Hughes's complaint about the Headingley, Leeds, wicket. That was the game when Australia was in the box seat and England won after following on, thanks to Botham's remarkable knock of 149 and Bob Willis's eight-wicket haul. (At one stage, the bookies had England 500/1 to win and Dennis Lillee and Rodney Marsh couldn't resist such odds. They had a bet, England won and the press had a field day.) Bradman played four Tests at Leeds, where he scored 334 in 1930, 304 in 1934, 103 and 16 in 1938 and 33 and 173 not out in 1948 – a total of 963 runs at an average of 192.06.

Bradman wrote: 'I always found Leeds playable.'

Merciless in his approach towards every bowler he confronted, Bradman would as soon give his wicket away as he would have flown to the moon. Just as the great West Indian sides of the 1970s and 1980s planned to target the better opposition batsmen, Bradman was like a Jack Russell on the hunt for rats – ever on a mission to destroy one particular bowler or the whole damned attack.

Bill O'Reilly, the bowler Bradman believed was the greatest of them all, always marvelled at the Don's batting when he was at the peak of his powers. 'That was the pre-war Bradman,' Bill said. 'And the pre-war Bradman was relentless, a young man who not only rattled off big scores and drove himself to make them bigger, but he took almost a fiendish delight in pulverizing an attack.

'Any bowler who gave him a hard time in his innings became a target for Bradman's special brand of punishment. A bowler unwise enough to publicly state that Bradman had a "weakness" was belted unmercifully. After the war Bradman was good, better than any other batsman, but not a patch on the Bradman of 1930, which makes sense. His powers had diminished as he neared the age of forty. He had slowed and you felt he sometimes was batting from memory. Some memory. He hit 2428 runs at 89.92 on the 1948 tour. I always have believed that Don Bradman, at any stage of his career, was worth three batsmen.'

Summing up

As we have seen, Don Bradman's Test batting average of 99.94 was so far ahead of Trumper's average that it seems folly to make a comparison. Yet Bradman himself seemed concerned that these comparisons between the two batsmen continually found some sort of public debate. Once I quizzed Bradman, asking him whether the comparisons irked him. He wrote to me:

No, it never irked me when the older players spoke so highly of Trumper and their views did not have any influence whatsoever.

You ask did it give me greater resolve 'to be the greatest batsman of all time'. I never, at any time, set out to be 'the greatest batsman of all time', nor did I ever have such an ambition. I merely tried to play as best I could and any comparable judgement of skill was for others to determine. I think I also had enough sense to realise each individual has his own particular skill and style and that you have to make the best you can of yourself. It is usually hopeless to try and copy others.

One of the most remarkable documents on the issue appeared in Michael Page's book, *Bradman: The Illustrated Biography* (Macmillan, 1983). Under the heading 'Who was Australia's top batsman – Bradman or Trumper?', there is a long and incredibly detailed discourse on the changing face of cricket when Bradman played and in the wake of Trumper's career. It discusses rule changes, size of stumps and covered wickets. Sir Donald counselled me to read this chapter in Page's book before I completed my own book on Trumper. I had read some five sentences of the chapter when it hit me: the style and detail in the words had me strongly suspecting that chapter was written by Bradman himself.

Part of it reads:

Bradman himself has always remained completely aloof from the argument. He was only a lad when Trumper died and obviously never saw Trumper bat. His only knowledge of his great predecessor was gained from the lips of those who had seen Trumper play and from reading books and articles.

And here is the statistical argument set in stone:

The only way to clarify the argument is by analysing the batting figures of both men and comparing the conditions under which they played, while first admitting that Trumper, by general consent, was the most stylish and graceful of batsmen.

Style and grace are lovely assets and pleasing to the eye. They play a worthy part to the attraction of cricket for spectators. But, of course, they do not win matches.

Sound familiar?

Trumper never faced the speed of Larwood, nor did Bradman have to contend with the magic of SF Barnes. They were both brilliant athletes with good throwing arms. Each was an accomplished pianist and they both loved the game of cricket with a passion. Undoubtedly each man was a genius and a legend.

Who was the better player: Bradman or Trumper? We will know for sure when the world greets the first time machine.

Five great quicks

Ray Lindwall

Stocky and strong, Ray Lindwall played first-grade rugby league and once ran 100 yards in a shade over 10 seconds. He was like a well-toned welterweight, ready to punch and counter-punch, and batsmen always suspected he had a knockout blow up his sleeve. He had what the old England cricketer Sir Pelham Warner called 'shades of pace'. This artist-cricketer changed his pace with all the subtle artifices any fast bowler of any era has achieved and he did what all great bowlers must do – broke the rhythm of the batsman.

At his zenith, he had the power to slay by thunder or defeat by guile. Lindwall bowled outswingers at genuine pace and, between these late away-curves, his searing, skidding bouncer. To the purists, Lindwall's bowling arm was too low, but that helped his bouncer, which came at the throat instead of climbing harmlessly over the batsman's head.

As a starry-eyed kid born in 1921, Lindwall always timed his after-school cricket in the street with his mates to occur at the very time that Bill O'Reilly walked the streets of Kogarah, in Sydney, on his way home. The instant O'Reilly turned into the street, there was young Lindwall in full flight. Just before World War II, Test great O'Reilly, then St George Cricket Club captain, took Lindwall under his wing. O'Reilly brought to the club the technology called 'electric-eye photography', which allowed the youngster to study his action on film in slow motion, and identify any technical faults.

After serving in the war with the 2nd AIF in New Guinea and the Solomon Islands, Lindwall's first Test was O'Reilly's last. They turned out for Bill Brown's 1945–46 one-off Test against New Zealand in Wellington. Australia scored 199 and the Kiwis replied with a paltry 42 and then 54. O'Reilly grabbed a match haul of 8/33 off 19 overs; his protégé 2/29 off 17 overs.

Lindwall was at the pinnacle of his powers when he spearheaded Don Bradman's attack on the celebrated 1948 Australian tour of England. Along with Lindwall, Bradman's Invincibles had a string of class bowlers, including Bill Johnston, Keith Miller and Ernie Toshack. In five Tests, Lindwall took 27 wickets.

Throughout the 1950s, Lindwall was Australia's spearhead, bowling his heart out against some of the greatest batsmen of any era – Len Hutton, Denis Compton, Garry Sobers, Everton Weekes, Clyde Walcott, Frank Worrell and Vijay Hazare.

In his last overseas tour, Lindwall bowled in tandem with New South Wales speedster Gordon Rorke, who bowled the first over. When he presented the ball to Lindwall, the great man looked at Rorke and said: 'Son, that ball is a bloody disgrace. The idea is to hit the pitch on the seam – every ball.' He demanded that the youngster stay with him until, with a combination of spit, sweat and polish, he had brought the ball back to the look of a fresh, young cherry. 'When I finish this over, I will hand you back this ball in the same condition and that's how I expect you to return it to me – every time!'

Lindwall played 61 Tests, taking 228 wickets at 23.03, with a Test best of 7/38. However, his 6/20 in the England first innings of the Fifth Test at The Oval in 1948 to demolish Hutton's men for a total of 52 was his *pièce de résistance.*

Arthur Morris loved being asked, 'Did you play in Bradman's last match where he got a duck?'

'Yes, I did play that game.'

'Oh, did you get any runs?'

'A few ... 196 to be exact.'

Morris's 196 plus Lindwall's demolition job on England with the ball denied Bradman the chance to bat again. He needed just 4 not out to end his career with a Test average of 100.

Dennis Lillee

Good judges describe Dennis Lillee as 'the complete bowler', who always kept one step ahead of the pack. On the Test arena, Lillee was never beaten. West Indian champion Viv Richards took the sword to all the international bowlers of his era. And from very first eye contact when Richards came up against Lillee it was like two irresistible forces meeting toe to toe: a heavyweight fight between two unrelenting combatants. Their contests were always take-no-prisoners affairs.

Lillee's well-documented battle to overcome near-crippling back injury and return from relative obscurity to dominate the Test arena proves his fighting qualities. Lillee did what it took to take you out, and sometimes he roughed you up along the way. The young Lillee was once castigated by Western Australia captain Tony Lock, who told him bluntly, 'Dennis, you are bowling like a fucking old tart.' Teammate and later Western Australia captain John Inverarity grabbed hold of Lock's description and, using the first letter of the words, he coined Lillee's nickname, FOT.

In December 1971, Lillee blitzed a strong World Xl batting line-up in Perth, taking 8/29 in Garry Sobers's team total of 59. He bowled magnificently in England in 1972, taking a record 31 wickets at 17.67 in the series, which was drawn 2–all.

In the three Tests against Pakistan in Australia in 1972–73, Lillee again bowled manfully. He also revealed his terrific sense of humour in Adelaide, when two Pakistani batsmen were continually meeting midpitch for a chat. Their midwicket pow-wows were becoming tedious, until we came to the ludicrous situation of Lillee standing, hands on hips, waiting for the batsmen to return to their positions.

Suddenly, Lillee let out a call: 'Book, book-begurk!'

It was the famous Lillee family chook call, known to many in Western Australian cricket circles but rather foreign to our Pakistani visitors. In fact, those two Pakistani batsmen thought the call was some sort of strange code from Lillee to keeper Rod Marsh.

Late in that summer, many believed Lillee's career was all but over when he sustained multiple stress fractures in his back. Some critics blamed captain Ian Chappell for what they called his over-bowling of Lillee, who bowled unchanged from the Paddington End for 23 overs in the Pakistan second innings for a return of 3/68. It made sense for Chappell to keep Lillee bowling, not just because the fast bowler was hell-bent on continuing. Lillee kept going because once he stopped and his back got cold he wouldn't have been able to return to the crease.

He underwent a long regime of intensive physiotherapy under the direction of Dr Frank Pyke, a Perth club cricketer, baseballer and footballer. Lillee's determination became legend, coming back to big cricket in 1974–75, perfect timing to partner Jeff Thomson against England Down Under when the speed pair destroyed the visiting team, Australia winning 4–1.

He played World Series Cricket for a couple of years and during that time worked diligently on his approach to the wicket and his delivery. If it was possible, he became an even better bowler in the technical sense. The famous 'caught Marsh bowled Lillee' dismissal appears on Test match scorecards 95 times. In 70 Tests, Lillee took 355 wickets at 23.92, with 23 hauls of five wickets. Lillee's best Test figures were 7/83 against the West Indies at the MCG in 1981.

But figures cannot tell of a bowler's strategy, the way a victim is stalked and finally put to the sword. If his body was a struggle out there – and it often was over his stellar career – Lillee called upon all his inner reserves and he often drove himself upward and onward by sheer willpower.

Wasim Akram

To me, cricketing heaven would be Wasim Akram and Shane Warne bowling in tandem to Victor Trumper and Don Bradman. As he came in to bowl, Wasim was a mirror image of Keith Miller, the great Australian all-rounder. While Wasim did not appear to make much use of his non-bowling arm, he excelled at the highest level with the ball – often on wickets which did not provide much in the way of pace and bounce. He could move the ball either way with the new or old ball. His efforts with the old ball were fabulous, for he learnt better than anyone how to rough one side of the ball in such a way that he could achieve what they call today 'reverse swing'.

This 'newfangled' reverse swing has been about for some 150 years. At the time WG Grace took guard, it was called 'going Irish', but it is more important in recent times because very few bowlers, among them England's James Anderson and South Africa's Dale Steyn, get the ball to swing in the conventional manner. In Lindwall's day, every side had a specialist swing bowler, so too in Lillee's day.

Once, Jeff Thomson wandered from the top of his mark to Lillee at mid-on and said: 'Hey, FOT, can you help? I'm holding the ball for an effing outswinger, but it is swinging the other way. How do I get the ball to move away from the bat?' FOT eyeballed him and said, 'Thommo, turn the ball around.'

Wasim had a style of his own. He'd shuffle to the crease, transfer his weight from back foot to front and, with an incredibly swift arm action, let fly with a searing bouncer, a late in-swinging yorker or a ball which he held back to lure the batsman into an indiscreet off or cover drive. The best Pakistani fast bowler since the halcyon days of Imran Khan, Wasim had the skill, drive and charisma to charm the cricket world.

He was a match-winner with the ball, but I recall him once batting with Imran and the pair both hit centuries on the

Adelaide Oval to thwart an Australian victory. Alas, all too seldom Wasim did excel with the bat, although he did hit a career-best 257 against Zimbabwe in Sheikhupura in 1996–97.

I have seen some fabulous left-arm pace bowlers in my time, including Alan Davidson, Ian Meckiff, Bruce Reid and Garry Sobers, but none of them at their top quite gets above Wasim. In 104 Tests, he took 414 wickets at 23.62, with 25 bags of five wickets and a career best of 7/119.

But mere figures never tell the full story. Wasim invariably worked his magic and brought the deadest of pitches to life. I can still see Steve Waugh shoulder arms to a wonderful inswinging yorker at the Adelaide Oval which would have scattered all three uprights. It was as palpably lbw as any in my memory.

Alan Davidson

Another gifted left-arm fast bowler was Alan Davidson, whose strength, smooth action and skill saw him complete a 44-Test career with 186 wickets at an average of 20.53. He bowled from a 15-pace approach and eased into a lovely side-on position just before delivery.

While he didn't have the bustle or rapid bowling arm of Wasim Akram, Davidson had a nice rhythm. Davo was immensely strong, with the shoulders of a colossus giving him super power behind every ball. He used his front arm to good effect and had the ability to swing in late to the right-handers or angle the ball away. Davo didn't aim to hit batsmen in the upper body with short-pitched deliveries, but knew if he could land a blow on the inner thigh it would count: 'There's not much padding in that area and if I could hit the fast bowlers there, they really did struggle to get into good rhythm when their time came to bowl.'

It was, of course, his ability to swing the ball which made his away angle so dangerous. So many of his Test victims were caught behind by the ever-reliable Wally Grout behind the stumps. Garry Sobers told me that Davo was 'lightning fast when the mood took him' and Keith Miller described Davo's bowling as 'deadly and devastating'.

His Test debut came against England in the first big match of the 1953 England tour. That Trent Bridge Test was drawn, but Davo could never forget his first victim – Len Hutton (43), caught by Benaud in the gully. He took some time to emerge from the shadow of Bill Johnston, one of the bowling stalwarts of the 1948 side. It was Johnston who showed him how to adjust his grip ever so slightly to achieve subtle changes of pace and swing. Davo recalled:

> *Bill was terrific to me on my first tour of England in 1953. I fielded mid-on to him in the county matches and he'd say to me, 'Ready, Davo?' For a beautifully disguised slower one, he pushed the ball back into his palm and he spun it in the orthodox fashion. The ball seemed to curve in and drop, thus creating a lot of mishits and scoops to me at mid-on.*

Davo was then just 21, and fielding to Johnston was an education in itself, for the old craftsman would talk of the batsman's weaknesses and implement his plan to dismiss him. 'Look at the way he moves forward and across, his weight going well to the off side. Get ready, Davo!'

The WACA Ground in Perth was the venue for the only hat-trick Davo ever got in first-class cricket. In the 1960s, sheep roamed in the outer, nibbling the grass under the old scoreboard, and Sheffield Shield matches didn't attract big crowds on any work day, even a Friday. I took a 'sickie' from my post at the Commonwealth Bank to watch Western Australia versus New South Wales in February 1963 on the very day Davo got his hat-trick. His first victim was John Parker, a solid right-hander, who lost his castle to an inswinging yorker. Next came the Western

Australia captain Barry Shepherd, a burly left-hander whose fighting qualities were admired throughout the cricket world.

Davo told me much later, as if the picture of Shep's dismissal was right there in his mind's eye:

> *I got him with a yorker that moved in late to knock out the leg stump. 'You bastard,' he said, but there was no malice in his words. I knew he was so disappointed to go early, because he carried the weight of the state on his shoulders whenever he batted for Western Australia. But he was gone, crossing with the new batsman, Russell Waugh, who walked briskly towards the centre, hell-bent on saving the team from the third wicket in three balls. I tried the inswing yorker and he came forward, getting an inside edge onto his pad, the ball ballooning to Norm O'Neill at silly point.*

Throughout his playing career and after, Davo has made a study of the bowling craft. He practised bowling deliveries with his fingers strategically placed along the seam, using his thumb as rudder. 'I think of the grip as a kangaroo – two fingers at the top of the ball are the kangaroo's legs, the thumb at the bottom of the ball is the kangaroo's tail. When a kangaroo wants to change direction, he stops, squats and his tail points the way. My thumb became the kangaroo's tail.' It was Davo's method and it worked for him.

He bowled with success against some of the greatest batsmen to play the game and must be rated up there with the great fast bowlers of any era.

Malcolm Marshall

Malcolm Marshall emerged from a pack of tremendous West Indies fast bowlers. As he started his international career, the likes of Andy Roberts. Joel Garner, Colin Croft and Michael

Holding were established, among others, to provide an armoury of fast-bowling riches for West Indies captains Clive Lloyd and Viv Richards to call upon. At one time, when the Windies were running amok in world cricket, one got the feeling that if a great fast bowler fell in a hole and broke a leg, another would suddenly appear, ready, willing and good enough to make his mark on the Test stage. With bowlers like Roberts, Garner and Holding, a batsman needed to be able to hook a bouncer and dig out a searing yorker. There was usually nothing in between. Any ball which was caressed between cover and mid-off would provoke a cold stare from the Windies captain.

Not so with Marshall. Here was a man who bustled to the crease with sparkling little steps, as if he was wearing dancing shoes. There was a twinkle and a bustle about him. Some purists thought his action too open. In fact, his action *was* open; Marshall was smooth in approach and action, but very chest-on at the point of delivery, yet he managed to get the ball to swing away late from the right-handers. In terms of pace, he seemed to always have a little in reserve – quite unsettling for a batsman because he knew that this man could take things – especially pace – to another level. His front-on action allowed him to bowl an outswinger or an inswinger from exactly the same position and that gave him an enormous advantage, because only top-class batsmen can negotiate controlled swing of that nature at genuine pace.

Like Wasim, he possessed a wickedly fast arm that took him at will from medium-fast to express. Marshall did not have the height of Garner or Holding; he was of average height with a broad chest and strong legs and, like Lindwall, his bouncer skidded at the batsman. Another very front-on fast bowler was South African Mike Procter. As much as the pair were different, they were the same in that they were at you at near express pace and their bouncer had your name written on it. Procter was deceptively quick and he had a quirky straight-down-the-pitch delivery and follow-through, and like Marshall was relentlessly at you. They were hunters. Procter played just seven Tests, but like Marshall he proved that you don't have to possess a copybook action to be a success.

Late in his career, Marshall developed a splendid leg-cutter and on an absolute SCG turner – the one on which Allan Border took 11 Test wickets – Marshall bowled 29 overs and took 5/31, a masterly piece of pace bowling on a wicket which provided nothing for any type of pace bowler. It was akin to a spinner getting a bag of wickets against a top-flight Test batting line-up on a greentop.

His strike rate of 46.7 was phenomenal. In 81 Tests, Marshall took 376 wickets at 20.94. He got 22 bags of five wickets, with a Test best of 7/22. His great courage was ever with him. His most astonishing and bravest performance came against England at Headingley, Leeds, in July 1984. Marshall had sustained a badly broken left thumb and was not expected to take any further part in the match. When the ninth West Indies wicket fell, some of the England players began to stroll towards the pavilion, but they stopped when they saw Marshall emerge from the shadows. He batted one-handed, enough to allow Larry Gomes to complete his century.

Then, with his left hand and wrist encased in pink plaster, Marshall demolished England with a take-no-prisoners 7/53, a feat which must have demoralised the England team. Could nothing stop this human dynamo? He excelled for the West Indies and for Hampshire, the county team he loved.

There was always something special about this bloke. I recall the 1979–80 season when Marshall rarely got a game for the Windies, but he was forever in the nets. Who is that whirlwind in the nets? We found out soon enough. He may well have been the greatest quick of them all.

Len Pascoe: white-line fever
from Bankstown

Born Leonard Stephen Durtanovich in Western Australia, Len Pascoe came to Sydney in the late 1950s. Off the field, he was one of nature's gentlemen, but once he crossed the boundary line he got white-line fever like no other cricketer who ever walked the Earth. Early in his career for New South Wales, Pascoe would charge in yelling all manner of threats. It was so funny, but your mood changed the instant he released the ball.

He grew up with Jeff Thomson and the pair of fast bowlers terrorised everyone at Punchbowl High School in the late 1960s. They bowled in tandem at school and for Bankstown. No club team wanted to face Thommo and Pascoe at Bankstown Oval. Sometimes they'd miss the start of a grade game, but within an hour of their arrival the opposition would be either battered, bruised and cowering, or bowled out, or both.

Alan Davidson, who had batted against Frank Tyson, said he was:

> ... *mighty quick, but I've seen all the fast bowlers since the war and Jeff Thomson, before he injured his shoulder, was 5 to 10 kilometres an hour faster than anyone.*
>
> *I saw Thommo as a 17-year-old bowling for Bankstown against Billy Watson and Warren Saunders. Watson was a great hooker. He belted Tyson all over the place when he scored a century against MCC in 1954–55, but this day against Thommo he struggled to get the bat up in time to*

fend off the ball. It was embarrassing to watch those blokes trying to survive.

As with Thommo, Len took some time to get recognition in New South Wales, seemingly because they did not conform to the 'rules'. They'd turn up to state squad training at the SCG in board shorts, totally ignore coach Peter Spence's insistence that they bowl at a target on the pitch and proceed to knock over stumps and their fellow players as if they were some sort of human hurricane. It would all happen quickly, then they were off seeking other amusements. The players at the nets would have a chuckle, but hope that Thomson and Pascoe didn't come back.

Lennie and Thommo were 'legends' in the Bankstown area, feared by all the opposition batsmen. During a period when Lennie was working for Bankstown Council, Thommo's fiancée was secretary to the Town Planner, Dave McInnes, who just happened to play A-grade cricket for Sydney University. One day Lennie was fielding at short leg and Thommo was about to bowl when Lennie rushed up to him and they exchanged words: 'I told Thommo that Dave McInnes, who was about to face the bowling, was taking his fiancée out. And I was telling Thommo all the things McInnes was doing to her. Thommo was trying to get back in her good books and I don't think he was too impressed with McInnes. Boy, did he give the batsman a working over.'

Thommo hit McInnes in the legs, the chest, the arms and the jaw. Eventually captain Dion Bourne sidled up to Thommo and said, 'Jeff, this is getting embarrassing. Can you just get him out?'

David Lord, a journalist and sports manager, handed the A-grade captaincy of the Mosman club to ex-England all-rounder Barry Knight. He could never forget what transpired that day at Bankstown Oval. Thommo and Pascoe had, as usual, terrorised the Mosman batsman and when Thommo bounced Johnny McKenzie, a number eleven who wore thick glasses, Knight saw red. When Thommo came to the crease, Knight demanded the ball. He ran in from a longer approach than normal, charged straight through the crease and when he was about 14 paces from Thommo he threw the ball with all the strength he could muster at the batsman's head.

Lennie Pascoe was at the non-striker's end. He grabbed his bat by the splice and, yelling 'you Pommie bastard!', started chasing Knight around Bankstown Oval.

Lord said it was always the same when Mosman played Bankstown:

You'd get in your car in a buoyant mood, for somehow this day would be different even though you knew you were about to face Thomson and Pascoe, the most dangerous pace attack in Australian club cricket. You'd be feeling on top of the world ... then you'd return looking like the old black telephone, blackened and bruised all down your left side from the pounding of that fearsome pair.

There was a Shield match at the SCG when Ian Chappell hit 150 in the first innings for South Australia, but got out hooking Pascoe for a duck second dig. Len took 7/18 in that second innings and when Ian walked into the New South Wales room to congratulate the opposition – especially Len – the big man was still very fired up. He jumped from the bench, yelling at the South Australia captain, and they ended up in the Members' Bar; Lennie had Chappelli by the throat and off the ground. Chappell was baiting Lennie, 'C'mon, mate, hit me.' When things calmed down, those in the packed bar gave the pair a standing ovation.

In 14 Test matches, Pascoe took 64 wickets at 26.06. His best performance was his 5/59 in the first innings of the Centenary Test at Lord's in 1980. His best mate Thommo was made twelfth man for the game and Lennie offered to feign a hamstring injury so he could play, but Thommo turned him down, saying he would pull out of the game if he did that.

Probably some of his best performances were in World Series Cricket. One time in the Caribbean with WSC, Ian Chappell accused Len of not training hard enough, intimating that Pascoe was more tourist than player. Len saw red. In the nets, he unleashed all his considerable power as Chappelli egged him on, cursing him, telling him that he was bowling half-rat-power. Cricket writer Phil Wilkins was behind the net and couldn't fathom the reason Chappelli was baiting Len, given the fast bowler was going over the front line by a mile and trying every ball to knock his captain's block off. 'It was the most amazing net session I've seen,' Wilkins said later. Chappelli hooked and cut and drove and never let up with his tirade against his fast bowler. Then, as he walked from the net, he eyeballed the steamed-up Pascoe, who stood with one arm on the net, sweat pouring from his face, and said: 'Thanks, Lennie, that's one of the best nets I've ever had.' The captain included Lennie in his team next day and Pascoe picked up four wickets.

Against the West Indies at Adelaide in 1980, Len reckoned on a ploy to upset Viv Richards. He'd deliberately go well over the front line to make the bouncer, which he knew would be called a no-ball, all the more menacing, and get the great man backing off, then employ the yorker. Viv wasn't pleased with the first ball.

The umpire Max O'Connell tried to step in, but Viv waved his hand, 'No, man. I can handle him.' Chewing his gum laconically, Viv waited for the next ball and slapped the top of his bat handle as Pascoe moved in. The attempted yorker was full and fast, but Viv gave it everything and the ball came back at Lennie at frightening pace, almost decapitating him as it passed on its way to the long-off boundary.

Lennie never changed the way he went about his business. He aimed to bowl fast and defeat the man with the bat. As he once said, 'A tiger never changes its spots.'

'Mr Mendis, do you wish to press charges?'

Former Sri Lanka opening batsman Sunil Wettimuny flew jet airliners for more than 30 years, experiencing storms, mechanical breakdowns and terrorist bomb threats. However, Wettimuny has never known fear like the time he faced the sheer pace of Jeff Thomson at The Oval on 11 June 1975. Australia won the toss and batted, belting the Sri Lankans to the tune of 5/328. Then captain Ian Chappell unleashed his fast men, Thommo and Dennis Lillee, on the Sri Lankans.

'We had never seen such pace and, with the way Thommo seemed to hide the ball behind his back, you couldn't pick it at all,' Wettimuny recalled. In his opening spell, Thomson hit Wettimuny twice in the inner thigh, and also delivered a cracking blow to the hipbone and a crunching hit to the ribcage.

Despite the aggression of Thommo and Lillee, the Sri Lankans batted bravely. We had thought our total of 328 was unbeatable, but our back-up bowlers were leaking runs too easily. I was going at six an over, Max Walker and Lillee at four an over, and Doug Walters at five. Only Thommo seemed able to restrict the scoring.

Chappell read the warning signs. At 2/150, the match was getting away from Australia. Duleep Mendis was batting stylishly on 32 when Chappell threw Thommo the ball for another spell. Poor Mendis. He played a couple of Thommo's deliveries, after which the fast man let fly. The ball rose from a good length like a striking cobra. Mendis tried valiantly to fend it off, but the ball hit him squarely on the forehead. He staggered and fell heavily to the crease.

Paul Rigby's immortal cartoon: 'Ashes to ashes, dust to dust, if Thommo don't get yer, Lillee must!'

There we were, peering down at the diminutive Mendis lying face down on the pitch. To our great relief, he stirred and turned over onto his back. His eyes were open, like saucers. Tears streamed down his face.

'How ya goin', mate?' someone asked.

Mendis opened his eyes wider, the tears continuing to stream down his face, and said, 'Oh, my god ... I am going now.'

Wettimuny, nursing his badly bruised ribs, watched his brave partner being carried off the ground on a stretcher. Thommo was booed by the crowd as the Sri Lanka captain, Anura Tennekoon, slowly walked to the crease.

'I took a long time to get to the wicket,' Tennekoon recalled. 'I stopped to see if Duleep was okay. Not a very pleasant situation, having to face Thomson after he had just knocked one of our men out cold.'

Wettimuny took a single off Walker's next over, which meant he was now facing Thommo again. 'I have this vivid image of what happened on Thommo's third ball of the over,' Tennekoon remembered. 'He hit Sunil flush on the instep and, as he hopped about in pain, Thomson threw down the wicket.'

Thommo saw things differently: 'I had the ball in my hand and, as the batsman hopped about, my teammates were urging me to throw down the stumps and run him out. I threw down the stumps at the batsman's end with Sunil miles out of his ground. I appealed and no other bastard among my teammates joined in on the appeal. They all stood about with their arms folded. I was done cold.'

He also remembers saying to Wettimuny, 'Look, mate, it's not broken. But if you face up to the next ball, it bloody well will be broken!'

After a lengthy delay, Wettimuny bravely stood up to face the next ball. It was an identical sandshoe crusher and screamed into his right instep, the exact spot where he had been hit the previous ball. This time he collapsed in agony and had to be carried off the ground on a stretcher. He was taken directly to join Mendis at nearby St Thomas' Hospital.

Wettimuny will never forget that day:

Never before or since did I know fear on a cricket field.
When I got to hospital, I discovered I had sustained a
hairline fracture of the rib, my right foot was broken, I had
a dreadful bruise on my inner thigh, my hip bone was
badly bruised and I was completely numb in my left leg.
I thought I was paralysed. The numbness stayed with me
for 12 hours.

A policeman who was not on duty at the World Cup game heard the tail-end of a radio report about two Sri Lankans being assaulted by an Australian cricketer at The Oval.

'Next morning, a policeman walked into my room,' Mendis recalled. 'He held his bobby's helmet under one arm and he asked, "Do you want to press charges against a Mr Jeff Thomson?"'

Mendis still marvels at Thommo's speed:

*I remember Sri Lankan players telling me later on of
the great pace of Imran Khan. Sure, Imran was a speed
merchant, but compared to Thommo, Imran came at you
at a gentle medium pace. If you go to the West Indies and
talk to the old fellows in the stands, they know the game
backwards and they have seen all the great fast bowlers –
Wes Hall, Charlie Griffith, Andy Roberts, Michael Holding,
Joel Garner, Curtly Ambrose – and when you ask them who
was the fastest of the lot, they will say, 'JR Thomson'.*

Thommo's legendary pace left its mark on many. Once, in
a Shield game, Thommo trapped Rick Darling lbw and the
batsman had to be carried off on a stretcher.

Pace like that concentrates the mind, as we learn from Mike
Brearley's words: 'Broken marriages, conflicts of loyalty, the
problems of everyday life, fall away as one faces up to Thomson.'

Jack Marsh – better than SF Barnes?

Long before Queensland Aboriginal fast bowler Eddie Gilbert knocked the bat out of Don Bradman's hand in 1931, another Indigenous speedster, Jack Marsh, was the champion bowler in New South Wales.

Test opening batsman Warren Bardsley said publicly in 1928, 'Jack Marsh was the best bowler I ever faced.' He added, 'Marsh was a tougher bowler to combat than SF Barnes, the great England bowler.' He also reckoned Marsh to be better than the all-rounder Monty Noble. Fate's cruel hand gave Noble the Test captaincy and 121 wickets at an average of 25.01, while Marsh was no-balled out of the game. Marsh was a black man and a black sportsman in the racist society of the early to mid-twentieth century had no hope of ever playing Test cricket for Australia.

Sadly, there are only scraps of information for us to use in coming up with some sort of idea about Jack Marsh's true ability.

In 1916, after news of Jack Marsh's untimely death, Australian cricket writer JC Davis (a good judge of a cricketer's skill) wrote this tribute to the fast bowler in the *Sydney Mail:*

> *Marsh possesses gifts like no other man in Australia – and*
> *probably no other bowler in the world – possesses: he*
> *curves the ball. He bowls a peculiar dropping ball and his*
> *break back on a perfect wicket is phenomenal for a bowler*
> *of his pace. Marsh could make the ball do stranger things*
> *in the air than any other bowler I saw.*

Jack Marsh was born to an Aboriginal woman on Yulgilbar Station at Baryulgil, on the Clarence River near Grafton. Jack and his brother Larry were exceptional runners and the station owner sponsored Jack and Larry to test their skill on the track in Sydney. They met up with the great Aboriginal sprinter Charlie Samuels at La Perouse and sprinted their way to track stardom between the years 1889 and 1895. The Marsh brothers competed in Sydney and Melbourne at all the big track meets.

Jack Marsh's talents went way beyond running; he was also a brilliant exponent of throwing the boomerang. Just as Charles Lawrence reckoned members of his 1868 Aboriginal cricket team might adapt their skills in footwork and throwing a boomerang to their bowling and batting, West Sydney cricket identity Alf Dent envisaged stardom for Marsh. If, as Dent reckoned, Marsh could make a boomerang 'talk', how good might he become at bowling a cricket ball. Marsh began with West Sydney in 1895.

Only an exceptional Aboriginal cricket talent could attract attention in the press of the day. In October 1895, Marsh featured in *Australian Cricket: A Weekly Record*:

> *We note with pleasure that J. Marsh has already taken 16 wickets for 44 runs for West Sydney in the second junior competition. For his club versus Adelphi, he secured 6/12, an excellent performance.*

In 1895, the Aboriginal people were 72 years away from getting the vote and there was a restrictive immigration policy in place known as the White Australia Policy, which became law at Federation in 1901. The policy not only stopped non-Europeans from entering Australia, it also further alienated the Indigenous Australians who had lived here for up to 100,000 years. One of the policy's strongest advocates, Alfred Deakin, became Australia's second Prime Minister in 1903.

By that time, Jack Marsh had already established himself in Sydney grade cricket. He played for the West Sydney and Marylebone clubs in the Moore Park competition in 1896. In 1897–98, Marsh played for South Sydney, taking 18 wickets at an average of 18.22. His 1898–99 summer in Sydney was not so successful, his 10 wickets coming at a modest 26.70 apiece. That moderate performance was significant because, if he'd had a bumper season that year, he might well have come under consideration to tour England with Australia in 1899. In those days, grade cricket was important, for the state and Test men played most matches and club performances counted.

In 1899–1900, he took 30 wickets for South Sydney at an average of 9.87. The following summer, he joined Sydney club, where he took 44 wickets at 11.75. Wickets flooded against his name: the year after, 58 wickets at 9.35; then 48 at 12.58; 50 at 11.65, until his modest 22 at 18.95 in his last summer of grade cricket. But Marsh played just four state matches for New South Wales, taking 24 wickets at an average of 22.37.

There seems little doubt that Marsh was a champion bowler, but with the White Australia Policy in place, how could a non-European represent Australia in a Test match? The black man in pre–World War I Australia was persona non grata. And the game of cricket does – or used to – provide an avenue to get rid of any bowler by simply branding him a chucker and having an umpire no-ball him out of the game.

In 1897, Marsh was bowling with his customary verve for South Sydney against Paddington on the SCG. One of the umpires, William Curran, caused a sensation by no-balling Marsh twice for throwing in his opening over. Marsh completed his second over by delivering underhand. Some of the wiseacres among the SCG members booed, because they thought Marsh's action fine and umpire Curran's action grossly unfair. However, the damage was done. Curran's no-balling of Marsh influenced others to oppose Marsh's advancement in the game.

Monty Noble scored an unbeaten century in that same match – ironic given that Noble's bowling was strikingly similar to Marsh's, and it was considered that only one bowler of the medium-pace variety was required for New South Wales, or for that matter the national side.

Jack Marsh was continually overlooked for state representation and received another setback in a state trial match. Playing for the State Colts versus New South Wales, Marsh first clean-bowled Noble with a ball which cut to the off, then he produced a magnificent outswinging off-cutter to knock Victor Trumper's leg stump out of the ground.

The ball swerved dramatically and late. Trumper was perfectly poised to execute his classic cover drive when the ball changed course completely, veering like a runaway colt. Instead of the delivery maintaining its away movement, upon pitching, the ball broke back alarmingly and found its way through the tiny gap between Trumper's bat and pad to hit the champion's leg stump. Trumper, then at the height of his powers, was clean-bowled by Marsh for one.

However, umpire William Curran, the man who had called Marsh for throwing in 1897, again called Marsh for what he considered an 'unfair' delivery and he announced that he intended to call Marsh again the next day.

On the morning of the third day, the *Sydney Morning Herald* commented:

> *Marsh, who was no-balled ... feels so confident that his delivery is fair, that he is prepared to have his arm so bandaged as to render it impossible to bend or jerk the elbow – which is generally accepted as constituting a throw. As a matter of fact, he has already demonstrated to some of the principal members of the Sydney Cricket Club that his delivery is absolutely fair. He caused a piece of wood to be tightly fixed along the arm, and bowled as fast as ever.*

> *Orders have been given for a splint for the arm, which will
> keep [it] absolutely rigid, and, if completed in time, will be
> worn for the balance of the eleven's innings.*

Umpire Curran claimed he was made to appear 'foolish' and
withdrew from the match. While Curran reckoned Marsh threw
the ball, every other umpire in Sydney grade cricket believed
Marsh's action to be completely fair. If Curran had it in for
Marsh, so too it seems did Monty Noble, for Noble voted against
Marsh's state inclusion in 1901. But he was outvoted by the other
two selectors, former Test player Tom Garrett and Ted Briscoe.

Marsh's first match was on the Adelaide Oval. He took 5/161
in South Australia's then record total of 575 and had no problem
with the umpires. Clem Hill, the only batsman to fathom Marsh's
disconcerting swing and cut, scored 365 not out.

Against Victoria, umpire Bob Crockett called Marsh three
times for throwing. Crockett mysteriously questioned Marsh's
'twist of the wrist', not his elbow, in explaining his decision to
call the Aboriginal bowler.

Then came the return game against South Australia at the
SCG in January 1901, where Marsh excelled, playing alongside
Victor Trumper. New South Wales scored 918 and won by an
innings and 605 runs. Jack Marsh took 5/34 off 16 overs in the
first innings, getting Clem Hill (55) and George Giffen (6), and
5/59 off 20 overs in the second dig. He again claimed Test left-
hander Hill (20).

The return match against Victoria at the SCG was to be played
over the Australia Day weekend of 1901. However, the death of
Queen Victoria saw cricket administrators postpone the match
a few days, to be played during the colony's week of mourning.
This proved to be the match in which officialdom effectively
kicked Marsh out of big cricket. In his first over, umpire Crockett
stunned the SCG crowd by no-balling Marsh three times. Marsh
was called a few more times but, despite the shock of his ordeal,

he managed to get through the defences of Warwick Armstrong and Peter McAlister to have Victoria tottering at 5/50. Victoria recovered to score 279 in its first innings, but poor Marsh was called no less than 19 times by his nemesis, Bob Crockett.

The crowd hurled a barrage of verbal abuse at Crockett, for they considered the umpire part of a conspiracy to keep Marsh out of the Test selectors' eye lest, horror upon horrors, they dare to pick a black man for Australia. There are claims that Marsh, in a fit of pique, deliberately threw three deliveries. Marsh allegedly hurled the ball at Frank Laver after the batsman had patted the ball back to him and Laver supposedly said, 'It's okay, Jack. There's plenty of times I've wanted to do the same thing.'

Jack Marsh never again played for New South Wales.

Upon Trumper's 1902 return to Australia from his greatest tour, a grand night was organised at the Sydney Town Hall for the Test hero. Among the 5000 people crammed into Town Hall, the NSW XI were special guests, including Jack Marsh. He was smartly dressed in a three-piece suit and when they were introduced he stood up to acknowledge the ovation. After waving his arms above his head, he bowed to each section of the audience and had the people in hysterics. No-one laughed louder at Jack Marsh's antics than Deakin, the man who had pushed so hard for the White Australia Policy. In 1868, the Aboriginal players in the team used to welcome the English batsmen who came to the crease with a collective whoop. Their enthusiasm was as infectious in 1868 as was Jack Marsh's love of the big stage in 1902.

The White Australia Policy was in full swing during the 1930s, when another Aboriginal fast bowler of class emerged, Eddie Gilbert. On 6 November 1931, Don Bradman faced the express speed of Gilbert. Queensland had been dismissed for a paltry 169 and New South Wales expected an easy path towards a substantial first-innings lead by the day's end. Wendell Bill fell for a duck and in walked Bradman, then at the zenith of his batting powers.

Bradman was intrigued by Gilbert's short approach, only a few paces. A mere slip of a man, weighing just 57 kilograms, Gilbert had long arms and was wiry, but his physique was nothing remarkable. Yet Gilbert was deceptively strong and he let the ball go as if it had been fired from a catapult. Bradman fended at the first ball, which lifted quickly to about chest height and slipped down leg side.

Gilbert's second ball caused Bradman to thrust his bat at the rearing delivery. It struck with such force that Bradman's bat was knocked clean from his grasp. No other bowler had ever done that to Bradman. The crowd gasped in amazement, as did Jack Fingleton, the batsman at the other end. Bradman played and missed the next Gilbert delivery, but succeeded in getting a touch to the fifth ball and was caught behind for a duck.

Because of his short approach to the wicket, the consensus among players and officials was that Gilbert simply 'had to be' a chucker. Years after Bradman got what he at the time described as 'the luckiest duck I ever got', he said:

> *That day, he was faster than Larwood at his peak. From the pavilion his bowling looked fair. But in the middle his action was suspect. He jerked the ball and only delivered it from a very short approach. It's very hard that way to generate such speed with a legitimate delivery.*

In the 1970s along came Jeff Thomson, who, like Gilbert, shuffled up to the crease and went whang. And Thommo was mighty quick. If the fast men of today bowl their very fastest deliveries at 160 kilometres per hour, that was Thommo's cruising speed. Gilbert and Thommo were very similar in that they had a short approach to the crease, but they both locked their front leg, so that their delivery was high and the ball was propelled as if fired by a catapult. They both delivered the ball from the highest position possible.

As with Jack Marsh, Eddie Gilbert was literally 'thrown' out of the game by an umpire. In a Queensland versus Victoria match at the MCG, umpire Andy Barlow no-balled Gilbert 11 times for throwing. At the start of the 1936–37 season, the Queensland Cricket Association wrote an amazing letter to the Queensland Protector of Aborigines:

> *At the meeting of the Executive Committee held last evening, the matter of Eddie Gilbert was fully discussed and as it was unlikely that he would be chosen for a Representative team this season, it was decided with your concurrence, to arrange for Gilbert to [return to] the settlement next week. With regard to the cricketing clothes bought for Gilbert, it is asked that arrangements be made for these to be laundered at the Association's expense and delivery of the laundered clothes to be made to this office.*

Eddie Gilbert returned to Barambah (now Cherbourg) and in 1948 was placed in protective custody in a mental asylum at Wolston Park, near Brisbane. Attempts were made to free Gilbert, but the Queensland Protector of Aborigines stated that he would only agree to release Gilbert from the asylum if Gilbert found 'suitable employment with a suitable person'. It was, of course, impossible for Gilbert to find work outside the asylum because he was forbidden to leave the place at any time, day or night. Gilbert died a broken man in 1978.

After the triumphant return of Joe Darling's 1902 Australian team, Jack Marsh took 58 wickets at an average of 9.35 apiece in the Sydney grade competition. Marsh once sketched a plan of the field and drew the places where his fielders would be standing. Then he went out to do battle with Noble, Trumper and Syd Gregory. Marsh had already explained to a friend how he would dismiss each of those eminent players. His plan worked exactly as he envisaged it.

While Marsh was hounded out of state cricket, no umpire other than the biased Curran, and Bob Crockett, objected to his action. But in the wake of his disappointment, Marsh returned to Bathurst. He bowled magnificently against the visiting England team in the summer of 1903–04, taking 5/15 against them for the Bathurst XV.

England captain Pelham Warner, later a leading Marylebone Cricket Club administrator at Lord's, said at the time that, 'Marsh's action is perfectly legal and Marsh is the best bowler in the world.'

Marsh was, according to Warner, as good as SF Barnes, the bowler many claim to be the greatest of all time.

The New South Wales and Test all-rounder Monty Noble reckoned Marsh was a 'chucker' and 'did not have class enough for representative matches'.

That comment from Noble came months before Warner described Marsh as the 'best in the world'.

Marsh had no hope in a society where Aboriginals didn't have the right to vote and were generally considered second-class. Even the game of cricket itself was deemed only suitable for 'Anglo-Saxons'. This sentence appeared in the *Queensland Times* in 1905: 'Cricket is our ONE national game – the ONE pastime we have all to ourselves … cricket is essentially and particularly the British game. It is suited to the genius of the Anglo-Saxon race, and, it would seem, to no other.'

Jack Marsh was never given his due as one of the great bowlers of all time. Soon after his brilliant spell against Warner's England team, Marsh fell on hard times and joined a travelling Royal Hippodrome, appearing on the same star billing as strongmen, martial arts exponents and wrestlers. In 1909, he was charged with attacking the owner of a grog shop.

In 1916, he was kicked and beaten in a street in Orange, in country New South Wales. Marsh was so badly beaten he couldn't crawl out of the gutter where his attackers had left him and died of his horrific chest and head injuries. Two men – John Hewitt and Walter Stone – were charged with manslaughter over Marsh's death, even though evidence pointed to Marsh's skull having been fractured by 'the toe of a boot' and they should have faced a murder charge. Both were acquitted. Judge Bevan summed up: 'As far as the kicking was concerned, Marsh might have deserved it because he had been offensive.'

And it was the best part of a century before a man of Aboriginal heritage, Jason Gillespie, was picked in the Australian Test team. Gillespie's paternal great-grandfather was a warrior of the Kamilaroi, one of the largest groups of Aboriginal people in eastern Australia.

The Battle of Bowral

In the summer of 1925–26, two youngsters starred in what became known as The Battle of Bowral. Bowral's 16-year-old sensation Don Bradman would pit his batting skills against the best bowler in the Southern Highlands, Wingello's spin king Bill O'Reilly, 19. In 1988, over a beer at the Pineapple Hotel, near the Gabba, Bill told me the story, which he had also done in his usual colourful prose in his 1985 book, *Tiger: 60 years of cricket*.

In 1925, he had been at Sydney Teachers' College and told fellow student Len Kelsey that after graduating he intended to spend a few weeks in the holidays playing for Wingello in the Southern Tablelands cricket competition. Kelsey warned his mate to keep a wary eye open for a young batsman named Don Bradman, whom he knew as a fellow pupil at Bowral High School, and who had been scoring runs like they were going out of fashion. Bill took Kelsey's words with a grain of salt; the efforts of some pint-sized kid didn't impress him.

One Saturday in December 1925, he boarded a train at Sydney's Central Station for Goulburn. The train came to a halt at Bowral and Bill heard his name being called by the stationmaster: 'Get your bag, O'Reilly, and get off the train!' He then explained, 'We're all down here to play Bowral this afternoon and you're going to get the new ball.' He told Bill that everything had been arranged: Bill's mum had packed all his cricket clothes and he would be taken to the ground straight from the railway station.

Bill clambered aboard a 1918-vintage T-Model Ford truck, where those already seated on the wooden benches briefed him fully on the growing reputation of a kid named Don Bradman.

It was, they said, because of Bradman's recent great form that they had decided on the absolute necessity of having Bill O'Reilly leading the Wingello attack. The truck duly arrived at the ground and the players dressed for the match in the shade of a couple of gum trees near the grandstand.

Bowral won the toss and batted and Bill O'Reilly got the new ball, not because Bill was fearsomely fast, but because he could consistently bowl at the stumps and if a batsman played and missed he was invariably clean-bowled, a fate which befell one of the Bowral openers midway through the third over of the match.

Bill eyed the incoming batsman, a diminutive figure wearing pads which were clearly too big for him, as he struggled to take normal steps. If the boy's pads looked too big, his bat seemed far too small and insignificant. But after a few balls Bill, whose ambitions in life embraced the ideas of becoming a schoolteacher and a good cricketer, realised that he had just confronted his first 'problem child'. This kid Bradman could bat.

Wingello's skipper, Selby Jeffrey, had been one of the first Anzacs to wade ashore at Gallipoli in 1915 and was the man who had arranged for O'Reilly to play. He always fielded at first slip and there was a good reason for this. Selby wore a sparkling white shirt, immaculate duck trousers and a black waistcoat, worn unbuttoned, over his shirt. The waistcoat was essential because it held his big-bowled bent-stemmed Captain Petersen pipe, his tobacco pouch, which fitted snugly into one pocket, with the tin box of matches in the bottom pocket and a penknife for cutting his plug of tobacco. It would have been hopeless for Selby to field in any other position than slip, because immediately he got out of the slowest of canters, his smoking paraphernalia would have been scattered in all directions.

O'Reilly reckoned he had a slice of bad luck that day, because he had Bradman dropped twice before he had scored 30. O'Reilly got a ball to turn and bite; the ball lifted awkwardly and Bradman, in his attempt to fend if off, edged the ball straight to Selby Jeffrey at slip. The ball came gently at waist level, but struck Selby in the solar plexus at the precise moment both Selby's hands were otherwise occupied. He was lighting his pipe!

'Sorry, Bill,' waved a cheery Selby. A few overs later, Selby turfed another ball off the edge of Bradman's bat. O'Reilly was again none too pleased as he watched his captain clutch vainly at the ball as it disappeared into a cloud of pipe smoke. The boy Bradman rode his luck and belted the Wingello attack into submission. Bill wondered where this mere slip of a kid hid the power of his strokeplay. On half a dozen occasions, Bradman hit the ball over the fence and at the end of the day's play he was 234 not out.

There wasn't much chat on the 30-mile ride home to Wingello in the back of the old truck. Bill was tossing up in his mind whether he should quit cricket and follow a career in tennis. He'd spent two years running for Botany Harriers, so athletics was another option. But as the new week unfolded and O'Reilly considered how he might tackle Bradman when they resumed hostilities the following Saturday, he realised that his love of the game of cricket was too great to give up in the face of one humiliating thrashing. That the belting came from a mere slip of a schoolboy hurt, but he was determined to show the boy who was boss the next week.

Bill's pride had been dented. He yearned to make amends. Every day he bowled at a gate in the family back garden. He had all week to reflect on his bowling and Bradman's dominance. Just how the contest panned out you will learn from my poem:

The Battle of Bowral
The Battle of Bowral in '25
Saw Bradman the boy come alive.
His first joust with Tiger, Goliath of spin,
200 not out, Don Bradman must win.
At 30 a leg-break caught the Don's bat,
An edged chance to slip; a drop and a drat.

Young Don escaped the chance of the flight:
First slip, the skipper, was lighting his pipe!
A flurry of fours and sixes to boot,
O'Reilly at day's end a sorry young coot.
The Don stood supreme, the hint of a grin;
Bill's belly on fire, his head in a spin.
Don so fluent, so strong and so keen,
Tiger's red hair stood out from his spleen.
The cocky young bat from Bowral had done
More than enough to ensure they had won.
At two-thirty-four, the Don left the field,
Raging O'Reilly refusing to yield.
All through the week Bill bowled at a gate,
Bradman the boy made the Tiger irate.
O'Reilly the demon had never been caned,
Don hammered Big Red, he cannot be blamed.
For Spin King O'Reilly to fume and to scheme,
The Don, bowled O'Reilly: 'Impossible dream?'
Fuming O'Reilly bowled full steam ahead,
He dreamed of revenge as he tossed in his bed.
Seven days of pure hell, no fitting reward,
For Spin King O'Reilly put to the sword.
Second day of the match yet to be played,
O'Reilly's revenge: no more to be flayed.
Townsfolk in droves arrived just in time
To see the young warriors: a battle sublime.
They saw O'Reilly bowl that first spinning ball,
Young Don tapped his bat, a wicket must fall.
Arms wheeling away in the hot noon sun,
O'Reilly moved in; his homework was done.
Don eyed with suspicion that O'Reilly first ball,
His footwork so keen, his score so tall.
The ball fairly buzzed, an ace and a trump,
It pitched leg perfect and hit the off stump!

The Tiger and the Fox

Between 1918 and 1939, Bill O'Reilly and Clarrie Grimmett reigned supreme as the greatest spin-bowling partnership of the age, and were arguably the best in Test history. O'Reilly, the Tiger, and Grimmett, the Fox, were both leg-spinners but they were as different in their approach to their art as were Trumper and Bradman in the way they went about their batting.

With arms and legs flailing in the breeze, O'Reilly stormed up to the crease with steam coming out of his ears. He was all-out aggression and he called himself a boots'n'all competitor. O'Reilly first came up against Bradman in the summer of the 1925–26 season (as told in 'The Battle of Bowral' in the previous chapter).

O'Reilly the wordsmith was inspired to write after meeting Henry Lawson in 1914, introduced by his father outside a pub near where now stands the Milsons Point Railway Station. Bill was nine, Bradman was six and Victor Trumper was still turning out for Gordon in Sydney grade cricket. In retirement from cricket, Bill would cover Test matches throughout Australia for the *Sydney Morning Herald* and *The Age*.

Bill O'Reilly was a tangible link to the cradle of cricket in Australia. One day in the 1920s, he was bowling his heart out in his usual fashion before the New South Wales selectors when the great old leg-spinner Arthur Mailey approached him: 'You must change that grip, son. Otherwise, I'm afraid, you'll never do any good at the game.'

Young Bill was hurt, but didn't show it. He thanked Mailey for the advice and said resolutely: 'I think I'll continue with this grip, thank you, Mr Mailey.'

'Good on yer, sonny. They tried to change me, yer know. Follow yer own instincts.' The voice came from a little, rugged-faced man with gnarled hands – none other than Charles Thomas Biass (the Terror) Turner. It was the same CTB Turner who was a legend in Australian cricket in the 1880s, the man who took 993 first-class wickets at just 14.34 runs apiece.

At the age of 85, O'Reilly told me with his typical defiance: 'I'd give my left arm to have a crack at Dean Jones! He stands with his legs three feet apart. He's got to be a real chance. I'd have liked to have bowled at Jones about every second Friday.' I suspect Bill might have fancied himself in dismissing the likes of Viv Richards and other West Indians, few of whom could fathom even ordinary leg-spinners.

Don Bradman reckoned O'Reilly was the best bowler of any type he ever saw or played against. He said O'Reilly had the ability to bowl a leg-break of near medium pace to consistently pitch round leg stump and turn to either hit the outside edge or take the top of off stump. Bradman wrote to me in 1989:

Bill also bowled a magnificent Bosey [wrong'un or googly] which was hard to pick and which he aimed at middle and leg stumps. It was fractionally slower than his leg-break and usually dropped a little in flight and 'sat up' to entice a catch to one of his two short leg fieldsmen. These two deliveries, combined with great accuracy and unrelenting hostility, were enough to test the greatest of batsmen, particularly as his leg-break was bowled at medium pace – quicker than the normal run of slow bowlers – making it extremely difficult for a batsman to use his feet as a counter-measure. Bill will always remain in my book the greatest of all.

Clarrie Grimmett was born in 1891, and round about the time O'Reilly came into this world in 1905, Clarrie tore a hole in his new blue suit clambering over the barbed wire at Wellington's Basin Reserve to watch Victor Trumper hit a famous hundred. In 1914, Clarrie sailed into Sydney from his native New Zealand seeking cricket fame, but it wasn't until after a long stint in Sydney, more fruitless years in Melbourne, and then a last throw of the dice in Adelaide that he found his haven for an unwanted bowler and the staging post for England.

It was in the Adelaide Test match of 1931–32 against South Africa that the Tiger and the Fox first joined forces. Clarrie had begun his Test career against England at the SCG in 1925, taking a match haul of 11/82 (5/45 and 6/37), and he had starred in Australian tours of England in 1926 and 1930. In Adelaide for the Tiger's debut Test match, Grimmett was the master spinner and O'Reilly the apprentice. That game was a triumph for Don Bradman, who scored 299 not out, and Clarrie Grimmett, who bagged match figures of 14/199.

Bill O'Reilly was amazed by the way Grimmett bowled: 'I learned a great deal watching Grum [the nickname Bill always used for his old spinning mate] wheel away. I watched him like a hawk. He was completely in control. His subtle change of pace impressed me greatly.' The pair played two Tests that series and a couple in the Bodyline series of 1932–33, before O'Reilly took over as Australia's number one spinner and Grimmett was dropped. However, the pair were back in harness for the 1934 tour of England – the Tiger's first England tour, Grimmett's third.

Here's how O'Reilly describes his partnership with Grimmett in 1934:

It was on that tour that we had all the verbal bouquets in the cricket world thrown at us as one of the greatest spin combinations Test cricket had seen. Bowling tightly and keeping the batsmen unremittingly on the defensive, we

Above: The 'Tiger', Bill O'Reilly.
Left: Clarrie Grimmett in full flight.

collected 53 [Grimmett 25, O'Reilly 28] of the 73 English wickets that fell that summer.

Each of us collected more than 100 wickets on tour and it would have needed a brave, or demented, Australian at that time to suggest that Grimmett's career was almost ended.

With Grum at the other end I knew full well that no batsman would be allowed the slightest respite. We were fortunate in that our styles supplemented each other. Grum loved to bowl into the wind, which gave him an opportunity to use wind resistance as an important adjunct to his schemes regarding direction. He had no illusions about the ball 'dropping' as we hear so often these days before its arrival at the batsman's proposed point of contact. To him that was balderdash. In fact, he always loved to hear

people making up verbal explanations for the suspected
trickery that had brought a batsman's downfall. If a
batsman had thought the ball had dropped all well and
good. Grimmett himself knew that it was simply change
of pace that had made the batsman think that such an
impossibility had happened.

O'Reilly was not alone in his reckoning that he and Grimmett
bowled in perfect harmony, each with a careful eye for the other.
O'Reilly was all-out aggression, whereas Grimmett was steady
and patient. While they possessed a stock ball which turned
from the leg, O'Reilly's deliveries came at a pace: his leg-break
spat like a striking cobra and his wrong'un reared at the chest
of the batsman. For any batsman in combat with the Tiger there
was no respite, no place to hide. In contrast, the Tiger's spin
mate, the Fox, wheeled away in silence. He was like the wicket
spider, spinning a web of doom. While he had a slightly lower
strike rate than O'Reilly, sometimes it took longer for Grimmett
to snare his victim. Perhaps the times he spun against the
weaker sides, such as the West Indies and South Africa, he
cashed in big time and boosted his strike rate considerably.

Despite their vastly different styles and methods of attack
they were both deadly foes. A man for Grimmett caught at
cover was just as out as a man who lost his off stump by a ball
pitching leg and hitting the top of off stump from O'Reilly.

Test bowling record

	TESTS	BALLS	RUNS	WKTS	AVG	B/B	BBM	S/R	5W	10W
Grimmett	37	14513	5231	216	24.21	7/40	14/199	67.1	21	7
O'Reilly	27	10024	3254	144	22.59	7/54	11/129	69.6	11	3

Grimmett and O'Reilly were much-feared bowlers in Australian
cricket and throughout the cricket world. They played lots of
Sheffield Shield cricket and club cricket, something which sadly

eludes today's top cricketers. The tight schedule today precludes our top men playing grade cricket and there are far more Test matches played in the modern era.

In 1991, Don Bradman wrote to me about Grimmett:

I always classified Clarrie Grimmett as the best of the genuine slow leg-spinners (I exclude Bill O'Reilly because, as you say, he was not really a slow leggie) and what made him the best, in my opinion, was his accuracy. Arthur Mailey spun the ball more – so did [Chuck] Fleetwood-Smith and both of them bowled a better wrong'un, but they also bowled many loose balls. I think Mailey's Bosey [wrong'un] was the hardest of all to pick.

Clarrie's wrong'un was in fact easy to see. He telegraphed it and he bowled very few of them. His stock-in-trade was the leg-spinner with just enough turn on it, plus a really good top-spin delivery and a good flipper (which he cultivated late in life). I saw Clarrie in one match take the ball after some light rain when the ball was greasy and hard to hold, yet he reeled off five maidens without a loose ball. His control was remarkable.

Grimmett invented the flipper, which Shane Warne at the height of his brilliant career bowled so well. Like Grimmett, Warne didn't have a great wrong'un, but he possessed a terrific stock leg-break and a stunning top-spinner. When O'Reilly asked SF Barnes where he placed his short leg for the wrong'un, Barnes replied: 'Never bowled the Bosey [wrong'un] ... Didn't need one.'

Warne played 145 Tests and took 708 wickets. Imagine if Grimmett and O'Reilly had played the same number of Tests as Warne. At the rate per Test they took their wickets, Grimmett would have snared 846 wickets and O'Reilly 770.

But supposing Grimmett had bowled the same number of balls as Warne – 40,705 – at his own 67.1 strike rate, he would have only 606 wickets, not 846 or Warne's 708. Conversely, if Warne had bowled as many balls as Grimmett, he would have taken 253 wickets, compared to Grimmett's 216. Or if he'd bowled O'Reilly's 10,024 balls, he would have taken 174 wickets compared to O'Reilly's 144.

How would Grimmett and O'Reilly bowling at their peak fare against the likes of Sachin Tendulkar, Brian Lara and Joe Root? Would Warne have dominated batsmen such as Wally Hammond, Frank Woolley or Len Hutton, as he did most batsmen of his era?

In reality, Grimmett played just 37 Tests and O'Reilly 27, but what an impact they had on world cricket. It is virtually impossible to compare spinners from different eras, although most would agree that the three best leg-spinners in Test cricket were Grimmett, O'Reilly and Warne.

Swann in full flight

Graeme Swann's brilliant career in Test cricket ended abruptly on 21 December 2013. He quit midway through the Ashes summer of 2013–14.

A few weeks before he announced his retirement, I met with Swann at the England team hotel in Adelaide, where he told me that his elbow was giving him grief and that he was not far away from giving the game away. In the wake of a terrific career, which netted him 259 Test wickets at 29.96, Swanny decided to call it quits because he just could not do physically what his mind was urging he must do to succeed.

Although he didn't harvest wickets in the same way he had in previous Ashes series in England, for a time during Australia's second innings in Perth his bowling was back to the Swann of old: fiercely spun balls complemented by an acutely dipping arc.

This was always Swann at his best. He spun to confuse and befuddle. And confuse the brilliant David Warner he did that torturously hot afternoon in Perth. Warner made a quick-fire 112, but Swann confused him a couple of times and should have had the left-hander out cheaply but for some deplorable keeping by Matt Prior. Two stumpings were missed off Swann that afternoon and he frustratingly wasn't rewarded in the shape of well-earned wickets.

Through his career, Swann bowled with excellent rhythm and his strategy was always to take wickets. Shane Warne admired Swann because of his attacking attitude. Swann could dry up an end, but it was never done by bowling flat, quickish offies as we see from other less-talented off-spinners. There were times when Swann bowled a little too straight, that is, he sometimes operated to a right-hander on a line of off to middle turning down the leg side.

I first saw Swann when he was in Adelaide with the England Cricket Academy. The then academy head Rod Marsh asked me to work with Swann, Worcestershire offie Gareth Batty and Northamptonshire's Monty Panesar. Out of that trio of budding England spinners, Swann was easily the most talented. Unlike Panesar, who never seemed to improve, Swann was like a sponge, soaking up spin knowhow, and he bowled his heart out.

It was probably round the time when Nasser Hussain was saying that any off-spinner of that time without the *doosra* would never make it at the highest level. Hussain's words were nonsense. Swann didn't need the *doosra* because he had all that was required in variety to defeat the best of batsmen. When I played A-grade for Mount Lawley club in Western Australia, I was the number seven man to get a bowl, because most spin was handled by Ron Frankish, a quickish off-spinner who had the *doosra* before the word was coined. Ron, as with all the rest in later years, had to bend and straighten his arm to deliver it. In those days, we called it a 'chuck'.

The *doosra* was not, in fact, a delivery for Swann. All off-spinners know full well that you have to bend and straighten your elbow to achieve that particular ball and some, like Swann, refuse to go down that track. Swann turned out to be the world's best off-spinner without the 'other one'.

He did, however, have a far better straight-on ball than most finger-spinners – the square-spinner. I showed Swann this ball, having already shown it to Daniel Vettori, who picked it up immediately. As with Vettori, the young Graeme Swann was intelligent and he too cottoned on straight away.

The ball is spun square and looks from the batsman's perspective like an off-break that is spinning, but not hard-spun, and his first instinct is to look for a ball that turns from the off. In fact, the square-spinner reacts just like a leg-spinner who releases the ball out of the front of his hand. Swann calls the square-spinner his 'flying saucer ball'. When released out of the hand, the ball rotates around the horizontal axis and upon pitching it tends to skid straight on.

Nathan Lyon's spin-bowling mentor, John Davison, could bowl this ball; I know because I showed him and he showed Lyon, who can bowl it pretty well. Swann used to knock over Marcus North with this ball and, in the 2013 Lord's Test, Chris Rogers let a ball from Swann go in the second innings. Much to his horror, the perfectly released square-spinner pitched on the line of off stump and crashed into off stump.

Swann seemed to revel against the left-handers. When he operated against the likes of Phil Hughes and Usman Khawaja in England he was like a wicket spider weaving a web over them, reducing their footwork to that of a man wearing gumboots trying to make his way through a six-inch-high sea of mud. Against the wiles of Swann those two left-handers looked completely out of their depth.

In his final couple of Tests, Swann was nowhere near his best. He was inconsistent, even being clouted to all parts by the likes of Warner and Mitchell Johnson, players who usually had to fight for survival against him.

The Australians claimed that their plan to attack Swann was the key to his poor wicket haul in the first three Tests in the summer of 2013–14. That was not the case at all. It was all due to his pain-racked elbow. Some 27 pieces of bone were taken from his right elbow in April 2013 and for a while after the operation Swann was in good spirits and the arm 'felt terrific'. But it became increasingly worse and, while he had hoped he might last the Australian tour, Swanny made a decision to retire out of big cricket immediately.

My mind always goes back to the days in the early 2000s when I coached him. I also had the odd session with Swann when

I coached at the England Cricket Academy at Loughborough. It was there in 2003 that I delivered a course on spin bowling for budding ECB Level Three coaches.

Over the years, Swanny and I have kept in regular touch via email. He told me a few months after he had retired:

I loved every minute of my test career. Coming in at a time when finger spin was seen as such a defensive, negative tool I was always sceptical about how far I could go attacking as much as possible, especially in a four-man attack. I'm glad I stuck to my guns and had guys like you watching out for me when things slipped in my technique.

It has been no big deal – just an old spinner mentioning things I might have seen with his action or his field placements.

His England captain, Andrew Strauss, once had a man on the point boundary for Swann and I had to stress how wrong that was for the off-spinner, because it sent a negative message to the opposition: 'I've got a man on the fence because I don't want to be cut for four.' That happened in Brisbane in 2010–11, but after we spoke about it on the eve of the Adelaide Test, Swann got his way and persuaded Strauss to bring the man up, saving one at point, and picked up a bag of wickets to complement Kevin Pietersen's double hundred.

He was comfortable with Strauss's captaincy, but not so with Alastair Cook who, he said, would threaten to take him out of the attack if he conceded more than 1 four in any over. Some of Cook's field placements for Swann in Australia in that last Ashes series were defensive in the extreme and the Australian players took so many easy singles under no pressure whatsoever. Cook's captaincy didn't help the offie, who was having enough trouble getting through his overs.

When in full flight, Swann was easily the best England spin bowler I've seen since Jim Laker. He could do a great job on slow turners that he encountered in England and India and on hard-baked tracks in Australia and South Africa. Apart from his class off-break bowling, Swann was a brilliant slip fieldsman and a very useful down-the-list batsman.

Swanny knew the value in a spinner doing a good job. That might mean building pressure from one end while the others got the wickets. He also knew how annoying it was to read some cricket writers who weren't in touch with the game sufficiently to know a good spell from a bad one. The only 'good' spell to these people is one which brings the bowler a bunch of wickets.

On my list of all-time off-spinners I have Graeme Swann at number three. India's Erapalli Prasanna I have as my best, with Jim Laker number two.

Swanny has a great sense of humour and every spinner needs that. Laker perhaps summed it up best. He took all 10 wickets in the second innings at Manchester in 1956 to make it a total of 19/90 for the match. After Frank Tyson took the first Australian wicket in the next Test, he quipped from gully: 'Got *nowt* to play for now!'

Swanny revealed his keen sense of humour in the wake of a run-in with the law. In April 2010, after a party, he was driving in West Bridgford, Nottingham, when he was arrested after providing a positive breath test. A few months later, he appeared before a magistrate and explained that he had been on his way to find a hardware shop to purchase screwdrivers in order to rescue his cat, which had become trapped under the floorboards. There were several adjournments due to his cricket commitments before he was finally cleared on the grounds that the blood sample could no longer be used in evidence. I can imagine Swanny telling his cat story deadpan.

It is sad that we will never again see Graeme Swann bowl for England. In full flight, he was brilliant. Well done, Swanny. A career well played.

Chuckers? What chuckers?
Is world cricket in denial?

Queen Victoria was barely three years old when there was a near-revolution at Lord's Cricket Ground. On 15 July 1822, John Willes dared to bowl round-arm for Kent against the Marylebone Cricket Club (MCC) on the famous ground and he was duly no-balled for an illegal action. Willes was outraged. He threw the ball down, mounted his horse and rode like the clappers through St John's Wood, never to play in a major match again.

The popular theory is that his round-armers came about when his sister, Christina Willes, was bowling to him in their Kentish garden and she found it impossible to bowl underarm, the legal bowling of the day, because of the voluminous skirts that were in vogue in the early part of the nineteenth century.

While Willes's action at Lord's that day found him lost to the game he loved, he had really started something. Within a few years, round-arm bowling became the norm.

However, 'Silver Billy' Beldham claimed that Willes had not invented the style, but had, as it were, 'revived what was forgotten or something new to the young people'. Beldam maintained that 'jerking', a quaint name for chucking, had plagued the game of cricket in the 1780s and it was soon outlawed by the Hambledon Club, the cradle of cricket at Broadhalfpenny Down, the historic cricket ground in Hampshire.

If 'jerking' or chucking was banned all those years ago, why is it tolerated by the International Cricket Council (ICC) today?

Chucking is undoubtedly a form of cheating. It is considered a terrible outrage by the majority of cricketers, who expect the game at every level to be beyond reproach.

Cricket had the odd chucker over the years, but umpires dealt with them. For most of cricket history, the umpires were in control and if they thought a bowler chucked the ball, they called 'no-ball'. It was part of cricket's order of things and it went smoothly for more than a century. Many of those bowlers who were called for chucking became pariahs.

In the 1960s, it was claimed that West Indian fast bowler Charlie Griffith threw the ball when bowling bouncers. Indian opener Nari Contractor had his skull cracked by a Griffith short-pitched ball in 1962. For six days, Contractor lay unconscious in a hospital bed, requiring two operations to remove blood clots in his brain. Thankfully, he survived. There were no helmets in those days and taking your eyes off the ball when a fast bowler was in operation was potentially a fatal mistake.

England's Tony Lock, a brilliant left-arm spinner, allegedly threw his quicker ball and he was indeed called for chucking. To his credit, Lock worked tirelessly to modify his action and late in his career he became a great mentor as captain of Western Australia. He was to take 302 Sheffield Shield wickets for Western Australia, at an average of 23.

In the summer of 1966–67, I was twelfth man for Western Australia against New South Wales at the WACA Ground in Perth. Twice I was fielding when Lock was bowling to the brilliant Norm O'Neill. In those days, there were eight-ball overs. Lock's first seven deliveries were driven at bullet velocity to me at mid-off. Last ball of the over, Lock let his old 'special' go. It swung late and yorked O'Neill. In the second innings, exactly the same thing happened.

After play, Lock waltzed into the visitors' dressing-room and O'Neill yelled: 'Hey, Lockie, you threw that one today. And you chucked me out in the first dig as well.'

Lock threw back his head and roared.

I was in the same spot in both innings, standing at mid-off, just a few metres from where Lock released the ball, and I thought Lock threw the ball on both occasions.

O'Neill again challenged him in a good-natured way, saying, 'C'mon Lockie I knew you chucked it, both times.'

'Well, Normie old son,' he said with a stammer, 'I ... I m-might have done ... chucked it. Let's have a beer!'

Many of the bowlers allegedly branded as chuckers were spinners, but the most controversial spinner of them all was the man who has taken the most Test wickets (800) of all time, Sri Lanka's off-spinner Muttiah Muralitharan.

When I first set eyes on Murali, I was certain that he threw, not just the *doosra*, but every single ball. And throughout his career I haven't wavered from that belief.

In my opinion, sports scientists should not be allowed within a bull's roar of a cricket ground. They are being used to measure the workloads of our fast bowlers, and the administrative bodies of Australia and elsewhere in the cricket world place bans on bowlers who exceed X number of balls in any one day or week.

However, their greatest coup has been conning the cricket world into thinking that 15 degrees of flex is the point when the human eye detects a throw. These biomechanics experts who came up with this illogical nonsense should be aligned with those who believe the world is flat.

At one time, it was advocated that 5 degrees of flex should be the benchmark to establish whether a bowler threw or didn't throw. Then, in its infinite wisdom, the ICC pushed the benchmark to 14 degrees. And anyone with any nous at all could see that this was a political move to accommodate one bowler ... Muttiah Muralitharan.

In the early 1990s, the ICC made a rod for its own back when it allowed Murali to play on, despite ICC referee and former South Australia and Test wicketkeeper Barry Jarman citing the Sri Lankan for a suspect action inside the first year of his record-breaking career.

The ICC turned a blind 'political' eye to the matter by allowing Murali to carry on, but ensured that referee Jarman never again officiated at a match in which Murali played. Jarman is adamant that the Sri Lankan threw then and continued throwing for the rest of his career, which netted him a further 757 Test wickets, for a final tally of 800 – 92 more than the brilliant Shane Warne, who never threw a ball in his bowling life.

Murali was under scrutiny from umpires the world over for the majority of his career. The reason, the experts asserted, that Murali's bowling gave the 'illusion' of his arm bending and straightening in the manner of a ball being thrown was due to 'an unusual hyperextension of his congenitally bent arm during delivery'.

Despite the controversy about Murali's bowling action, the first time an umpire found the courage to call him happened during the Australia versus Sri Lanka Boxing Day Test at the MCG in 1995. Umpire Darrell Hair stunned the Sri Lankan when he called him for throwing. Hair later said that, given the opportunity, he would not hesitate to call him again. He described Murali's action as 'diabolical'.

Cricket's officials couldn't agree on the legality of Murali's action. Almost as if they circled the wagons and retreated inside the *laager* of utter denial, other umpires were reluctant to call Murali for throwing, thus isolating umpire Hair. Subsequent biomechanical tests cleared Murali's action. These tests revealed that Murali did not extend his arm any more than other bowlers with legal actions.

However, the tests never completely cleared Murali in the eyes of his critics. If it looks like a throw, if the arm bends and straightens in the manner of a throw, chances are it is a throw.

Certainly, the testing is far from foolproof, because the bowlers who are tested are rarely found to be chuckers. During the testing, they keep their arms as straight as they can and never bowl as they would in the heat of battle.

The Sri Lankan civil war began in 1983, with the Tamil Tigers battling to establish an independent state in the north and east of the country. Some people in Sri Lanka and in Australia suggested to me that Murali was allowed to continue in top cricket, bowling with his usual jerky action, purely because of the war and the fact that Murali was the lone Tamil playing for the Sri Lanka cricket team. His presence, some asserted, prevented the Tamil Tigers from attacking any team which included him.

This theory is, of course, only conjecture. After 26 years of bloody conflict, the war ended in May 2009. Murali began his Test career in 1992 and played his last match, versus India, at Galle in July 2010.

Pakistani off-spinner Saqlain Mushtaq pioneered the 'other one', called the doosra. It is a ball delivered with a seeming off-break action, but upon landing the ball turns like a leg-break.

When I played, I experimented with trying to get such a ball into my repertoire. However, I discovered the only way to achieve it was to chuck it.

Frankly, I have never seen a bowler actually legally bowl a *doosra*. It *has* to be thrown.

Murali had his *doosra* questioned, and so have a long list of so-called elite off-spinners, including Harbhajan Singh, Shoaib Malik, Marlon Samuels, Mohammad Hafeez, Saeed Ajmal, Shane Shillingford and Johan Botha.

Amazingly Botha, who played with a decidedly dodgy bowling action in South Africa before joining South Australia, advocated in 2014 that the degree of flex in bowling actions be increased from 15 degrees to 25 degrees. In essence, it seemed the then South Australia captain was calling for a licence to throw. His action had been under scrutiny, so he must have reckoned that when you are under the pump you carry out a pre-emptive strike and take the attack to the 'enemy'.

Thanks to the interference of the 'world is flat' brigade, the ICC came down with a set of tiered tolerance thresholds of allowable elbow extension: 10 degrees for fast bowlers; 7.5 degrees for medium-pacers; and 5 degrees for spinners. Now bowlers have to be within the 15 degrees range.

For hundreds of years, scientists believed the world to be flat. Now modern science is trying to convince the cricket world that a throw is not a throw.

I don't buy all this nonsense. A throw is easily detected by the naked eye and the no-balling of chuckers used to be the best way to rid the scourge from cricket.

Today there are more bowlers who appear to chuck every ball than at any time in my experience.

Back in 2006, I was chatting to Doug Walters in Colombo, where I was running a spin-bowling program for the Sri Lanka Cricket Board. I told Doug about a bloke who turned up at our senior session. We had scanned the island for spinners and this fellow materialised. He was with Ajantha Mendis, the finger-flick spinner who later played for his country. They were both from the Sri Lankan Army.

Mendis's mate was an off-spinner who spun off the thumb. He had a Murali-like action, but if anything he could spin it more than Murali. We had him tested by those biomechanics experts at the Western Australia University in Perth. Their verdict: 34 degrees of flex.

Until the technology can test bowlers in the heat of battle during a game, the biomechanics will continue to be hoodwinked by bowlers with dodgy actions. Until that time, the ICC should return to allowing the umpires to take back control of what happens on the field. If an umpire believes a bowler is chucking the ball, they should have the power to call him for throwing.

Should this remote possibility happen, umpire Darrell Hair's courage will be vindicated.

Rangana Herath: sings a song of spin

When he smiles, his whole face lights up like a Christmas tree. Sri Lanka's brilliant left-arm spinner Rangana Herath can disarm the most watchful batsman, because he has myriad shades of pace and breadth of turn to befuddle and bemuse. Rangana followed in Murali's footsteps. He played his first Test bowling in tandem with Murali at the spin-friendly Galle cricket ground in September 1999, but he had to wait until he was 31 in 2009, when Murali called it a day, to assume the number one spinner's spot in the Sri Lanka Test team.

I first laid eyes on the chubby, happy spinner in 2006 when I was running my Spin Australia coaching program for the Sri Lankan Cricket Board in Colombo. His success comes from good technique and a gift for spinning a ball, but most of all he has done brilliantly because of his inexhaustible work ethic. We trained most days of the week, save one day set aside for an All Spin Match, which the Sri Lankan spinners loved, for they are hugely competitive.

Ricky Ponting echoes what the players of yore will tell you: 'I never saw a player get better by doing less work.' Watching Rangana Herath go about his work in the nets was a heart-warming sight for the coaches, and more than that for the younger bowlers rubbing shoulders with him. His work ethic inspired them; and so did the example of his clever variations, which had the batsman groping or hurrying his shot. There is no respite from Rangana's bowling on any wicket showing only the slightest hint of turn. He is not a huge turner of the ball.

However, his stock ball is hard-spun and he has myriad different shades of pace to confuse the most competent batsman.

His Test debut was against Australia at Galle in September 1999. On that occasion, he bowled in tandem with the mercurial Sri Lankan wicket-taker, Muttiah Muralitharan. He took 4/97 off 34.3 overs of tantalising left-arm spin, his first victims Steve Waugh (19), Ricky Ponting (1), Shane Warne (10) and Damien Fleming (16). Rangana and Murali (5/71 off 38 overs) took nine of the 10 Australian wickets to fall; tailender Colin Miller was run out for six.

Watching Rangana at training, you knew he was special. A solidly built little bloke, standing just 5 feet 5 inches (165 centimetres) tall, there was, I thought, a need for him to drive up higher over his braced front foot at delivery, because he tended to bowl flat. From that time in 2006 when I suggested that he work hard to achieve a higher release point, his bowling improved out of sight.

While his stock ball is hard-spun, if he bowls a flat trajectory, he knows how to regain the desired just-above-the-eyeline shape by reaching up a little higher on his front foot at delivery. That technique helps Rangana stay for a split second longer on his front foot and helps him achieve maximum revolutions on the ball. Study the best spinners in modern times – Shane Warne, Murali, Saqlain Mushtaq – and you will note that they all spend a long time on the front foot. In recent times, Australia's Nathan Lyon is beginning to emulate these bowlers with similar technique.

Rangana also bowls what some journalists in the Indian subcontinent call a 'mystery' ball. It is, in fact, not a mystery at all, unless the mysteriousness is all about a batsman's inability to pick the direction of spin. He merely turns his hand over and the ball is released out of the front of the hand with a hint of leg-cut on it. Easy to pick, this one, but so too are off-breaks, leg-breaks, inswingers and outswingers – all stock deliveries that get the majority of wickets for the great spinners and fast bowlers.

Left-arm orthodox spinners don't always do well in Australia. There have been exceptions, such as England's Hedley Verity in the Bradman era between the wars, our own Bert Ironmonger, England's Tony Lock and Derek Underwood and New Zealand's Daniel Vettori. Too often, overseas spinners of this type bowl to a 6–3 field – to right handers, they would have six off-side fielders and three leg-side – usually bowling on or outside the right-hander's off stump. This is the field that left-armers bowl to in county cricket.

It is the field that brought Monty Panesar down in Australia. I will never forget speaking with Panesar about the line he bowled here. When the ball beats the bat, it misses off stump. The wicketkeeper throws back his head, everyone applauds and Monty is lauded for what is only a moral victory. Had he beaten the right-hander's bat when operating to a middle and leg line, the ball would have had every chance of hitting off stump or the pads, with more likelihood of a wicket. A wicket beats a moral victory any day. The 'Panesar line' is pretty much a fruitless way to go.

Little wonder Shane Warne said of Monty, when he'd played his 30th Test, 'Panesar has played one Test 30 times.'

Rangana bowled to a more attacking 5–4 field in Australia and was rewarded with wickets most of the time.

Mudiyanselage Rangana Keerthi Bandara (MRKB) Herath was born in the small lush village of Waduwawa, Kurungegala, situated on the southeastern tip of the Northwestern Province of Sri Lanka on 19 March 1978. Rangana and his older brother, Deepthi, often watched cricket with their friends on the family's black and white television set. After they'd had their fill of watching, they rushed outside and played their own 'Tests' on the backyard grass under the Thambili palms. Rangana was a natural left-hander, but Deepthi had to change to left-handed so that he wasn't breaking windows when he hit to the leg side.

When Rangana wasn't smashing deliveries from Deepthi into the trees, he'd hang a ball in a sock from a mango tree and hit it for hours at a time. At school, Rangana often opened the batting. Early on, he bowled little medium-pacers, but his coach offered sage advice: 'Rangana, bowl spinners. You are too short to be a pace bowler.'

His first job was working for a card centre during the domestic off-season and he played for the Sampath Bank's mercantile team in partial exchange for employment. There he met the brother of the international cricketer Chandika Hathurusingha, the former Sri Lanka all-rounder. His brother told Chandika, 'You have to see this fellow in my office who bats like Sanath Jayasuriya and bowls as well.' However, when Rangana came to train at Chandika's club he was impressed more with his bowling than his batting. Afterwards, he said, 'That was the last time I ever listened to my brother when it came to batting.'

Rangana worked diligently on his left-arm spinners and his batting and made his first-class debut for the Kurunegala Youth Cricket Club in the 1996–97 season. But after his Test debut in 1997, he was pretty much an afterthought in the Test selectors' minds, since Murali was doing the job all on his own.

In 2006, I was speaking enthusiastically about Rangana to a Sri Lankan Cricket Board official and he said sternly: 'Oh, he cannot get wickets. Went on a tour of India with Sri Lanka A and hardly got anyone out.' A look at the scores from the tour showed that batsmen on both sides pasted all the bowlers on hard-as-granite 'roads' of wickets. I stuck to my guns and pushed his case whenever and wherever I had the chance to talk to those who might have influence on selecting the Sri Lanka team.

Rangana reminded me of Shane Warne – not in the technique of his craft, of course not; one's a finger-spinner, the other a wrist-spinner. It was his insatiable desire to be up for the contest. The same as Warne, he revelled in the challenge and, like Warne, Rangana has always had a mischievous glint in his eye.

On 29 May 2016, Rangana Herath became the third Sri Lankan bowler to take 300 wickets in Test cricket history after Muttiah Muralitharan and Chaminda Vaas. At the time of writing (February 2017), Rangana had taken 357 Test wickets at an average of 28.31 with 28 hauls of five wickets in an innings and seven bags of 10 wickets or more in the match. In October 2016, due to an injury to regular skipper Angelo Mathews, Rangana was appointed captain of Sri Lanka for the tour of Zimbabwe, thus becoming the oldest player to lead a Test squad for the first time from any country since England's Tom Graveney.

Whenever Rangana tours Australia with the Sri Lanka team, I get to Adelaide Oval or the city's Intercontinental Hotel to meet him. At the oval, we have a brief chat and at the Intercontinental Hotel we have a lengthy chat over a beer. When he laughs, his entire face glows with health and joy.

Rangana is married to longtime partner Senani Herath and they have two young sons. There are no airs or graces about Rangana. He is his own man and has never forgotten where he came from or those who helped him along his life journey. 'You always remember the people who helped you when times are tough, isn't it? For me, the bank was like that ...'

At the top of his bowling mark, Rangana flips the ball from hand to hand. He is not the most athletic of bowlers. There is a generous tubbiness about him. As he starts his approach to the wicket, his legs move up and down, slowly gathering momentum, like a Puffing Billy from another era. At first he ambles, then there is a hint of a jog. Just before delivery, he assumes a nice side-on position and his midriff turns to face the batsman. The ball leaves Rangana's hand with the seam in perfect position. You know the ball is hard-spun for the revolutions give off a distinct buzzing sound. Some balls seem to hang, others drop dramatically, some spin, some do not, rather they skid on straight.

In Sri Lanka in 2016, Rangana destroyed the Australian batting during the 3–nil Test whitewash. During the Second Test at Galle, Rangana took a hat-trick, dismissing Adam Voges, Peter Nevill and Mitchell Starc in the Australian first innings. He became the oldest Test player to get a hat-trick and the first left-arm orthodox spinner since England's Johnny Briggs achieved the feat against Australia in 1892. In that bleak series for Australia, Rangana took 13 wickets in the final Test to take his tally for the three-match series to 28.

Five great all-rounders

Garfield St Aubrun (Garry) Sobers was undoubtedly the game's best all-round cricketer. As cricket's lion, he heads my pride of the five best all-rounders I've seen: Sobers, Keith Miller, Imran Khan, Ian Botham and Mike Procter.

Garry Sobers

Because of his mercurial all-round ability, Sobers must be crowned the greatest player in cricket history. Statistics don't always tell the full story, but Sobers's stats aren't half bad: 93 Tests, 8032 runs at 57.78, with 26 centuries and a career best of 365 not out. Bowling left-arm fast, wrist or orthodox spin, Sobers captured 235 wickets at 34.03, with 6 five-wicket hauls and a career best of 6/73. He also took 109 catches, some at backward short leg which were seemingly impossible. During a charity match in Adelaide, Sobers took a catch off my bowling at short midwicket. There was not the hint of a sound. Another catch ... again no sound. Twice the ball had disappeared into a pouch of fur: Sobers was the epitome of the iron fist in the velvet glove. Don Bradman reckoned Sobers's 254 against Australia for the Rest of the World team at the MCG in 1971 was 'the best innings I've seen in Australia'.

Sobers had a sense of history and of fair play. When South Africa played South Australia at the Adelaide Oval in 1963–64, he sidled up to his state captain, Les Favell, and asked, 'Is it okay, skipper, if I wear my Test cap?' Favell said he couldn't care what cap Sobers wore, but he was intrigued as to why his great all-rounder wanted to don the West Indies cap. With a not-so-subtle swipe at the injustices of the Apartheid system, Sobers said: 'I believe it's time these Springboks got a good, long look at the West Indies cap I am wearing.' Sobers got a big hundred.

There have been a few better batsmen than Sobers, and superior bowlers; however, as a complete package – batsman, bowler, fieldsman, cricket thinker – Garry Sobers reigns supreme. There was a feline grace and ease of motion about the man which bordered on the poetic; Sobers in action was something to behold.

Keith Miller

Second to Sobers in terms of skill and an innate ability to perform when needed, Keith Miller was the man. Miller was right out of *The Boy's Own Annual*. He was a war hero and a supreme athlete, with the star quality we usually associate with stage and screen.

In 55 Tests, Miller hit 2958 runs at 36.97, with 7 hundreds and a best score of 147. He took 170 wickets at an average of 22.97, with a career best of 7/60 among his seven bags of five wickets or more in an innings. Statistics don't reflect the whole Miller tale, for he batted and bowled on whim and the needs of the side. If Australia was in trouble, Miller lifted a few gears and got the job done.

Leonard Hutton, one of the greatest England batsmen of all time, always found Miller a handful. He told me in Adelaide in 1984 that the best bowler he ever faced was SF Barnes, when Barnes was 62 and Hutton a boy of 16. But on the Test stage, 'The most dangerous bowler was undoubtedly Keith Miller. He'd just as likely bowl me a slow wrong'un first ball of a Test match as he would an outswinger or a searing bouncer. Keith was the greatest bowler I ever faced in Test cricket.'

In 1969, 50-year-old Miller turned up to take part in a coaching film. All he had to do was bowl three balls at an unprotected set of stumps. He walked past me where I stood some seven paces back from my mark and said, 'Ahem, son, I'll pitch leg and hit off.' His first and third balls did precisely that; the ball was propelled at a speed at least as fast as then Australian fast bowler Graham McKenzie. The seam was perfectly upright and it pitched on both occasions on the line of leg stump and broke like a Shane Warne leg-break to hit the top of off stump. Remarkable.

Imran Khan

Imran Khan was a warrior cricketer if ever there was one. He was blessed with great strength and a calm temperament. Imran could lift as a batsman or bowler and was a born leader. In 88 Tests, Imran hit 3807 runs at 37.69, with a highest score of 136 among his 6 hundreds. With the ball, he took 362 wickets at an average of 22.81, taking five or more wickets in an innings 23 times.

While he batted with skill and good judgment, especially when needed to guide his country out of the mire, it was Imran's bowling which fired the imagination. Imran succeeded with his pace bowling on all surfaces, even on the bone-dry, parched pitches which powdered to the touch like some riverbed in Biblical times after 40 years of drought. Imran loved a challenge and was at his best against the best of batsmen, who provided the greater challenge. Like a good-quality red wine, Imran got better with age. In his final 50-odd Tests, he averaged a shade above 50 with the bat and just 19 with the ball.

Imran could be operating at a pace round medium-fast, then, without any obvious change in approach or action, he could deliver at savage express pace. When he was quick, he was seriously quick, as he proved in Australia in the 1976–77 series. His stirring match figures of 10/77 against England at Headingley in 1987 gave Pakistan its first Test series win against the old enemy on their home soil. At the MCG in 1992, he top-scored in leading Pakistan to World Cup glory against England.

After his illustrious cricket career, Imran was often in the headlines and the natural leadership he showed on the field is a trait which has stayed with him in his political quest to try and steer Pakistan towards a democracy of sorts.

Ian Botham

Ian Botham has an outstanding all-round record. In 102 Tests, he scored 5200 runs at 33.54 with 14 centuries, and he took 383 wickets at 28.40 with 27 bags of five wickets or more and a career best of 8/34. Botham was probably lucky to have struck an Australian team mostly without its better players. Just after Botham began his career, Australia and the West Indies lost their best players to World Series Cricket, and then came the rebel tours of South Africa. But Botham batted and bowled with great belief.

He was a better batsman than bowler. He took the opposition bowlers on and hit with explosive power, especially straight. As a bowler, he seemed to bowl well within himself, then every now and again he would drive through the crease with amazing energy and produce a pearler of a delivery. It was this element of surprise which had batsmen guessing and often led to another Botham wicket. He wasn't in the class of Kapil Dev or Richard Hadlee as a bowler, yet he was a better bat than either man and a brilliant slip fieldsman.

Perhaps Botham's magnum opus came at Headingley in 1981. After scoring 50 in England's first innings, when Australia enforced the follow-on, he flayed Dennis Lillee, Terry Alderman and Geoff Lawson to the tune of 149 to turn the match on its head and – thanks to an eight-wicket haul by Bob Willis – won a match which had been so far gone that the bookies were offering 500/1 against an England victory.

Botham was never far away from the headlines throughout the 1980s, and his good work in raising funds for charity via his long and arduous walks earned him a knighthood.

Mike Procter

My fifth choice is a little controversial in that Mike Procter played little international cricket. In just seven Tests, he averaged a modest 25.11 and took 41 wickets at 15.02. Procter came at you like a raging bull. He was full-on, bustling towards the batsman with a determined glint in his eye. At delivery, he was very front-on, not unlike Malcolm Marshall. He seemed to bowl off the wrong foot, the ball coming on to you in a big rush. His pace was around Marshall's speed, but Procter's deliveries usually came in at a right-hander. He bowled huge, dipping inswingers and clever leg-cutters.

In England in 1972, I saw on TV Procter complete an unusual hat-trick, in that each ball was bowled from around the wicket and every batsman was plumb lbw. All three batsmen were caught across the crease dead to rights.

As a youngster, Procter spent a season on the Lord's ground-staff with Barry Richards. Both were denied long and successful Test careers with South Africa because of Apartheid. He played for Rhodesia, South Africa, Gloucestershire, Natal, Orange Free State and Western Province. It was with Gloucestershire that Procter really blossomed.

Because of the prevailing attitude throughout the free world about the horrific Apartheid system in South Africa and the likelihood his country might face an international sporting isolation, Mike Proctor knew his days of Test cricket were numbered. Due to South Africa's subsequent sporting ban, Procter played just seven Tests, but despite this fact I believe he was among the greatest all-rounders of his time.

In 401 first-class matches, Procter scored 21,936 runs at 36.01 with 48 hundreds and a highest score of 254. He also took 1417 wickets at 19.53, with 70 bags of five wickets in an innings and 15 of 10 wickets in a match.

Procter reckons his loss of a long and successful Test career was little compared with the suffering of 40 million non-whites in South Africa. Apartheid was an evil political system which not only separated the various races of the nation, but decreed that the minority non-whites held on to the reins of power. South Africa had as its Prime Minister John Vorster, who was interned in South Africa during World War II because of his pro-Nazi stance.

In April 1971, Nelson Mandela was spending his seventh year in a cell at Robben Island. At the same time, a cricket match between Transvaal and the rest of South Africa was about to start at Newlands in Cape Town, 12 kilometres across the water from where Mandela was cracking rocks. The players knew the Vorster Government had decreed it would prevent the South African selectors from picking a non-white player in the national team for the coming tour of Australia. After one ball was bowled, four players – Procter, Graeme and Peter Pollock and Denis Lindsay – walked off the field and issued a press statement supporting selection on merit regardless of skin colour. From that moment, Mike Procter and the others could walk tall forever.

The day they booed Bradman

By his own recollection, Don Bradman was booed by the crowd just once in his fabulous cricket career.

In 1926, 18-year-old Don Bradman had not long left Bowral to play with the St George Cricket Club in Sydney. He boarded in the district with one of the New South Wales Cricket Association's leading administrators, Frank Cush, and one day he dropped in to see Mick Bardsley (Test opener Warren Bardsley's brother) for a dental check.

Bradman later explained that the dentist told him he had pyorrhoea and must lose one of his double back teeth. But in fact he had six teeth extracted, three on each side. Nursing a bruised and swollen face, young Don caught the bus home and lay on a sofa, a large bowl at his side. When Mrs Cush returned from shopping, the bowl contained so much blood that she rang for the doctor, who advised that the youngster should withdraw from the grade match due to start next day.

However, Bradman recounted:

*I was captain and I didn't want to let the team down, so
I played, I won the toss and sent the opposition in to bat
because I felt weak and not up to batting. For the same
reason I put myself at first slip, much to the annoyance of
the crowd, who knew I was the best cover fieldsman and
wasn't any good in the slips. You guessed it. I put down two
catches in the first 10 minutes, but worse was to follow. We
bowled them out by 4.30 pm and we had to bat. I dropped*

*myself down the batting order, hoping our early batsmen
would stay in. They didn't. By ten minutes to six we had
lost eight wickets and I could not any longer refuse to bat.
So I walked out to be roundly hooted by the spectators (the
only time I can remember) who knew nothing of the drama
being enacted behind the scenes.*

At stumps St George was still eight wickets down, 40 runs
behind Marrickville's first innings score. Bradman and leg-
spinner Frank Ward had survived the first day of the match.

Inevitably, Bradman completed his century (116 not out)
the following Saturday, then St George bowled Marrickville out
cheaply a second time to win the match outright.

'I went from villain to hero.'

While behind the scenes Bradman may have divided loyalties
among the players, he was ever the idol of the fans purely on
the strength of his sheer consistent brilliance. The only time he
fell foul of the crowd was that Saturday in 1926 when St George
turned out against Marrickville. What lived in the memory for
the spectators and the other players who featured in that game
was the crowd's reaction to Bradman batting so low in the order.

Don Bradman, a shadow drive.

Clarrie and the Don

The St George teammate who was Bradman's batting partner the day he was booed (see the previous chapter, 'The day they booed Bradman') was the leg-spinner Frank Ward. He left St George at Bradman's behest and in the 1936–37 season became a teammate of the Don's in the South Australian team.

When the 1938 Australian team to tour England was chosen, Ward was in the squad, but Clarrie Grimmett – who had taken a record 216 Test wickets – was not. Grimmett had his heart set on the 1938 touring team and blamed Bradman for influencing his fellow selectors to omit him. He never again played for Australia. Grimmett's exclusion greatly annoyed his spin twin Bill O'Reilly, who wrote, 'I have always placed that dereliction of selection responsibilities on a par with the omission of Keith Miller from the tour of South Africa in 1949. I was heartbroken when Clarrie was passed over for the 1938 tour.'

In 1988, Bradman put up a lame argument to justify the Test selectors' decision to omit Grimmett in 1938:

Bill O'Reilly was our spearhead, while Fleetwood-Smith was our up-and-coming spinner, and then you had Grimmett and Frank Ward.

Grimmett was at that stage, I think, 46 years of age. Now that is pretty old for a tour of England and he had already been dropped from the Australian team as far back as 1932. So, whatever happened, O'Reilly was going to be number one; Fleetwood-Smith was going to be number two and whoever the next spinner was would have to be number three, and you didn't have room for four.

I don't think people realised just how well Frank Ward did on that tour. I think he took 92 wickets and he was high up in the bowling averages. But the important thing that has been overlooked is the strike rate. And it is very important on a tour of England that you get the opposition out quickly. It gives you less time in the field and more opportunity to rest. Now, Ward bowled 526 overs on tour, taking 92 wickets, and his strike rate was that he got a wicket every 5.7 overs. That was better than Grimmett achieved on any of his three England tours and it was a better strike rate than O'Reilly achieved, as great as he was, and I think Frank was one of the great successes on the tour because he filled the gap very well indeed.

I believe now, after all these years, that we still did not make a mistake in taking Frank instead of Grimmett in 1938.

Grimmett had toured England in 1926, 1930 and 1934 – taking hauls of 116, 142 and 109 wickets respectively. As Bradman said, Ward on his one tour collected 92 wickets, but Bradman avoided talking about Test wickets. In the 13 Tests he played in England over those three tours, Grimmett took a total of 68 wickets, while Ward failed to take a single wicket in his one Test at Nottingham in June 1938, bowling 30 fruitless overs and conceding 142 runs.

Bradman's stance at that time mystified cricket followers and many, including his Test cricket peers, found it difficult to forgive. However, the animosity between Bradman and some players who toured with him to England probably stems back to 1930, when the 20-year-old hit a record 334 in a day in the Test at Headingley. For his fabulous batting effort, a wealthy Australian soap manufacturer, UK-based Arthur Whitelaw, gave Bradman a staggering £1000, the equivalent now of $80,000 to $100,000. When Bradman pocketed the lot without so much as offering his teammates a shout at the bar, the likes of Alan Kippax, Vic Richardson and Bill Woodfull were livid.

In 1935–36, Bradman missed the South African tour, which Richardson led. The side went through the tour undefeated, Grimmett took an amazing 44 wickets at 14 runs apiece and Richardson's captaincy was loved by all the players under him.

While the side was in South Africa, Bradman captained South Australia. The next summer, Richardson was stripped of the state captaincy in favour of Bradman, and while Grimmett played for South Australia, so too did Frank Ward and he ended up grabbing Clarrie's Test spot.

Grimmett didn't enhance his cause with Bradman. He always maintained that Victor Trumper was the greatest batsman he had seen and bowled against in a match, although the only time Clarrie bowled to Trumper was for a single over in a match between his Wellington team and an Australian XI led by Arthur Mailey at the Basin Reserve in 1914.

In the wake of that disappointment, Grimmett was offered £2000, plus expenses, to sail to India and coach His Highness the Rajah of Jath. He gladly accepted the offer, for £2000 was a veritable fortune in 1938, and was more than double the fee Don Bradman's tourists received for the England tour.

Apart from coaching the Rajah of Jath and his younger brother, Grimmett also took a young, enthusiastic all-rounder under his wing – the promising 23-year-old Vijay Samuel Hazare. At training in India, Grimmett threw tennis balls from close range at him and Hazare always maintained that the Australian's coaching and encouragement helped him tighten his defence and learn to execute his strokes efficiently.

The old leg-spinner always considered himself a pretty good batting coach. Once he handed me his Jack Hobbs autograph bat and asked me to play a drive. Upon my saying I couldn't bat and wanted to learn about bowling, he replied, 'Ah, I taught a young man to play the back cut on the boat to England in 1930 ... and Don Bradman was a fast learner!'

Just before war broke out, Hazare wrote to Grimmett:

Let me note here that this little success of mine in the cricket sphere is entirely due to your valuable instructions which I will never forget, at least in this life. I will also be thankful to you if you will in future, as in the past, kindly help me by giving necessary instructions.

World War II hampered Hazare's progress and he didn't play his first Test until June 1946, against England at Lord's. Down Under on India's 1947–48 tour, he hardly troubled the scorers with the bat until the Fourth Test in Adelaide.

As well as Lindwall and Miller, Hazare had to negotiate the left-arm medium-fast stuff from Ernie Toshack, the off-spin of Ian Johnson and the leg-breaks of Colin McCool. Hazare played grandly. He walked to the wicket with India a precarious 5/133 in the first innings and with Dattu Phadkar (123), hit 188 for the sixth wicket. Following on, India was 4/99 in the second innings when Hazare came to the wicket. He batted like a man possessed, playing deft cuts and pulls and wristy shots off his toes which appeared to gain pace the further the ball travelled, not unlike the magic of VVS Laxman when he was in peak touch.

After he made his two majestic centuries – 116 and 145 – the crowd rose as one and among them was Hazare's mentor, a little man in a suit and grey felt hat, his hands clasped in victory above his head where he stood in the press gallery near the players' change-room high in the George Giffen Stand. This little man was none other than Clarence Victor Grimmett, at the Adelaide Oval to see his protégé Vijay Hazare.

Hazare's double in Adelaide gave him hero status back home and huge respect in Australia. Bradman was moved to say, 'Hazare is the most graceful batsman it has been my pleasure to watch.'

Clarrie Grimmett would have seen the irony that the man Bradman 'dropped' would become Vijay Hazare's mentor. After his majestic Test-match double, Hazare was invited to Grimmett's Adelaide home and at the dinner table, Clarrie raised a glass to him: 'Vijay, a toast. You have made me a proud man today.'

Alec Bedser: cricket colossus

Alec Bedser's 'pitched leg, hit off' delivery to clean-bowl Don Bradman for a first-ball duck at the Adelaide Oval in February 1947 was, Bradman claimed, 'the best ball I ever faced'. It was as good as the Shane Warne ball to dismiss Mike Gatting at Manchester in 1993, but we don't have TV footage of Bedser's delivery, so we are left to rely on the memory of witnesses. I'll take Bradman – the best judge of cricket and a cricketer of my experience – as a reliable enough witness.

Bedser proved to be one of the Don's toughest combatants on the Test stage. He was also one of his best mates. Australians warmly remember Bedser as a strongly built medium-fast bowler who was possessed of a never-say-die attitude in the best British bulldog spirit.

In 1939, Alec was enjoying the first of more than 15 seasons with the Surrey county side. But Bedser's cricket was rudely interrupted by the outbreak of World War II. Among many RAF servicemen trapped at Dunkirk in 1940, Bedser was evacuated from that dangerous coast by a miracle flotilla of little boats. Over the next few days, Alec and his inseparable twin, Eric, volunteered to go back to Dunkirk to rescue soldiers still trapped there.

The Bedser twins were demobilised just in time to turn out for Surrey in the 1946 county championship. Alec played for Surrey between the years 1939 and 1960. He played 51 Tests from 1946 to 1955, taking 236 wickets at an average of 24.89, 15 times taking five or more wickets in an innings, with 7/34 his best.

In 1953, he took a then record 39 wickets (at an average of 17) in the Ashes series against Lindsay Hassett's Australians, as the mainstay of an attack which eventually brought Australia undone in the Fifth Test at The Oval – England winning back the Ashes it had lost to Bill Woodfull's team in 1934.

Bedser bowled late-dipping inswingers, then developed the leg-cutter, which lifted him above the ruck of other medium-paced bowlers. The old-timers I have spoken with place Bedser second to Maurice Tate among the great medium-paced bowlers. However, Tate bowled on faster pitches and when he got the ball to cut, it moved swiftly, allowing little time for even the smartest of batsmen to withdraw the bat.

(Late in his life, Sir Donald Bradman told me that he could detect late movement and that he turned the blade edge-on to avoid snicking a catch to keeper or slip. Then again, that was Bradman. Such a ploy by mere mortals would no doubt turn out disastrously.)

Alec Bedser made his Test debut against India at Lord's in June 1946. It was a memorable debut, for Bedser took 7/49 off 29.1 overs in the Indian first innings. He followed that with 4/96 off 32.1 overs in the second innings. Bedser immediately established himself as a man of iron; a bowler who would trundle away through thick and thin. In the Second Test at Old Trafford, Bedser again went berserk with the ball, taking 4/41 and 7/52.

The Indian visit was a precursor to England's much-awaited tour of Australia, the first since Gubby Allen's team of 1936–37. After six long years of war, the Australian public were hungry to watch Test cricket. There had been huge speculation about whether Don Bradman was going to play, or concentrate on building his stockbroking business. Alec Bedser was looking forward to bowling to the great batsman.

Bradman's first innings against England in Brisbane in the summer of 1946–47 (his first since the Oval Test of 1938) was the subject of great controversy when the Englishmen were adamant that Bradman had chopped a ball off the bowling of Bill Voce straight to Jack Ikin in the gully and was out for 17. Bradman stood like a statue waiting upon umpire Jack Borwick to adjudicate, while the bowler and fielders gathered in a group. The consensus among the players was that Bradman got an outside edge, the ball flew comfortably waist-high to Ikin, who took the catch cleanly. Umpire Borwick thought Bradman had jammed the ball into the pitch and it was a bump ball. Bradman went on to score 187.

Alec Bedser copped a pasting, with 2/159 off 41 overs. It was in that Australian innings of 659 that Bedser decided he needed to develop a ball which left the right-handed batsman – a leg-cutter, the very delivery which would bring him eternal fame in Adelaide a few weeks later.

In 1999, Alec wrote me a letter explaining how he came to develop the leg-cutter:

> *Most fast bowlers pre-war bowled outswingers because of the lbw law. [At that time,] the ball had to pitch [in line] stump to stump before an lbw appeal was upheld. Inswingers were rather frowned upon by the so-called experts ... Not many were bowled, so Don never really had to cope with the late-inswing bowling and especially difficult was such a bowler who could also get the ball to move from leg to off after the ball pitched. I needed to develop such a ball. Today, they call this a leg-cutter and because of the big seam on the ball these days it deviates upon pitching. Balls just after the war had hardly any seam, so I found I had to actually spin the ball. I found my big hands helped the process and that I did not have to change my action at all.*

The Second Test in Sydney in December 1946 saw Bradman (234) and Sid Barnes (234) hit a record 405-run fifth-wicket stand. Bedser knew how good Barnes was off his pads and he decided that the Sydney Test was the best place to try his new delivery.

> *I didn't want the ball to swing in, so I held it across the seam as if gripping the ball for a leg-break. When it pitched, it went away off the track like a big-spinning leg-break. Obviously I had spun the ball. Sid looked down the pitch and said, 'What's bloody going on?' I walked back for the next ball, again holding the ball across the seam, and Peter Smith, an older Essex player fielding at mid-on, observed my grip and said, 'You can't hold a new ball like that!' Next ball, I held it the same way and again it skipped off the pitch, just like a leg-break. It took me another 18 months to achieve the accuracy I wanted. Developing that ball confirmed what I had always believed – that bowlers should try things and think for themselves.*

Bedser finally dismissed Barnes, but his 46 overs would return him a dismal 1/153.

Then came Adelaide, where Denis Compton scored a century in each innings for England and Arthur Morris also got the coveted double for Australia. Keith Miller also hit an unconquered 141, but it was Bedser's inswinging leg-cutter to clean-bowl Bradman for a duck which will live forever in cricket folklore. Bedser described it: 'When I bowled Don at Adelaide, the ball swung in after pitching round leg stump, moved from leg to off and hit the off stump. Don must have missed it by six inches.'

Bradman was amazed by the delivery: 'The ball was, I think, the finest ever to take my wicket. It must have come three-quarters of the way straight on to my off stump, then suddenly it dipped to pitch on the leg stump, only to turn off the pitch and hit the middle and off stumps. It was too good for me – similar to the ball Bill O'Reilly bowled me with in a match at Bowral in 1925.'

Bedser went on to dismiss Bradman six times in Test matches, twice for a duck, but said he was always mindful that the post-war Bradman was nowhere as good as he was between the wars. 'I never saw him play before the war, but I have spoken to many who did. Jack Hobbs always said he was a better player before the 1914–18 war, but Hobbs still managed to score 100 hundreds after he had turned the age of 40. Maybe Don was not as brutal after the war, but he was still bloody good!'

Former Test captain and Australian team coach Bob Simpson has good reason to thank Bedser. He recalls:

Alec was tremendous to me. In 1954–55 with Hutton's side, Bedser was out of favour. Whenever I was twelfth man for New South Wales in Sydney, Alec would come into the dressing-room and say, 'C'mon, young Simpson, come to the nets and I'll bowl you a few.'

The thing which impressed me about Alex was his huge size, the most penetrating of blue eyes and his huge hands. He kept smashing me on the leg with his big off-cutters, but it was a terrific experience facing him. In the return match with MCC, I got 98 for New South Wales.

Later, when my career was over and I was Australian coach, Alec would often see me and offer advice on some of our pace bowlers. He was always spot-on with advice. Alec Bedser had a very shrewd cricket brain, identified talent well and knew how a problem could be rectified.

Apart from dismissing Bradman five times in succession during the 1948 Australian Ashes series, Bedser defeated the great Arthur Morris 18 times on the 21 occasions he bowled to him. Glenn McGrath did a similar job on England's Mike Atherton, but Morris was a world-class player and Atherton was a plodder who was lucky to play in an era when England had such a weak array of batting talent.

Knighted by Queen Elizabeth at Buckingham Palace in 1997, Alec quipped after the ceremony, 'I'm the first English bowler to be knighted since Sir Francis Drake!'

Keith Miller, superstar

Keith Miller was cricket's swashbuckler; he had film-star looks and was a war hero. His shoot-from-the-hip, frantic life stemmed from his days as a night fighter pilot. John Arlott once wrote that Miller seemed to be 'busy living life in case he ran out of it'.

In 1953, rumour had it that Miller was linked romantically with Princess Margaret. The Australian team was touring England that very year of Queen Elizabeth's coronation and Lindsay Hassett's men were invited for cocktails at Buckingham Palace. When the bus arrived, Hassett observed Miller making a beeline towards an area away from where officials awaited the team. Hassett asked: 'Where are you going, Nugget?' 'Oh, it's okay,' Miller replied, 'I know another entrance here.'

During the war, Miller flew night-time missions over Germany and Occupied France in his Mosquito. His love of classical music compelled him on one mission to turn his Mosquito back to the war zone. Taking a slight detour, Miller overflew Bonn, Beethoven's birthplace. Miller once flew up the straight at Royal Ascot, and another day he buzzed the Goodwood track.

But war is deadly serious. It respects neither friend nor foe, and Miller lost many of his mates during the war. When he was based near Bournemouth, every Friday night he and his mates from the RAF base met at the Carlton Hotel in Bournemouth. One Friday night, Miller couldn't make the regular appointment and when he returned he found that a German Focke-Wulf fighter-bomber had bombed the church next to the hotel, causing the spire to collapse directly onto the pub's bar, instantly killing his eight mates. For more than 50 years, Miller returned to England every year and he always spent time with a relative of each of his mates killed that night in 1943.

After the Battle of Britain and year-long Blitz, there were still regular German bombing raids, but throughout the war, the English were still staging cricket matches at Lord's. On weekends off, Miller often flew to London to play cricket there. Described by Sir Pelham Warner as the 'cathedral of cricket', Miller initially was none too taken with it, describing it as 'a crummy little place', but it eventually 'grew' on him.

At war's end in 1945, the British people were nursing their wounds. Some of the old guard were back in English cricket. Len Hutton, Bill Edrich, Wally Hammond, Cyril Washbrook and Denis Compton would form the nucleus of the batting line-up for the post-war England cricket team. The great Yorkshire left-arm spinner, Hedley Verity, had fallen in battle. England was crying out for a new hero. Their hero came in the guise of Keith Ross Miller, the young, handsome Australian airman, on loan in England for the war.

Miller had come into cricket as a batsman. He hit a debut 108 against a South Australian team which included Clarrie Grimmett in the 1939–40 season, his first and last Shield match until after the war. Grimmett was at the nets before the match and Miller impressed him with what he saw as 'a natural bowling action and a young man who loved to bowl'. Clarrie told Miller: 'You'll like bowling more than batting, for it will fascinate you throughout your career.'

It was in the immediate aftermath of the war that Miller first came under notice as a champion cricketer. His all-round flair, his attacking batting and brilliant fast bowling made an instant impact in world cricket when he impressed as an all-rounder in the 1945 Victory Tests, an unofficial 'Test' series between England and Australia. The Australian team was led by affable Lindsay Hassett and included batsmen Dick Whitington (South Australia) and Keith Carmody (New South Wales), the man who invented the so-called 'umbrella field'.

Miller was like a runaway colt as a medium-fast bowler, yet he assumed an aristocratic air when he batted. He loved the attention and always beamed as he strode towards the wicket, then stood relaxed and upright in his stance at the crease. Miller scored 514 runs in the series, including a brilliant 185 at Lord's, where he hit leg-spinner Eric Hollies for 7 sixes, one of the hits crashing into the top of the Lord's Pavilion.

Miller was selected as a member of Don Bradman's 1948 Invincibles, who swept through England like William the Conqueror on an earlier 'tour'. Another team member, Sam Loxton, loved to talk of the 48ers: 'How good was the '48 side? I'll tell ya how good. The little fella [Bradman] would walk briskly onto the ground, and he'd pick up the ball left by the advancing umpires. He'd toss the ball high over his head and whoever caught the ball opened the bloody bowling ... that's how good we were!'

On a 14-hour flight from Taiwan to Johannesburg, Miller told me about players and officials and lots of war stories. I quizzed him about rumours that he purposely allowed a ball from Trevor Bailey to hit his stumps first ball in the 1948 match against Essex, because he considered the English 'had suffered enough'. Miller was adamant. 'No, I was bowled fair and square,' he said firmly. I did read where the ball from Bailey was straight, pitching round middle and leg stumps, and Miller shouldered arms. Mind you, getting Miller for none was a good thing for the Essex attack, as the score was by then 3/364 and Australia made 721 in the first day's play.

Another rumour he pooh-poohed was about the time he refused to bowl when Bradman tossed him the ball during the 1948 Lord's Test. In diving at slip to accept a Denis Compton snick off the bowling of Ray Lindwall, Miller yelled, 'Hell, I think my back's gone.' Ian Johnson was standing next to Miller in the slips and at the end of the over the pair walked towards Bradman, who – as a matter of course – had thrown the ball to Miller, as he wanted a change in the bowling. Miller mentioned his back to Bradman and immediately the Don replied, 'If you have any doubts at all, I'll give the ball to Bill [Johnston]. Don't take a chance, Keith.'

On Bradman, Miller said:

> *Len Hutton told me that Bradman was a 'far better player'*
> *in the 1930s than he was when I saw most of his batting on*
> *the 1948 tour. In 1948, he was pretty much a father figure.*
> *We all looked up to him and marvelled at his batsmanship.*
> *Here was a guy nearing forty, yet he ran about the field like*
> *a two-year-old and just kept making runs. If Bradman was*
> *'better' in the 1930s, he must have been some player.*

In December 1948, Bradman made the last of his 117 first-class centuries in what was called the 'Bradman Testimonial Match'. Keith Miller told me of the game, where he decided to bowl a few short ones, 'just to test his reflexes'.

'First one was a medium-fast bouncer. It didn't get up too far, but Don was swiftly into position and he smashed it like a rocket past mid-on,' Miller recounted. 'Fast bowlers don't like that treatment, so I charged in for the next ball and gave it my all. It was a tremendous bumper, straight at his head, but he simply swung into position and cracked it forward of square, almost decapitating Sam Loxton on its way to the fence.'

Once, when Miller was sitting with a young Richie Benaud at the Adelaide Oval, Benaud said, 'You know, Keith, I wish I had been given the chance to bowl to Don Bradman. I came into the side just too late.' Miller coughed and replied, 'Ahem, Richie my boy, your not having to bowl to Bradman was your luckiest break in cricket.'

Between 1948 and 1956, Miller and his fast-bowling mate Ray Lindwall formed an opening partnership which ranks with that of Jack Gregory and Ted McDonald in the 1920s and Dennis Lillee and Jeff Thomson in the 1970s.

Keith Miller on the drive.

★

Richie Benaud regarded Miller as 'the best captain never to have captained his country', for Miller led by instinct and by example. Miller never captained Australia, but he did lead New South Wales in the 1950s, when it was the powerhouse of Australian cricket.

In November 1955, New South Wales struggled to 215 for the loss of eight wickets on the first day of a Sheffield Shield match with South Australia. At stumps, Miller declared the innings closed. He then celebrated long and hard the birth his first son, Denis, and he was decidedly late by the time he got to the SCG. His New South Wales teammates were already on the ground when Miller arrived, and Alan Davidson had already measured out his run-up.

When Miller set his red eyes on the pitch, they positively opened wide, for the wicket was as green as a tree frog. 'Ahem, Davo, I think you can do a job for us today. Try the other end, and I'll have a go here.' Within a few overs, South Australia was dismissed for 27. Miller took a career-best 7/12. South Australia's opener Dave 'Noisy' Harris batted twice before lunch that day and bagged a pair!

Miller treated his men as equals. He believed they all knew where they should be fielding, and there was little need for him to wave his hands or 'direct traffic'. Once on the field, Miller would say 'scatter' and the players knew instinctively where they should be going.

When Bob Simpson first played for New South Wales, Miller asked him where he fielded and he told him first slip. 'Then first slip it is, Bobby,' Miller declared. Simpson developed into the greatest first slip fieldsman of all time.

Miller was like Shane Warne, a champion, charismatic and a risk-taker. Yet as with Warne, Miller must have been regarded by administrators as too great a risk to be handed the Test captaincy. A great pity.

The 'baby' of the 1948 side

Neil Harvey danced yards down the wicket to get to the pitch of the ball from slow bowlers, with one bowler quipping, 'He kept coming so far along the track towards me that I thought he must want to shake my hand.' Yet he was never out stumped in Test cricket despite having batted against some of the finest spinners of any era.

Not only did he conquer all manner of spinners, he succeeded against some of the greatest fast bowlers to walk the Test stage. Against fast bowlers, he was quick to read length; he would go back deep in his crease to pull, cut or hook, and when the ball was up he would transfer his weight to drive with a beautiful flourish of the bat, or, when the mood took him, he would execute a late cut or whip off the pads with exquisite timing, something approaching a feline touch, a gentle caress to the fence.

Arguably the best Australian batsman since Don Bradman, Harvey played 79 Tests, scoring 6149 runs at 48.41, with 21 hundreds and a highest score of 205. His batting delighted thousands of fans world-wide. 'Neil was the greatest Australian batsman of any Test I played. He revelled in a challenge,' said former Test champion and Test teammate Alan Davidson.

As mentioned in 'Backyard Test matches', Harvey grew up in a cricketing family in Fitzroy, Melbourne. He played two Tests in 1947–48 against India and scored his first Test century (153) in the Fifth Test of the series in Melbourne. Then, at the age of 19, Neil found himself picked for the team which toured England and became known as the Invincibles. Speaking about Harvey's selection, Bradman opined, 'He has the brilliance and daring of youth, and the likelihood of rapid improvement.' Harvey was an acrobatic fielder, and Jack Fingleton said he was 'by far the most brilliant fieldsman of both sides, who was to save many runs in the field'.

From the outset of the tour, Neil absorbed as much information as he could from the old campaigners such as Arthur Morris, Lindsay Hassett, Keith Miller, Ray Lindwall and Bill Johnston. However, he struggled to come to terms with the slow, seaming English tracks and he felt he needed some wise counsel. He asked his room-mate, Sam Loxton, if he would ask Bradman what he was doing wrong. Loxton always called Bradman 'George', his middle name, so he asked, 'George, what's young Harvey doing wrong?' Bradman looked Loxton in the eye and said matter-of-factly, 'Sam, you go and tell your little mate that if he doesn't hit the ball in the air he can't get caught.'

In a tour game against Surrey, Australia wanted to finish the run-chase quickly so they could watch Australian John Bromwich play in the Wimbledon tennis final. Harvey volunteered to open and promised Bradman that he would reach the target quickly. Australia chased down the target of 122 in just 58 minutes and 20.1 overs. Harvey ended unbeaten on 73 and the Australians arrived at Wimbledon on time.

In the wake of an injury to opener Sid Barnes, Harvey was picked to bat at five in the Leeds Fourth Test. After England had amassed 496 in the first innings, Australia had slumped to 3/68, with Bradman one of the dismissed batsmen. Harvey, the youngest member of the squad, joined Keith Miller. Australia was more than 400 behind and if England were to remove the pair, they would expose Australia's lower order and give themselves an opportunity to take a large first innings lead.

Upon Harvey's arrival in the middle, Miller greeted him cheerfully and said, 'Okay, mate, get up the other end. I'll take the bowling for a while until you get yourself organised.' Harvey said, 'Mate, that will do me.'

I couldn't get up the other end quick enough. I watched him play a few overs and I thought, 'This is good', and then they brought Laker on to bowl. The third and the fifth balls of Laker's over disappeared over my head, on the way up, and they both finished in the crowd for six ... I can honestly thank Keith Miller for the confidence he gave me during our partnership ... and it did so much for my future cricket career.

The pair launched a counterattack, with Miller taking the lead and shielding Harvey from Jim Laker, as the young batsman was struggling against the off-breaks that were turning away from him. This allowed Australia to seize the initiative, with Harvey joining the counterattack, hitting consecutive boundaries against Laker. By the time Miller was out for 58, the partnership had yielded 121 runs in 90 minutes, and was likened by *Wisden* to a 'hurricane'. Jack Fingleton wrote that he had 'never known a more enjoyable hour' of 'delectable cricket'.

Loxton came in at 4/189 to join Harvey, who continued to attack the bowling, and the partnership yielded 105 in only 95 minutes. Harvey was eventually out for 112 from 183 balls, bowled by Laker while playing a cross-batted sweep. His shot selection prompted Bradman to throw his head back in disappointment.

Loxton's fierce driving bagged him 5 sixes and 9 fours in his 93 and the high rate of scoring helped to swing the match into a balanced position when Australia was finally dismissed for 458. On the final afternoon, Harvey was at the crease with Bradman (173) when Morris (182) and Miller (12) were out. He got off the mark by hitting the winning boundary as Australia successfully completed a Test world record run-chase of 3/404 in less than one day.

As Bradman's team broke up in the 1950s due to retirements, Harvey became Australia's senior batsman. In South Africa in 1949–50, Harvey was forced to shoulder more responsibility in the batting order with Bradman's retirement and Sid Barnes taking an extended break. Harvey rose to the challenge. He started the tour well and was highly productive in seven first-class matches leading into the Tests. Harvey made 178 in the first innings of the Second Test at Cape Town, which set up a first innings lead of 248 runs, to guide Australia to an eight-wicket victory.

This was followed by an unbeaten 151 in five and a half hours at Durban, regarded as one of his finest Test innings. Having been dismissed for 75 on a wet wicket in the first innings, Australia had slumped to 3/59 in pursuit of a victory target of 336. On a crumbling, sticky pitch, the Australians were having extreme difficulty with the spin of Hugh Tayfield and faced defeat. Harvey adapted his game to play a patient innings, Tufty Mann and Tayfield began to tire in the heat and Harvey began to score more quickly. He registered his slowest ever century on his way to guiding his team to an improbable victory by five wickets.

Harvey amassed four centuries in consecutive Tests in the series. He scored six centuries in his first nine Tests, totalling 959 runs at 106.55.

Following his success in South Africa, Harvey batted regularly at either number three or four. The triple-figure average from his first two Test seasons could not be maintained when Australia hosted the 1950–51 Ashes series – he managed only three half-centuries then. The 1951–52 season, with the West Indies touring Australia, was even less productive.

Harvey started the 1952–53 season having failed to score a century in ten Tests over almost three years, but in that season's series against South Africa in Australia, he accumulated 834 Test runs at 92.66.

Harvey totalled 1659 runs at 63.81 for that first-class season, the second-highest tally for a season in Australian history, just 31 runs behind Bradman's record. In the last match of the season, the Western Australian captain declared early on the last afternoon to allow Harvey another innings so he could break the record. Harvey muttered, 'I wouldn't want to break a record that way,' and managed only 13.

In 1953, he became only the third Australian in a quarter of a century to score 2000 runs on an Ashes tour. Bradman (three times) and Stan McCabe (once) were the others. After the first three Tests were drawn, Harvey returned to Headingley, the venue of his famous innings five years earlier. In a low-scoring match, he top-scored for the entire match with 71 in the first innings as Australia took a 99-run lead. Australia looked set for victory and retention of the Ashes at the start of the final day, but time-wasting and defiant defence from the English batsmen left Australia a target of 177 in the last two hours. This would have required a scoring rate much higher than in the first four days of the match.

Harvey scored quickly and Australia was on schedule for a win, at 111 in 75 minutes. English medium-pacer Trevor Bailey then began bowling with the wicketkeeper more than 2 metres down the leg side to deny the Australians an opportunity to hit the ball, but the umpires failed to penalise them as wides.

The match ended in a draw, Harvey describing Bailey's tactics as 'absolutely disgusting'. England wicketkeeper Godfrey Evans said the tourists 'were absolutely livid' and he agreed that they were right in claiming that Bailey's bowling was 'the worst kind of negative cricket' and that he had 'cheated them of victory'. England won the Fifth Test, taking back the Ashes after 19 years in Australian hands.

The 1954–55 season saw England tour Australia. Harvey made 162 in the First Test in Brisbane after Australia was sent in, helping to compile 8/601 to set up an innings victory. In the Second Test in Sydney, Australia needed 223 to win on a poor wicket against the lethal pace of Frank Tyson and Brian Statham. The express Tyson was bowling with the help of a tailwind and the slips cordon was over 50 metres behind the bat. Harvey stood firm while Tyson scattered the stumps of his partners, and he farmed the strike ruthlessly, protecting the tailenders and counterattacking the England fast bowlers. He played all the shots, including a hook for six that landed to the right of where my grandfather and I were sitting in front of the Noble Stand and thudded into the visitors' dressing-room.

Bill Johnston came in at 9/145, with 78 runs still required. Protected by Harvey, he only had to face 16 balls in 40 minutes and they almost produced an unlikely Australian victory. England won by 38 runs when Johnston gloved a Tyson delivery down the leg side to the wicketkeeper. Harvey had played what many observers thought was the greatest innings of his life, a defiant, unbeaten 92.

Australia's 1956 tour of England proved a disaster for Ian Johnson's team. It was an English summer dominated by off-spinner Jim Laker and his Surrey teammate Tony Lock, who repeatedly dismantled the tourists on dusty spinning pitches specifically tailored to cater for the home side. At Old Trafford, Jim Laker took a record match haul of 19/90 on a spiteful, spinning wicket which prompted former champion leggie Bill O'Reilly to bellow from the press box: 'Why, I'd get 12 wickets on that poor excuse of a wicket without bothering to remove my coat.'

Australia was routed by an innings in what is known as 'Laker's match', to concede the Ashes 2–1. The debacle at Old Trafford was part of a three-week trough during which Harvey scored only 11 runs, including three consecutive ducks in a 17-day period that yielded not a solitary run.

As expected, the Australian team's leaders, Ian Johnson and Keith Miller, retired from cricket after the tour. Harvey replaced Johnson as Victorian captain and was the logical choice as successor to the Test captaincy, as the most experienced member of the team (48 Tests).

However, both Harvey and Benaud had been criticised for their attitude towards Johnson in an official report to the board about the 1956 tour. Harvey was surprisingly overlooked for the captaincy, which went to Ian Craig, who had replaced Miller as New South Wales skipper. Craig was only 22 and had played six Tests. Harvey was named vice-captain to Craig for both the 1956–57 non-Test tour of New Zealand and the 1957–58 tour to South Africa.

The day after the captaincy announcement, the Harvey-led Victorians met Craig's New South Wales team at the SCG in the last match of the Shield season. Harvey admitted to being irked by the board's snub and felt that it was because of his blunt nature. The men were cordial at the toss and Craig sent the Victorians in to bat. But as Harvey and Craig had gone out to toss, Victorian batsman Colin McDonald had been practising and hit a ball into his face and broke his nose. Harvey asked for a gentleman's agreement to allow a substitute for McDonald. Craig refused, citing the importance of the match.

New South Wales players Richie Benaud and Alan Davidson noted a rare angry reaction from Harvey, who walked briskly back to the dressing-room, donned the pads and walked onto the arena with the determined look of a man going to war. Benaud said that Harvey 'proceeded, with a certain amount of anger, to play one of the best innings I have seen in Sheffield Shield'. Harvey made 209 and he later said it 'gave me as much pleasure as any innings I had ever played'.

Davidson recalls:

Harv smashed us all over the place. I bowled the first ball, it was quick and moved late from leg stump to a little outside off and I thought, 'Hey that's a beauty!' Harv moved back and across and hit the ball like a rocket in front of point for four. In fact, it was hit with such power the ball struck the pickets and rebounded 10 metres back into the playing area. We started the match at 11 am and at 2 pm I took the second new ball. The Victorians, thanks to Harvey's extraordinary showing, had reached 200 by that time.

177

Some players remained resentful of Craig's dubious elevation ahead of Harvey during the 1957–58 tour of South Africa, but appreciated that Craig had not promoted himself and that he was fair and open to input from teammates. Despite the disagreement as to whether Craig was deserving of the captaincy, the team proceeded smoothly without infighting. The team labelled the worst to leave Australian shores came home 3–0 victors in the five-Test series.

Prior to the Fifth Test, Craig had wanted to drop himself due to poor form, which would have made Harvey captain. Peter Burge, the third member of the selection panel and a Harvey supporter, was comfortable with this, but Harvey ordered Burge to retain Craig.

After returning from South Africa, Harvey embarrassed the Board of Control when he frankly discussed his financial situation during a television interview. He revealed that the players earned only £85 per Test and that he was almost broke, despite being an automatic selection for Australia.

Harvey received a job offer and moved to New South Wales. As a new player, he was behind vice-captain Richie Benaud in the state's pecking order, despite being the Test vice-captain. With Craig unfit, Harvey was appointed to captain an Australia XI in a warm-up match against the touring Englishmen, indicating that the selectors were considering him for the Test captaincy. Harvey scored a duck and 38 and the Australians lost heavily, by 345 runs. Benaud was made Australian captain ahead of Harvey.

In 1958–59, as Benaud's deputy, Harvey helped materially in Australia's surprise 4–0 series victory to reclaim the Ashes, though his batting form was modest. During the 1959–60 season, Australia undertook an arduous tour of the subcontinent, with three and five Tests against Pakistan and India, respectively.

In Dhaka, East Pakistan (now Bangladesh), Harvey made 96 on a matting pitch over rough ground in the First Test, mastering the medium pace of Fazal Mahmood, to set up an Australian win. In the course of the innings, Harvey had to overcome fever, dysentery and physical illness, which forced him to leave the field six times to recompose himself. Gideon Haigh has called it 'one of his most dazzling innings'. During his stay at the crease, his partners contributed 48 runs while seven wickets fell.

After the Second Test in Lahore came down to a run-chase for Australia, with Harvey and Norm O'Neill on schedule to win before time ran out, the Pakistani fielders began to waste time, swapping the cover and midwicket fielders very slowly each time one of the batsmen took a single. To counter this, Harvey deliberately backed away from a straight ball and let himself be bowled, throwing his wicket away for 37. This allowed Benaud to come in and bat with O'Neill so that the two right-handed batsmen would give the Pakistanis no opportunity to waste time. Australia won the match with minutes to spare.

Harvey began his final tour to England in 1961 and Benaud's regular absences due to a shoulder injury allowed him to lead Australia for a third of the tour matches. This included most of the first month of the tour. During the season, Harvey and Benaud led aggressively to force results through attacking strategy and a determination to avoid time-wasting.

His injury forced Benaud out of the Second Test at Lord's, meaning that Harvey finally captained Australia at the highest level. Davidson agreed to play carrying an injury, and this meant that Australia's two best bowlers were injured.

Played on a controversial pitch with a noticeable ridge running across it, which caused irregular bounce, The Battle of the Ridge was one of the great Test matches. Davidson took 5/42 and bruised many of the English batsmen with the irregular bounce as the hosts were bowled out for 205. Australia then replied with 339, in large part due to Bill Lawry's 130, during which he sustained many blows.

In the second innings, Harvey's captaincy moves proved to be highly productive. He gave the new ball to Graham McKenzie, a young paceman playing in his first international series, who responded by taking 5/37. Harvey brought the part-time leg-spin of Bob Simpson into the attack when Ray Illingworth had just arrived at the crease and moved himself into the leg slip position. Illingworth edged Simpson into Harvey's hands for a duck. England fell for 202, leaving Australia a target of 69.

Australia slumped to 4/19 on the erratic surface. Harvey sent Peter Burge out to attack the bowling, a tactic that worked as Australia won by five wickets. Harvey described the win as 'probably my proudest moment. We really got on the French champagne that afternoon. I knew it'd be my only Test match as captain and, being at Lord's, I decided to make the best of it.'

Having stated his intention to retire at the end of the 1962–63 summer, Harvey applied to the Australian Cricket Board for permission to work as a journalist while also playing cricket. The application was refused, but Harvey wrote some bitter criticism of England captain Ted Dexter at the end of the series. Following a complaint from the Marylebone Cricket Club, the board said that it deplored Harvey's comments.

Harvey made his 21st and final century in the Fourth Test at Adelaide, then returned to his adopted hometown of Sydney for his farewell match. With the series level at 1–1, the Ashes were still alive, but the game turned into a dull draw. In the two English innings, he held six catches to equal the world record, a reminder of his prowess as one of Australia's great all-round fielders.

Harvey was an Australian selector from 1967 to 1979 and from 1971 was chairman of selectors. It was a tumultuous period in Australian cricket, when captain Bill Lawry was acrimoniously sacked a few days before the Seventh Test of the 1970–71 series against England after a dispute between players and Australian officials. Lawry was not informed of his fate and learnt of his omission on the radio, when he was still one of Australia's most productive batsmen.

During that crucial selection meeting, Harvey clashed with Sir Donald Bradman over Lawry. Bradman wanted the Victorian to retain the captaincy, but Harvey, who plugged for Ian Chappell to take over the captaincy, thought retaining Lawry as one of the rank and file was not the way to go. A few years later when playing golf with Chappell, Harvey said: 'I got you the captaincy.'

Harvey may well have thought Lawry might have been a disruption to Chappell's leadership on the upcoming Australian tour of England. I doubt that, for I believe had Lawry toured England, along with Graham McKenzie and Ian Redpath, Australia would have won the Ashes.

It was the Australian Cricket Board's dreadful planning for the 1969–70 tour to Ceylon (now Sri Lanka), India and South Africa and Lawry's taking responsibility for the Australians refusing to play a fifth Test in South Africa, which led to the pay dispute, which led to the formation of World Series Cricket (WSC) in 1977 and generated a mass exodus of players.

Bill Lawry was a victim of circumstance. His name was in the selectors' little black book after the events in South Africa. Against Ray Illingworth's 1970–71 Ashes team, his captaincy lacked imagination; admittedly, he had two aging fast bowlers in Graham McKenzie and Alan Connolly, but his use of the spinners was left wanting. It was time for change. The selectors saw their chance. Axe Lawry, make Chappell captain and start again with a clean slate.

When WSC hit world cricket, Bob Simpson, after 10 years in retirement, was recalled at the age of 41 to captain the Test team. Following the rapprochement between the Establishment and the WSC players, Harvey left the selection panel, the WSC representatives feeling that Harvey's anti-WSC comments made him prejudiced against the selection of former WSC players.

In later life, Harvey was known for his blunt and critical comments towards modern players, believing the standard of cricket in earlier times was superior. He criticised modern-day batsmen, noting that players in earlier eras had to play on sticky wickets. 'These guys who play out here are a little bit spoilt in my opinion. They play on flat wickets all the time and they grizzle if the ball does a little bit off the pitch, and whatever ... But we had to put up with that.' He also lamented the decline in player conduct in the modern era, in particular criticising the advent of sledging.

After Steve Waugh's team set a world record of consecutive Test victories, Harvey named three Australian teams that he thought to be superior. In response to the suggestion that Waugh's men were the best team in history, he replied 'No, far from it.' He attributed the wins to weak opponents, stating, 'I don't think they're up to the world standard they were years ago,' and that the 1980s West Indies team was far superior. He also criticised the Australian team for publicly praising the skills of their opponents, believing that they did so to aggrandise their statistical performances against teams he considered to be weak.

In 2002, Harvey called for Mark and Steve Waugh to be dropped from the Australian team, claiming that they were a waste of space. He stated, 'Money is the only thing that keeps them playing ... If they earned the same money as I did when I was playing, they'd have retired at 34 as I did, and Australian cricket would be the better for it.'

When Steve Waugh was close to being dropped during the 2002–03 series against England, Harvey wrote off a half-century made by Waugh by saying, 'He's playing against probably one of the worst cricket teams I've ever seen.'

Harvey vociferously called for Shane Warne and Mark Waugh to be banned from cricket after it was revealed that they accepted money from bookmakers to give pitch and weather information and the Australian Cricket Board privately fined them.

*

Neil Harvey was regarded by *Wisden* as 'the finest outfielder in the world' during his career. His right-handed powerful, swift and accurate throwing caused many run-outs. Norm O'Neill and Harvey formed a formidable pairing in the covers, helping to restrict opposition batsmen from scoring in the region.

He bowled right-arm off-spin from a three- to four-pace approach on rare occasions, taking only three wickets in his Test career. Away from the field, Harvey had a quiet and unassuming manner, in complete contrast to his dynamic batting, and his non-smoking, non-drinking set him apart from the prevailing cricket culture of his period. Harvey was known for his respect for umpiring decisions and for never appealing for lbw when he fielded in the slips.

Harvey retired as Australia's most capped player and with a tally of runs and centuries second only to Don Bradman. He was of the firm belief that any bowling could and should be hit, and gave the impression that the balls were reaching the boundary with a minimum of power. According to Johnny Moyes, 'the sight of his slim figure, neat and trim-looking, always capless, coming to bat brought new hope for spectators. He will never prod a half volley or decline the challenge of a long hop ... he will go looking for the ball which he can hit for four.'

Harvey's attacking style often led to criticism that his batting was risky, with England captain Len Hutton feeling that he played and missed too much, while dour all-rounder Trevor Bailey quipped, 'I wonder how many runs Harvey would make if he decided to stop playing strokes with an element of risk about them.' Harvey was nevertheless happy to continue his flamboyant strokeplay.

Davo, the great all-rounder

Alan Keith Davidson was born in the small country town of Lisarow, near Gosford, New South Wales, in 1929. He was naturally fit through hard work on the family's rural property, chopping wood or carting hay, and when he wasn't working on the farm he was playing football or cricket.

In his playing days, before a Shield or Test match in Adelaide, at the crack of dawn Davidson helped leading horse trainer Colin Hayes wash and groom the racehorses after their early run along Semaphore Beach. 'I loved working with Colin's horses,' Davo recalled. 'I didn't let Sir Donald know ... because he was chairman of Australian selectors. Imagine if I got kicked by a horse one morning and couldn't bowl for the last two days of a Test match.'

He learnt to bowl on a pitch he burrowed out of the side of a hill on the family property. 'Although it proved to be a good, flat surface, when I missed the stumps I had to chase the ball down the hill,' he told me.

The young Davidson began his cricket as a hard-hitting down-the-list batsman and a left-arm orthodox spinner, but when his uncle wanted a pace bowler for the Gosford team, he volunteered to do the job and rarely bowled spinners again. In the summer of 1948–49, he met Richie Benaud and so began a lifelong friendship.

He became the mainstay of Australia's attack and was one of the great fast bowlers of his era, as related in 'Five great quicks' elsewhere in this book. He could also lay claim to having been one of Australia's best all-rounders. He moved fast in the field for a big man and was a superb catcher in almost any position. Davo held on to some breathtaking catches. And after one amazing catch, a journalist called him 'the Claw.'

His all-round gifts extended to his batting, although, as Keith Miller noted, 'He was never run-hungry as a batsman. He merely batted according to the tempo of the game.'

Davidson reached his all-round peak during the 1960–61 home series against the West Indies and was regarded as the key player in Australia's victory. In the First Test in Brisbane, Davidson, despite a broken finger on his bowling hand, became the first player to take 10 wickets *and* accumulate more than 100 runs in a match. He took 5/135 and 6/87 and, after scoring 44 in the first innings, made 80 in a counterattacking seventh-wicket partnership of 134 with captain Richie Benaud. Australia was seeking victory in the run-chase rather than attempting to survive for a draw. Although Davidson was run out for 80, it was largely due to his all-round efforts that the match became famous as the first tied Test in history and set the scene for the positive cricket by both sides in that series.

His batting was also a major contributor to Australia's Ashes win in 1961. With the series 1–all, the Australians were heading for defeat on the last day of the Fourth Test at Old Trafford. With their score at 9/334, they led England by a slender 157 runs when number eleven Graham McKenzie joined Davidson. Their 98-run last-wicket partnership (McKenzie 32, Davidson 77 not out) gave Australia a big enough lead for Richie Benaud (6/70) to bowl England out in its second innings. Operating around the wicket for the most part, Benaud aimed at the rough outside the right-hander's leg stump. His clean-bowling England captain Peter May around his legs, after having the dangerous Ted Dexter caught behind, was the turning point in the game.

Davo admires a host of cricketers before and during his era, but he will never develop eyes in the back of his head. For instance, he says, 'You know, I reckon to watch half an hour of Mark Waugh at his best was the best batting you could see in terms of grace and style.'

Richie Benaud: a legendary life

When I was growing up in Sydney in the early 1950s, Richie Benaud was every kid's hero. A good-looking bloke, leg-spinner, hard-hitting batsman, great gully fieldsman, Benaud to us kids had it all. His cricket attire was always immaculate. When playing junior cricket, we'd unbutton our shirts in true Benaud style and we simply had to wear Brylcreem in our hair; and that first shave one day would have to feature Smoothex, both products promoted by Benaud on advertisements in newspapers and on television. In our backyard 'Tests', my brother Nick was the eldest so he was always Australia and invariably had Benaud as his captain. I was left to make do with 'England', although he made a concession: I could have Victor Trumper opening with Len Hutton.

I first saw Richie play when my grandfather took me to the Second Test of 1954–55 at the SCG, when 'Typhoon' Tyson bowled England to a 38-run win. I followed Benaud's career through the mid- to late 1950s. In 1955 my parents relocated the family from Sydney to Perth, so the next time I set eyes on my hero was at the WACA, where Benaud's Test touring team played Western Australia before boarding the boat for England in 1961.

I skipped work at the Commonwealth Bank in Tuart Hill, a suburb of Perth, caught up with two old schoolmates, walked from town to the ground and clambered over the high cyclone fence, topped by barbed wire, to enter the ground, just behind the high corrugated-tin side wall of the curator's hut.

That summer of 1960–61 had been full of excitement. On the last day of the Australia–West Indies First Test in Brisbane,

Terry Jenner and I were at the WACA Ground for training with the Western Australia Colts squad. As we left the nets for the change-rooms, we noticed players walking from the main ground. It was tea time in a match involving the Governor's XI. Magically, a gleaming black Rolls-Royce cruised slowly alongside where we walked on the lawn. The vehicle stopped and the back door opened.

'Boys, it's the last over in Brisbane … Australia should win it. Hop in the back and listen with me.'

We didn't hesitate and accepted the invitation to sit in Western Australian Governor Lieutenant-General Sir Charles Gairdner's car to listen to the last over of the Test.

That day, chasing 233 runs to win, Australia had been 6/92 when Benaud joined Alan Davidson. At tea, Australia still needed 130 runs with four wickets in hand. As they walked off, Sir Donald Bradman said to Benaud: 'What are your thoughts?'

'We are going for a win.'

'Good to hear it,' Sir Donald smiled.

Like warriors going to battle, Benaud and Davidson strode to the wicket after tea hell-bent on turning the match Australia's way. Despite fast bowler Wes Hall's extreme pace and bounce, the pair cut, hooked and drove the fast man. They also climbed into all the others, hitting a record 134 for the seventh wicket before Davidson fell. Benaud (52) dropped a ball at his feet and called for a run. Davo reacted swiftly, but not quickly enough, for little Joe Solomon swooped at midwicket and threw the wicket down with Davo stranded. When Davidson lost his wicket, Australia was 7/227, with just six runs required off Hall's last over for victory. In those days an over in Tests in Australia comprised eight balls.

Ball one: A rising ball from Hall hit Wally Grout on the thigh, and Benaud charged down the track to steal a leg bye. Seven balls left; five runs to win.

Ball two: Hall bounced Benaud and the Australian skipper, attempting to hook, got a faint touch on the glove and West Indian keeper Gerry Alexander accepted the catch down leg side with a cry of joy. Australia now 8/228. Six balls left; five runs to win.

West Indian captain Frank Worrell had forbidden Hall to bowl a bouncer to Benaud. The Australian was not expecting a short ball, but short it was; fast, dangerous and to Benaud, eminently hookable. Instinct took over and his attempting to hook Hall for the winning runs was typical of his reaction, totally in line with the assurance he gave Bradman.

Ball three: New batsman Ian Meckiff pushed the ball to point. No run. Australia was still in the box seat with five runs required off five balls.

Ball four: Hall strayed down leg side. Meckiff swung hard at the wayward delivery, but missed the ball altogether. Grout seized his opportunity and raced towards the batting end. Alexander gathered the ball and threw at the non-striker's end. The ball missed its target and Meckiff got home. Four balls left; four runs required for victory.

Ball five: Grout tried to keep a rising ball from Hall down, but it hit on the splice of his bat and ballooned to Rohan Kanhai at square leg. In the calamity of the moment, Hall also wanted the catch. He charged towards Kanhai, the pair collided and the ball fell to the ground, and the batsman scampered for a run. Three balls left; three runs required to win.

By now Benaud and others in the Australian dressing room, including Norm O'Neill, were on the edge of their seats, chain smoking. Everyone had to stay in their seats. The tension was unbearable. Ken 'Slasher' Mackay was more superstitious than most cricketers and he insisted on following dressing-room tradition when a batting side was in a tight spot. 'He wouldn't let us move from our seats for fear of divine intervention,' Benaud said later. Benaud remained silent as he sat glued to the tense battle in the middle.

Ball six: Hall pitched up and Meckiff swung with all his might. Meckiff's crude swing of the bat saw the ball career towards the midwicket boundary for what seemed a certain four and everyone thought it was the winning hit. However, there was a thick mat of long grass in the outfield, which proved decisive because the ball stopped just inside the boundary fence with Conrad Hunte in swift pursuit. Hunte had a rocket arm and he fired the ball into keeper Alexander's gloves right over the bails. Grout was run out for 2, Australia 9/232; one run to win.

Years later, with typical Benaud precision, he recalled the scene: 'The Hunte throw was magnificent – it was not one side or the other, not right, not left but directly over the top.'

Ball seven: Spinner Lindsay Kline came to the wicket to join Meckiff. They decided to run whatever happened the very next ball. Hall pitched up, Kline pushed square of the wicket and Meckiff took off. So, too, did little Solomon. He picked up and threw, hitting the stumps with Meckiff short of his ground.

In the confusion that followed, none of the players seemed to know what happened. Some of the West Indians thought they won, most of the Australians thought they'd lost the match.

Soon enough everyone realised that the match was indeed history in the making: the first Test match tie ever.

Great credit went to Benaud, for when all seemed lost he went all out for a win.

The game set up what was one of the greatest Test series of all time.

The spirit in which that match, indeed the entire series, was played was due to the attacking captaincies of Australia's Richie Benaud and the West Indies' Frank Worrell.

Fast bowler Des Hoare, who played in the Adelaide drawn Test, was not picked for England due to a midwicket 'confrontation' with West Indies opener Conrad Hunte. As Hunte ran to the non-striker's end to complete a three, Hoare stood in his way, there appeared to be physical contact between the pair and after the match Hoare was seen in conversation with Australia's chairman of selectors, Sir Donald Bradman.

Only a couple of days before sailing to England for the Ashes series, Hoare played as a lower-order batsman for Western Australia against Benaud's Australia team. Benaud bowled in tandem with left-arm wrist-spinner Lindsay Kline and neither could make any impression on him. He played stoically, hitting a century, a small reward for being dumped forever from Test cricket.

In England, Benaud's bowling shoulder worried him and he missed the Lord's Test, which Australia won under the captaincy of Neil Harvey.

At Manchester, England was cruising towards victory at 1/150, Ted Dexter in full command, when Benaud decided to go around the wicket with the intention of landing his deliveries in the rough outside the right-handers' leg stump. Over the course of the match, the right-handed fast bowlers had helped create the rough. They included England's fast men Freddie Trueman, Brian Statham and Jack Flavell on that fascinating last day.

Benaud immediately had Dexter caught behind, then bowled Peter May around his legs. By the time the ninth England wicket had fallen, Benaud had captured 6/71.

The new ball was due and Benaud's deputy, Neil Harvey, said, 'Rich, put on Davo. Let's finish it.' But Benaud ignored Harvey and took the ball for the next over. Australia had plenty of runs to play with and a seven-wicket haul beckoned. Harvey was unimpressed. The second ball of the over was hit to him at cover point and, instead of returning it to Grout over the stumps, Harvey deliberately threw the ball to the midwicket boundary for four.

'Now, will you put Davo on?' he said with a grimace.

Next over, Davidson clean-bowled Brian Statham and Australia won the match easily.

*

It was on my first tour of England in 1968 that Richie gave me his dillybag with the formula for skinned spinning fingers.

The Benaud Cure

INGREDIENTS:
1 bottle of oily calamine lotion
1 packet of tissues
1 packet of emery boards
1 packet of boracic acid powder

When a spinner loses skin off his main spinning finger, he can apply methylated spirits to harden the skinned area. However, if the skin goes too hard, it will split and the problem will remain for a long time. The idea, Richie explained, was to allow the affected area to be fairly hard but flexible.

The unaffected skin next to the skinned area needs to be on much the same level, so that's where the emery board comes in. You cut away any dead skin and file to ensure there are no little bits that the seam can catch and rip. You mix the boracic acid powder with the oily calamine lotion and work it into a paste, and spread the paste thickly on the affected area. Leave for an hour and repeat.

The Benaud cure worked nicely for me. It doesn't work for all, but I pass on Richie's formula to young spinners where I can.

In the Australian summer of 1968–69, I was twelfth man for the Fifth Test at the SCG. Bill Lawry's team won the match. Richie had no doubt been in the Windies dressing-room with both teams sharing a drink, as was tradition after the last day of a series. As he was about to walk out, he noticed me by the window and stopped to tell me, 'A tour of India is a most important part of a young Australian cricketer's education.'

How right he was: the cricket challenges of spinning wickets, the umpiring, the poor-quality accommodation, the weather and fanatical spectators all created a totally different cricket environment. Apart from the negatives, I loved the spinning wickets and thrived, getting 28 wickets at 19 runs apiece. The record wicket tally for an Australian bowler in a Test series in India is 29, jointly held by Alan Davidson and Richie Benaud. I was glad not to have bettered their record. They were my heroes and I'm happy to sit in behind them.

On my second England tour in 1972, I got to know the Benauds better. Richie and Daphne were found at the Knightsbridge flat of their friends John and Dumpy Morley. They were grand hosts and often had a few of the Australians to a Sunday roast when the team was in London. The Benauds knew a wide range of people from all walks of life in Australia, England, South Africa, West Indies and New Zealand.

John Morley was an antiques dealer and his pride and joy was a blue Ferrari, which he enjoyed driving rather fast on any motorway to be found. One day 'up north', he was clocked by two Yorkshire policemen at 170 miles per hour. The police gave up the chase and decided to take a slip road to a good pub nearby, thinking that, as they were out of their jurisdiction, a 'few beers would go down a treat'. Just as they approached the pub carpark, they noticed a distinctive blue Ferrari parked near the pub front entrance.

They rushed into the pub and asked, 'Who owns the blue Ferrari out front?'

'I do,' Morley said confidently.

Both policemen walked towards Morley, thrust out their hands and one said with a big smile: 'Congratulations, that's the first time we've caught someone going 100 miles per hour over the speed limit.'

In 1972, Daphne Benaud worked for the Australia team management. She proved brilliant in her organisation. The players found her an absolute delight, with Daphne sending back to Australia all manner of correspondence and recorded tapes for our families. Richie and Daphne enjoyed the company of the Australian players – the characters, the brilliance of some and the mayhem of others. They particularly enjoyed my clumsiness.

On the morning of the first ODI at Lord's, Richie offered to help me in the nets. I had developed a bad habit of running on the wicket on my follow-through. Unfortunately, I'd had a few too many at the previous night's team dinner and was a bit the worse for wear when I met him in the nets. I suspect my immediate improvement was due partly to Richie's inspiration and partly to a stumble or two left, into the safety of the practice net.

England won the toss and batted. I fielded at third man and Geoffrey Boycott guided one down through the gully. I had the ball in my sights, but there was a slight misjudgment – I ran right and the ball stayed left.

There were a few other instances of clumsiness which would have raised a wry smile from Richie and Daphne, including walking through the stumps when retrieving my cap from the umpire. After 12 overs, I had 2/24: Man of the Match award stuff ... if Chappelli had let me bat first drop.

Richie was always immaculately dressed, never a hair out of place, and whenever I met him, he'd always find something wrong with my attire, such as my tie being askew. One day, I thought I'd be absolutely beyond reproach. I had my suit dry-cleaned, shirt laundered, new shoes ... just for the Sydney Test match. I saw Richie in the distance and confidently approached. He smiled generously and thrust out his hand.

Then, to my utter horror, he pointed to the middle of my tie and there it was ... a tomato pip. Some things never change.

In 2016, my fiancée, Patsy Gardner, and I caught up with Daphne at the SCG Test. There the subject came round to my clumsiness and Patsy told her, 'There was a Rowdy moment at the airport. All to do with a plate of food flipping over.'

In 1976, Australia had just beaten Clive Lloyd's West Indians 5–1 on home soil. In March of that year, Richie Benaud was the manager of the International Wanderers tour of South Africa. The side was: Greg Chappell (captain), Mike Denness, Ian Chappell, Phil Edmonds, Gary Gilmour, Alan Hurst, Martin Kent, Dennis Lillee, Ashley Mallett, John Morrison, John Shepherd, Bob Taylor, Glenn Turner, Derek Underwood and Max Walker. A South African Invitation XI opposed us in three unofficial 'Tests'. Among the South Africans were some greats: Barry Richards, Graeme Pollock and Clive Rice. In accordance with Benaud's stipulation that the team should include a number of non-white cricketers, Tiffie Barnes, Winston Carelse, Baboo Ebrahim, Devdas Govindjee, David Jacobs and Farouk Timol were selected in the host team's squad.

We won the first 'Test' in Cape Town, drew the second in Johannesburg and lost the final match in Durban, thanks to an inspirational bowling performance by the left-arm spinner Baboo Ebrahim. His performance in that match warmed the hearts of all, even the Wanderers. He took six second-innings wickets to humble our side.

Six years earlier, on the eve of the First Test at Cape Town, Baboo had turned up to the Australian team's training and asked if he could bowl to Lawry's men. Ian Redpath told the young Ebrahim that he could, despite the protestations of a burly white security guard who bellowed, 'He can't bowl to your men. That man is black.' Baboo bowled to the Australians and immediately impressed. He was better than the two spinners South Africa played in that Test match, off-spinner Michael Seymour and left-armer Graham Chevalier.

Benaud had brought the team to South Africa to help that country's non-white cricketers and to help through sporting endeavour to break down barriers. He particularly agonised over Ebrahim and other players there might be like him. Here was a brilliantly gifted spinner denied the chance to play for his country in an official Test match because of the colour of his skin. For the duration of our short tour, Benaud especially requested that there be no restrictions on where people, regardless of colour, could stand or sit to watch a game. He also insisted that bars in all parts of the ground be open to people of any race or colour. In 1970, when the Australian team played its first provincial match of the tour in Pretoria, no non-white person had been permitted to enter the ground.

One teammate was the jovial West Indian and Kent all-rounder John Shepherd. How, in Apartheid South Africa, Shep got on the tour was a bit of a mystery. Perhaps he was on the same pass that the Japanese obtained to canvass business opportunities: they were presented with an 'honorary white pass'.

In Johannesburg, Benaud had booked the team into a restaurant for a meal. Everyone was neatly, albeit casually, dressed – slacks, open-necked shirts and sports coats. The restaurant manager approached one of the tables where John Shepherd was sitting and began an extraordinary tirade. 'Get out,' he yelled at Shep. 'No tie, no service. You are not welcome here. Leave the premises immediately.'

Incensed, Benaud confronted the restaurant manager: 'Don't concern yourself. We are all leaving and we plan to eat at a civilised establishment.'

Whether the tour achieved any lasting good for the non-whites of South Africa's is debatable. Apartheid was a such a dreadful, heartless policy that only people power could ever overturn minority rule. Eventually, protests over many years, trade sanctions, isolation and international sporting ostracism prevailed.

However, the International Wanderers tour proved to the masses, black and white – through the example of Baboo Ebrahim's bowling in Durban – that a black South African was as good and often better than a white man in the game of cricket. Rebel tours from the West Indies and Sri Lanka followed a few years later to emphasise that point.

Benaud's team had paved the way.

Richie Benaud was a brilliant all-rounder and captain. There was a sort of aloofness about him, but as you got to know him better, it was more shyness. How can a shy person host on television, you might ask? Well, it happens. Billy Birmingham, The 12th Man, does all his funny work in a studio and tells me he hates speaking in public.

Born in the shadow of the Blue Mountains at Penrith, New South Wales, on 6 October 1930, Richie inherited his father's love of cricket. In the summer of 1922–23 his leg-spinning father, Lou Benaud, took all 20 wickets for 65 runs playing for Penrith Waratahs against St Marys. In 1940, at the age of 10, Richie went to see a match at the SCG for the first time. As he sat alongside his father, Richie became engrossed with South Australia's Test legend Clarrie Grimmett's bowling in the Sheffield Shield match against New South Wales.

He marvelled at the two wickets Grimmett got with what Richie thought to be a shorter, faster leg-break which skidded on straight; but, in fact, it was the flipper, which Grimmett had invented. South Australia and Test leg-spinner Bruce Dooland was shown the delivery by Grimmett and Dooland in turn revealed the secret to Benaud.

It takes time to develop a flipper, as it is propelled by squeezing the ball out when holding the ball between finger and thumb –

an action much like flicking your fingers while holding the ball. When at the Cricket Academy under former Victorian batsman Jack Potter's tutelage, Shane Warne was shown the flipper and he became a master of that delivery.

In 2004, Mark Nicholas was involved in putting together Richie Benaud's Greatest XI for a DVD produced by Mark's brother, Ben. The team he chose was: Jack Hobbs, Sunil Gavaskar, Don Bradman, Viv Richards, Sachin Tendulkar, Garry Sobers, Adam Gilchrist, Imran Khan, Shane Warne, Dennis Lillee, SF Barnes.

Some time later, Nicholas asked Richie if there was anything he would change if he had the chance to play out his career again. 'Yes, I would like to have been coached by Shane Warne and had the opportunity of bowling at the other end to Warne.'

And just to illustrate how heroes can have their own heroes, Richie's dad, Lou, was Richie's hero, and Richie Benaud was a hero to Ian Chappell, who always cherished his advice. 'Whether it was in business, or cricket, or life in general, he was the person I always approached,' Chappelli said.

In 1963, soon after Chappell had scored his maiden first-class century – 149 versus Benaud's New South Wales at Adelaide Oval – he travelled to England to play a season of Lancashire League. When he arrived at the Ramsbottom Club, there awaiting him was a new Gray-Nicholls cricket bat, courtesy of Richie Benaud.

Richie was always generous of spirit to emerging players and always made time to help a young bowler or journalist. He was mentor to so many on the Channel Nine commentary team. Nowadays, the likes of Mark Taylor, Michael Slater, Michael Clarke and Ian Healy are mainstays and they still have the likes of veteran commentators Ian Chappell and Bill Lawry to bounce off.

There are so many stories about Richie – his sporting brilliance, his television genius, his loyalty and friendship. Those who dress up as 'Richies' to attend the Tests will help keep his name in lights, but he never needed any help on that score.

For years, he worked for a Sydney tabloid newspaper and became efficient in covering all manner of events – council, parliament, police rounds, cricket and feature articles. It didn't make his move into television seamless; what made his move brilliant was his staying behind in London after the 1956 Australian tour and undergoing a three-week commentators' course with the BBC.

His philosophy of 'less is more' regarding television commentary was brilliant. Richie believed that a commentator should not say a word unless he can add to the images, or: 'Don't tell them what they are seeing; tell them what they don't see.'

David Hill was the imaginative founder and head of Channel Nine's Wide World of Sports. When he first met Richie, he lost the power of his speech: 'My mouth opened and closed, but nothing came out. It was like being in the presence of an immortal.'

From the outset of World Series Cricket (WSC) in 1977, Kerry Packer approached Benaud to become his strategic adviser and also the lead television commentator. His enormous input behind the scenes and in front of the camera with WSC has been well documented.

Richie and his wife, Daphne, were a magnificent team. Packer recognised Daphne to be a hard worker, problem solver, lateral thinker, loyal staffer with twinkling eyes and an infectious laugh that lit up a room.

From humble beginnings, Richie Benaud became a brilliant Test cricketer, a wise and courageous captain, newspaper columnist, author, television commentator par excellence, teacher, confidant. That's a whole lot of wonderful attributes in one human being.

Richie once said to Keith Miller. 'You know, I wish I'd got the chance to bowl to Don Bradman.' To which Miller replied: 'Son, that was your one lucky break in cricket.'

My lucky break in cricket was knowing Richie Benaud. He enriched our lives in so many ways.

Marvellous.

Spinner Kline: fame as a batsman

Lindsay 'Spinner' Kline, a talented left-arm wrist spinner for Victoria and Australia, was a gentle man with a fabulous dry sense of humour. He played 13 Tests, taking 34 wickets at an average of 22.82, including a Test match hat-trick against South Africa at Cape Town in 1957–58. Ironically, he is chiefly remembered for two batting performances:

At the Gabba in November 1960, in the First Test of the 1960–61 series against the West Indies, Spinner featured with his great mate Ian Meckiff in a brief last-wicket stand. He was facing as Wes Hall came in to bowl what was to be the last ball of the Test. The scores were level. Australia needed just one run to win. Spinner pushed the ball to little Joe Solomon close in at point and took off. Meckiff hesitated, then ran full pelt for safety, but Solomon threw down the stumps from side-on and the game was over.

Confusion reigned. The West Indies team danced in glee. They thought they'd won the match. Norm O'Neill and the Australians thought they'd lost.

In the wake of the first tie in Test history, Spinner said drily, 'There was me running for a win and there was Meckiff running for a tie.'

On 1 February 1961, on the last day of the Fourth Test, the series stood at 1–all, with the one tie. As Australian wickets tumbled to the West Indian attack, Norm O'Neill and twelfth man Johnny Martin took the team number eleven, Kline, to the nets at the back of the Adelaide Oval for what they hoped would be a confidence-boosting net.

For the next 15 minutes, Martin and champion batsman and part-time spinner O'Neill repeatedly clean-bowled Spinner, who hardly got a bat to any ball. So bad was his batting effort that a woman watching at the back of the net yelled, 'You're hopeless, Kline! Waste of time you going out there.'

When Des Hoare was clean-bowled by Frank Worrell for a duck, the score stood at 9/207. The 'hope of the side' gathered his gloves, pulled on his baggy green and was making his way down the steps through a throng of South Australian Cricket Association members when a man yelled in jest, 'Won't be long now, Lindsay.' All the members roared.

With a mixture of splendid defence, two cracking boundaries, and the patience of Job, Kline defied all the West Indians could throw at him and his senior partner, the indefatigable Ken 'Slasher' Mackay, for an hour and 40 minutes. Led by the explosive fast man, Wes Hall, who seemingly pushed off from the sightscreen for every delivery, the greatest all-rounder in history, Garry Sobers, medium-pacer Frank Worrell and spinners Lance Gibbs and Alf Valentine, the Windies attack-bowled a total of 120 eight-ball overs in that final innings.

But they failed to break that last pair. Mackay finished unconquered on 62. Through fear of getting an edge, he bravely allowed the last ball of the day from Hall to hit him fair on the chest.

Spinner Kline made his highest Test score – 15 not out – in this his last Test. His mates would later scold him over that innings, saying, 'How come you scored only 15 in a whole session? Terrible batting, Spinner!'

And Australia completed a great escape, to leave the series level with one Test to play.

Doug Walters – a touch of Bradman

Doug Walters was more than a fabulous batsman of the 1970s; there was a touch of genius about him. When he scored 155 in his first Test innings, Ian Wooldridge wrote in the *London Evening Standard*:

> *Today from the moment he met Titmus' second ball a yard out of his crease and struck it cleanly into the long-off fence, it became impossible to avoid the comparison with Bradman. Walters is straight, correct, deceptively strong, unashamed to loft the ball into the air, unimpressed by any reputation and totally run-hungry.*

He played a number of Bradman-like innings. In Australia's first innings of the Third Test against the West Indies at Port-of-Spain, in Trinidad, in March 1973, Doug belted 112, which included a blistering century in the middle session, when he took Lance Gibbs's off-spin apart on a turning wicket. Doug was the best player of off-spin I've seen. His bat came at you on an angle and the more the ball turned the more it was likely to find the middle of his bat. Even Erapalli Prasanna, arguably the best offie of them all, struggled to defeat Doug Walters.

At Port-of-Spain, Greg Chappell had departed for 56 right on lunch. Then, against England at the WACA in December 1974, Chappell was dismissed just before tea and, as they passed on the field, Greg said: 'Douglas, this time I've given you a bit of a sighter.' Doug was 3 not out at tea.

'Right from the start, I middled the ball and felt in total control,' Doug recalled. 'I'd look about the field and visualise gaps, then I found myself playing the ball almost in perfection.' To fully appreciate what Doug was saying, you need to know that he is the most self-effacing cricketer on the planet. He never brags and rarely talks about himself, so Doug's clear concept of his batting domination that day was something to behold.

Round about the time I had scored 60 I thought I had a realistic chance of scoring a hundred in a session. I was seeing the ball that well. I felt so good, so confident, that I believed I could make somewhere in the vicinity of 130 in the session. I was on three at the resumption after tea and in the 60s when drinks were taken.

Australian captain Ian Chappell was enthralled by the way Doug was batting. It reminded him of the magnificence of his footwork in that sensational knock in the Trinidad Test. At drinks, Chappelli said to our twelfth man, Terry Jenner, 'TJ, check with the little fella and see what his chances are.'

When TJ handed Doug a drink, he asked, 'How's it going?'

Doug smiled, 'I think I've got a chance.'

That was the extent of their conversation. Doug realised that his mates in the Australian dressing-room knew he was on course for another Test match hundred in a session. But how could we have known the frustration Doug was experiencing in the middle? Although he was in the best batting form of his career, Doug's frustration was with Ross Edwards at the other end.

Rossco was trying to give me most of the strike, but the more he tried, the more he grabbed the strike for himself. A century in a session was very much on my mind. My form was too good to miss this chance. I felt I played only one false shot in the entire knock and that was in the last over of the day when I was on 93. I needed 10 runs to complete the hundred in a session, so if Bob Willis was going to bounce me, I was going to hook. I hooked the first bouncer and I got a glove, the ball careering over Alan Knott's head for four. It was the only ball I played in that session which missed the middle of my bat. I guess I was feeling like Don Bradman must have felt when he played that great innings at Lord's in 1930.

Indeed, Don Bradman hit a classic 254 in the Second Test at Lord's in 1930 and he described it thus when we were discussing Walters' batting technique in Adelaide one July day in 1991:

Every ball I faced in that innings I played exactly as I wanted. It was the nearest thing I had ever come to batting perfection. Even the ball Percy Chapman stood on his ear to catch me off Jack White at cover I had hit sweetly and it was only an inch or so off the ground.

While Doug was hell-bent upon scoring the required 10 runs off Willis's last over, Ross Edwards at the non-striker's end was getting uptight. He thought Doug should put up the shutters and live to fight another day. Ross went down the wicket to give Doug sage advice. Doug nodded slowly, apparently absorbing this patently obvious Edwards wisdom, and then he ambled back to take strike at the Pavilion End.

Moments later came Doug's mistimed hook; the glove and near-miss over Knott's head – the one indiscreet stroke of his innings. Ross Edwards remembers it well: 'For a number of balls I had been walking down the pitch swearing at him. I had virtually given up trying to talk some sense into him. I ended up yelling out, swearing, calling him an idiot.' While Doug was thinking a hundred in a session, his ultra-conservative batting partner, an accountant, was thinking survival and the law of averages.

As he tapped his bat to face Willis's last ball, Doug's score stood at 97. Given that he was 3 not out when play for the final session began, he knew he had to hit the final ball for six to achieve what he had set his mind upon achieving. Back in the Australian dressing-room, the players were having little side bets. We all knew that if anyone in this cricketing life could hit a six off the last ball of the day to achieve 100 runs in a session it was Kevin Douglas Walters.

Doug gambled on the last ball being dropped short, so as Willis got into his delivery stride, Doug was well and truly back and across. If the delivery was directed at him, he'd hit it over square leg; anything wide of off stump he'd uppercut over third man. That was the Walters plan.

Willis charged in with that familiar, bustling approach, arms and legs flailing, his fuzzy hair dancing in the strengthening wind, as if chased by Perth's summer afternoon breeze they call the Fremantle Doctor. Doug recalls:

Willis dropped short all right and I was already in position to pull the ball. How sweet the feel and sound of my bat striking that short Willis delivery. It was one of those times when the bat hits the ball at precisely the right moment. I hit it right in the screws. The ball sailed away nearly bisecting the two guys at backward square and thudded over the boundary line. Six! You bloody beauty.

Doug walked from the ground to a standing ovation.

However, we in the dressing-room, still trying to come to terms with what we had just witnessed, decided to duck back into the showers at the back of the room. We were all out of sight when Doug entered the dressing-room. A look of mild surprise momentarily swept over his face, but he did as he usually did, whether he scored a duck or hit a century. Doug slowly removed his baggy green cap and his gloves. He sat on the bench and lit up a cigarette. Then he looked about him. There was a long period of silence. Then we all rushed from behind the shower door and there were plenty of handshakes all round and even more cans of beer for this little genius of the willow.

It is a pity England never saw Doug at his best. He so often fell to the medium and medium-fast bowlers on the slower, grassier English wickets. I had a theory that his reflexes were so swift that he actually adjusted to any seam away and was able to catch up with the ball only to edge it to slip or gully. When the ball seamed away on Australian pitches, Doug missed it completely, simply because the ball moved at great pace, much greater than the ball would seam in England. On the English tracks, Doug's fabulous reflexes were his downfall, for he adapted to the movement and usually edged the ball. His instinctive and lightning reflexes enabled him to swiftly react to any movement on the slow English tracks and Doug agreed that was, in fact, why he failed so often on the slower English wickets. I ran that theory past Sir Donald, who dismissed it straight away, saying in his unmistakable jockey-like squeaky tone, 'You'll have to do better than that, son.'

One of the reasons Doug was so popular with his teammates was his dry humour. In the Melbourne Rest of the World 'Test' in 1971 – the game in which Garry Sobers hit a magnificent 254 – Australia was left in the position of trying to save the match on the last day.

On the night of the fourth day, Doug's mate, former Test keeper Brian Taber, was in town and he planned to take Doug to a dinner party, a quiet meal and a few beers. Chappelli got wind of the plan and told Taber, 'Now, Tabsy, look after our little mate.

He might have to bat us out of trouble tomorrow.' Well, Tabsy forgot all about taking care of Dougie and he left the party round 3 am. Doug was still there, enjoying a cold one or two. When the host decided it was time to draw stumps, he accompanied Doug outside. They were greeted by bright sunlight.

'Gee, it's still light. I guess I'd better get back to the pub and some sleep, I've got to bat tomorrow.'

'No, Doug,' the host corrected him, 'you've got to bat today!'

Doug got back to his Melbourne hotel round 8 am and he sidled up to the desk in the foyer and asked the receptionist, 'Can I have an early call for 8.30, please?'

'Oh, that will be 8.30 tonight, sir?'

'No, young lady, I mean 8.30 this morning. I have to play cricket later today and you don't want me to turn up to the game without having had any sleep, do you?'

That very day, Doug quickly shook off the cobwebs, scoring a century before lunch on the last day of the MCG match against Garry Sobers's World Eleven.

Once his famous sense of humour backfired. A few days before the Brisbane Test match of November 1968 against the West Indies, Doug had to undergo a fitness test. He was confident he'd be right for the big game, but he made the fatal mistake of telling the doctor, 'Well, so long as I don't have to open the bowling for Australia, I'll be right for the Test.'

Doug knew his captain, Bill Lawry, would never contemplate opening the bowling with Walters, but the doctor missed the joke and ruled him out of the Test match. Doug hit 76 in the Second Test at the MCG and he went on to hit a Bradman-like 699 runs at an average of 116.50 in the four games he played in the series.

He might not have played at Sydney had he told administrators of a bad fall he sustained on the eve of the match. There was a flight of 30 steps leading to the door of Doug and his wife

Caroline's Sydney home. Wearing thongs (flip-flops to those in other parts), Doug somehow got his feet caught and fell down the steps, badly bruising his lower back and backside, but he wasn't going to tell anyone remotely connected with the medical fraternity. Doug scored 242 and 103 in that Fifth Test.

Ian Chappell always gives thanks that the Test tours he experienced were so much the better for Doug Walters being a part of them. As he recalls, Bill Lawry won't forget the training day at the Wanderers Cricket Ground in Johannesburg when he gave Doug a bucket of balls and sent him to the middle of the ground. Doug was instructed to hit high catches to those of us dotted about the boundary line. The Phantom had taken great pains to inform us that the rarefied atmosphere in Johannesburg (some 6000 feet above sea level) made the ball travel much further and we needed to learn how to judge high catches. Doug must have had a dozen cricket balls in that bucket. He proceeded to hit every one of those twelve balls high into the air, way over our heads and into the grandstand.

'You're right, Phanto,' Doug yelled, his face deadpan like the best of poker players, 'the ball does travel a lot further here in Jo'burg.'

In 74 Tests, Doug hit 5357 runs at 48.26 with 15 centuries and a highest score of 250.

On four occasions, he hit a century in a session in first-class cricket – twice in Tests, once against the Rest of the World and once against Central District (New Zealand) in 1974, when he scored the hundred without one single boundary. Mere statistics don't do the man justice. He got runs when they were needed and when on song there was a touch of genius about him; sometimes even a touch of Bradman. Irrepressible Doug Walters.

Gary Gilmour, the last amateur

Gary Gilmour was a super-talented cricketer. A left-hander, he was a fabulous attacking bat and a medium-fast bowler with the ability to swing the ball in late from outside off stump. In terms of raw talent, Gilmour's ability was up in the stratosphere where only the legendary reside. He was like a very raw Garry Sobers. Truly, Gilmour possessed that sort of amazing talent, but those who played against him and alongside him rarely saw him use that talent to full advantage.

In January 1972, Gary hit a debut 122 for New South Wales against South Australia on the SCG, flaying all bowlers to all parts of the ground.

There were glimpses of his pure genius, like the day at Headingley in 1975 when he took 6/14 off 12 overs (6 maidens) to destroy England in the semi-final of cricket's first World Cup. He swung the ball alarmingly and late. Most of his deliveries were late-swinging in-duckers to the right-handers, but he got one to angle away from Tony Greig and the resultant snick was caught in fantastic fashion by a diving Rodney Marsh. In the same game, Australia was 6/39 and still needing 55 runs when Gilmour came in to partner Doug Walters, both of them hitting out boldly, and they knocked off the runs.

He played only five matches in that World Cup, yet he took 16 wickets at an average of 10.31, with an economy rate of 3.09 and a strike rate of 20.0. In the final at Lord's in 1975, Gilmour took 5/48, his wicket haul comprising Alvin Kallicharran (12),

Rohan Kanhai (55), Clive Lloyd (101), Viv Richards (5) and Deryck Murray (14).

During that match, Lloyd hit a few furious drives back past the bowler and Gilmour was asked at a press conference: 'How do you bowl to Clive Lloyd?'

'With a crash helmet on.'

Gilmour played 15 Test matches, hitting an unremarkable 483 runs at 23.00 with 1 century and taking 54 wickets at an average of 26.03, bagging three hauls of five wickets in an innings. The figures don't tell, by a long shot, just how much ability this man possessed. He was likened to Alan Davidson – next to Keith Miller the nation's greatest all-round cricketer. Davo was very much a mentor to Gilmour and encouraged his protégé over his short international career.

Gary – or Gus, as he was affectionately known – wasn't all that keen on doing all the running and physical jerks which have sneaked into the game since round the time Kerry Packer's World Series Cricket took the Establishment by the scruff of the neck and shook the living daylights out of it. This was in the grand quest to grab television broadcasting rights and in the process it made the players become much more 'professional'.

One of Gus Gilmour's best mates was the legendary Doug Walters. They toured England together in 1975 and later New Zealand. It was in New Zealand that Gus scored his one and only Test century and he did so in partnership with Walters in the summer of 1976–77.

The team stayed at the Avon Hotel in Christchurch, where there happened to be a well-stocked bar, and during the Test match Australian team manager Roger Wotton had a beer with Walters. They were joined by Gus Gilmour and late into the night Wotton rang vice-captain Rodney Marsh to tell him that Gilmour and Walters were still in the bar. Rodney assured Wotton that Doug and Gus knew exactly what they were doing.

Next day, Walters and Gilmour, the not-out batsmen, were both on the board with a handful of runs.

Doug always says that, after Richard Hadlee's first couple of overs, which somehow missed the edge, he mysteriously started to find the middle. Gus also found a similar enlightenment and the pair went on to thrash the hapless Kiwi attack mercilessly. Walters scored a Test career high 250 and Gilmour scored his maiden Test century, 101.

Gilmour played WSC for the odd good pay-day, but just prior to the WSC 1977–78 season, he went to South Africa with an International Wanderers team, managed by Richie Benaud. There were a number of Australians in the team, including the Chappell brothers, Dennis Lillee, Martin Kent and yours truly, as well as England's Derek Underwood, Mike Denness, Dennis Amiss and Keith Fletcher, West Indian John Shepherd and New Zealanders Glenn Turner, Lance Cairns and John Morrison. We played a South African XI including the great Barry Richards, Graeme Pollock and Clive Rice. Gilmour, nursing a torn hamstring and batting at number ten, turned the match on its head by hitting a whirlwind 85 when all hope was lost. Thanks to Gus, we snatched that match from the jaws of defeat.

'Red Ink' O'Keeffe

It seems just a few days back when Kerry O'Keeffe delighted all and sundry with his dry wit and raucous laughter as a cricket commentator on the ABC. His comments were often obscure and had little to do with the game, but they made people roar laughing. His giggling eccentricity became popular with fans throughout the cricket world and, in this age of taking political correctness to a ludicrous degree, O'Keeffe slipped through the net on many occasions.

From 1938 until the 1980s, 'The Voice of Cricket' in Australia was Alan McGilvray. His words transported you to the game in your mind and painted a picture that some think was better than any television image. He had a variety of expert comments men, such as Victor Richardson, Johnny Moyes, Lindsay Hassett and Norm O'Neill.

McGilvray did have a sense of humour and delighted in some of the classic quotes by England's legendary John Arlott and Brian Johnston on BBC radio and Australia's Richie Benaud on Channel Nine. Arlott once described a batsman's technique as 'like an old lady poking her umbrella at a wasp's nest'.

Johnston observed Neil Harvey during a tense Test match at Lord's, 'standing at leg slip with his legs wide apart, waiting for a tickle'. When England captain Ray Illingworth took himself out of the attack in another Test, Johnston said, 'Illingworth is relieving himself in front of the pavilion.' Benaud's voice did not falter the time he said on Channel Nine, 'Laird has been brought in to stand in the corner of the circle.'

McGilvray, however, would have taken umbrage at O'Keeffe's irreverent words, along with that hysterical laughter which often drowned out the man on the microphone sitting next to him. During an India–Australia match at the SCG, this exchange took place between Harsha Bhogle and O'Keeffe:

Bhogle: How do you think Gillespie looks today?
O'Keeffe: Not too good. He looks stiffer than a triple scotch.
Bhogle: Stiffer than a triple ... scotch did you say?
O'Keeffe: Yeah. He's that stiff.
Bhogle: Kerry, how many stiff ones did you have last night?
   As the commentary box erupted in hysterical laugher,
O'Keeffe: I'm 54, Harsha ... ONE!

Kerry O'Keeffe came to the ABC microphone a few years after McGilvray had retired. Times have changed and the majority of ABC listeners loved Skull's banter, the same way many prefer a hamburger with the lot drowned by a litre of Coca-Cola, rather than grilled salmon and vegetables, matched with a fine sauvignon blanc.

During the second year of World Series Cricket, Ian Chappell's team toured the West Indies. Every morning, Skull had a fitness-building run about the streets with his roommate, medium-pacer Mick Malone. Skull got used to Mick always crying wolf and yelling, 'Look out.' Skull would stop or jump to the side and Mick would roll about laughing. One day, however, was different. As the pair approached a crossroad, Mick really did spot danger and yelled, 'Look out!' Skull simply laughed and kept going. He awoke in a Barbados hospital, his left leg plastered from toe to groin. His leg was broken in three places.

A few years before, in 1974, Skull and I were playing for Australia against Auckland at Eden Park. This was the game in which Skull recorded the highest score of his first-class career.

Skipper Ian Chappell had rested Doug Walters, so Rodney Marsh and Kerry O'Keeffe got a lift in the batting order. Skull walked purposefully to the wicket at the fall of the fifth wicket (5/138). Auckland had a couple of Test bowlers: medium-fast Bob Cunis and left-arm orthodox spinner Hedley Howarth.

They also had a brilliant fielder in Mark Burgess. For any batsman, Burgess in the field was a man to watch very carefully. He was lightning fast across the turf and he had a deadly accurate, bullet-like throw.

I came to the crease at the fall of the ninth wicket. Skull had played strokes to all parts of the field and taken his score to the 80s by the time I reached the crease. He was on track to score his maiden first-class century.

'I'll be there at the end, Skull,' I said confidently. 'Stay with me!'

At times, off the last ball of an over, I sacrificed a single so Skull could keep strike. Steadily, Skull's score mounted. Eventually, he cracked Cunis beautifully through the covers to the fence. O'Keeffe, 99 not out. There were four balls of the over to go.

A midwicket conference ensued.

'Nothing silly ... no run-outs, Rowdy.'

'Now, Skull, this is vital,' I warned him. 'Watch that man Mark Burgess at cover point. He's dynamite. Whatever you do, *don't* run if it goes anywhere near Burgess.'

Skull was a deadly serious character in 1974. In later years, he could laugh at himself, but I have the feeling that what was to come would not feature on the Kerry O'Keeffe top list of funny events.

Incredibly, the very next Cunis delivery saw Skull push the ball a foot to the left of Burgess and charge down the wicket for his 100th run. Didn't Skull listen to anything I said? I could see Burgess swoop and assumed that Skull had made his ground easily, because I caught a glimpse of a red leather sphere heading straight towards the wicketkeeper's end – the very end I needed to make good my ground. I dived and slid in a cloud of dust, but my bat stuck fast in the dust and I watched the bails being whipped off by the wicketkeeper.

O'Keeffe reached his ground easily, not out 99. Given the way batting averages are worked out, a 'red ink' is indeed advantageous. 'Red Ink' O'Keeffe mumbled his way off the ground as I wiped blood from both elbows. We arrived to a silent dressing-room that soon erupted in laughter.

I looked up from where my wounds were being treated and asked, 'Hey, Skull, what's your highest first-class score?' Skull never got a first-class century.

Boycott's genius on a black pudding

When he was gearing himself up for another Ashes campaign, on 8 May 1972, Geoff Boycott – whose very surname conjures up images of stoppage and inertia – played a knock so grand on a lump of black pudding masquerading as a wicket that it defied belief.

In the wake of bad weather, the scheduled Australia versus Yorkshire three-day match at Bradford was abandoned and in its stead the players agreed to play two one-day games. So bad was the state of the bowlers' approaches that their run-ups were restricted to 15 paces. In game one, Yorkshire batted first and amassed 176 runs for the loss of six wickets in 50 overs.

Later that day, the heavens opened up to ruin the match, but already the day belonged to Boycott. The ball was seaming and spinning all over the place. Often the ball did too much and evaded the edges of quality batsmen until they finally nicked one, but not Boycott. He batted like a man possessed. I doubt whether Don Bradman, Viv Richards or Brian Lara at their zenith could have played an innings of better quality than Boycott did that day on that shocking surface. The Yorkshire and England opener drove with extraordinary skill past mid-on and, when the ball was slightly short, he moved back and hit crisply through cover. He cut and pulled and once advanced down the track – yes, Boycott coming at you in the heat of battle was about as likely as Prince Charles batting three for England – and hit me clear over the football stand.

Early on that day, Bob Massie got one to move away from

Boycott and the ball skewed past slip to the third man boundary. There was Boycott rushing up the track yelling, 'Nowt off the edge, I turned face, I turned face.' He certainly had that ability and his batting that day bordered on a miracle of explosive power.

I once cornered the great Australian all-rounder Keith Miller and asked him for his opinion of Boycott the batsman.

He admired Len Hutton's cricket too and, when I pressed him about the relative merits of Hutton and Boycott, Miller said: 'Both were fine players. Hutton had a far greater range of attacking strokes, but defensively I reckon they were pretty much on a par.' Then he looked at me and added, 'But, for heaven's sake, don't tell Boycott!'

I read that great Yorkshire spinner Hedley Verity used to worry Bradman on a good track. On a bad one, as was the case in the Second Test at Lord's in 1934, he dismissed him twice (36 and 13), in taking 15/104 (7/61 and 8/43) in the game.

The writers of yesteryear say that Victor Trumper was the greatest player of all time on a bad wicket. In January 1904, Trumper hit 74 out of an Australian total of 122 against England at the MCG on a 'sticky dog' – the treacherous surface that results after torrential rain on an uncovered wicket is followed by a fierce baking in the sun. Most deliveries landing on the turf of a 'sticky dog' don't merely sit up like a begging mutt; they rear menacingly. For the statistically minded, in that 1904 Test England's Wilfred Rhodes, who bowled left-arm spin very much in the manner of Verity, took a match haul of 15/124.

That MCG pitch in 1904 was arguably more difficult to bat on than the 'black pudding' Bradford pitch of 1972, but either surface would have proved exceedingly difficult for any batsmen of any era and would have required amazing ability to merely survive, let alone play an array of strokes which beggared belief

Another unusual instance of daring batting occurred in the First Ashes Test of 1968 at Old Trafford. Bill Lawry – that other veritable 'corpse in pads' – emerged from his refuge of stodginess and took the long handle to England off-spinner Pat Pocock, who was threatening to 'do a Laker' on us. The angular Australian, who usually didn't play a lot of shots, decided to throw all caution to the wind and launched an attack on Pocock, savaging 34 runs off him in just six overs – power-hitting which included two slog-sweep sixes against the spin over midwicket. Lawry's assault set the pattern for what turned out to be a terrific Test win. As with Boycott, Lawry could drive, hook and cut with the best of them, but all too rarely did either man bat with such aggression.

Despite his wonderful batting on the black pudding wicket at Bradford, Boycott struggled in the 1972 Ashes series. In the Second Test at Lord's, when Bob Massie took a debut Test haul of 16/137, England hit 272 in its first dig, with Boycott playing and missing a Massie outswinger on 11, then being completely beaten next ball by a big inswinger which destroyed his castle. Australia replied with 308, Greg Chappell hitting a technically perfect 131 and tailender Dave Colley effectively belting a quick-fire 50.

England batting a second time saw Massie again grab eight wickets, but Boycott fell unluckily to Dennis Lillee. The ball struck him high on his left pad and flew high over his shoulder, only to fall to ground and spin back towards the stumps. Boycott whirled around trying to find the ball, only to watch helplessly as the ball bounded into the leg stump with just enough force to remove one bail. Boycott, bowled Lillee, 6.

An enraged Boycott stormed off the ground and legend has it he spent the next hour circling the big table in the dressing-room muttering to all and sundry: 'Blerdy Colley slogs for 50 and I'm out playing properly for 6. There's no blerdy justice in this game.' There is also a rumour that Boycs had a handsaw brought to the dressing-room and cut his bat in two.

In the wake of that big Australian win at Lord's, England's shrewd captain, Ray Illingworth, decided to show the team a film of Massie's bowling to watch how the bowler's swing had caused their downfall. Unfortunately, the film proved a monumental cock-up, for it showed Massie bowling left-handed and left-handed John Edrich batting right-handed. The meeting was abandoned and the players decided to have a few pints instead, probably what should have happened in the first place.

In the 1970–71 series Down Under, when Boycott batted magnificently to help England regain the Ashes, Edrich came down the track in the Sydney Fourth Test and said: 'Boycs, I've worked out which way Gleeson's spinning them.' The finger-flick bowler John Gleeson had some of the English batsmen in a flap because they couldn't read the direction of spin, although in truth most of Gleeson's deliveries hit the turf and carried on gun-barrel straight.

Boycott looked Edrich in the eye and said: 'I worked Gleeson out two Tests ago, but don't tell those boogers back in the dressing-room!'

That same Ashes summer saw our wicketkeeper, Rodney Marsh, regularly sidling up to Boycott after a day's play for a chat and Bacchus managed to get all the inside knowledge from Boycs on the England batsmen – other than Geoffrey himself. Sadly for Australia, we didn't have the requisite firepower in attack to make any impression on what was a very strong England batting line-up.

A few weeks before that Ashes series began, England played a four-day match against South Australia. Boycott hit an unbeaten 170-odd before Illingworth declared. At the end of the day's play, the South Australian team could see Boycott in the nets, still batting and smashing the bowling of a group of eager young aspirants.

The great South African Barry Richards, who played that summer for South Australia, watched Boycott in the nets and said, 'I'll show him what batting's all about tomorrow.' True to his word, Richards batted in sensational fashion, hitting a flawless 224 against an attack which included John Snow, Ken

Shuttleworth, Basil D'Oliveira and Derek Underwood. Donald Bradman would later say that Barry Richards and Jack Hobbs were the greatest opening batsmen he'd ever seen.

He's always been good company, has Geoffrey. Recently he said of Australian Test off-spinner Nathan Lyon: 'He wouldn't get me mum out.' Boycs may be proved wrong there, but there is one certainty, given that Boycs will be Boycs: Geoff Boycott will do it and say it in his own inimitable way.

Parky – on Bradman and company

When Michael Parkinson was 13, he rode his bike from Barnsley to Leeds to watch the 1948 Australians. That day, 27 July, Don Bradman hit an unconquered 173 to set up a famous victory, but for Parky the day fired his lifelong love for the game of cricket.

Parky, of course, went on to become a successful journalist and won global fame as a television host on *Parkinson*. Over the years, he interviewed an amazing array of talented people; however, a few of them became those who 'got away'. Frank Sinatra was one superstar who slipped his grasp. Parky told me once:

> *Frank Sinatra was the greatest star of them all and I wanted to have him on my show. At a party in Los Angeles, I was introduced to him and as I was about to leave the party I went up to the great man and said, 'Mr Sinatra, I have to go.'*
>
> *'That's fine,' Sinatra said, 'goodbye, David.'*
>
> *I thought, 'That's me buggered, that's me snookered, I'm not going to do any good here at all.'*

An aggrieved Parkinson continued, 'I got closer to the Kid from Hoboken than I did the Boy from Bowral.' The ideal time for an interview – 'to get the whole story, where Bradman could tell the cricket world his innermost thoughts about Bodyline and how he set about to destroy bowlers' – would have been during Parkinson's visit to Australia in 1979.

Had Parky managed to persuade Bradman to be a guest on his show, 'I would have asked him about his fame. Being famous is a bit like having the measles – it's a minor affliction and the rash soon disappears. But for some it never goes away; they and their family are on public display forever.'

What other guests would he have invited to accompany Sir Donald? 'None. Bradman stands alone,' Parky said firmly.

He regretted not getting to interview Bradman then because, 'By the time Ray Martin did an interview with the Don (then in his 88th year) in 1996, it was far too late ... He went to his grave without the world getting the chance to see the definitive Bradman interview on camera.'

He added wistfully:

On the odd occasion, I have glimpsed him in the distance and he vanished before I could reach him – like a mirage. Once a host showed me the teacup Sir Donald had been drinking from. The liquid was still warm and I felt like an explorer who had just found a fresh imprint of the Abominable Snowman.

Parkinson believes that the best interview he did with anyone purely on the game of cricket itself was with cricket and wine writer John Arlott, who maintained that 'today, cricket is taken too seriously and life too casually. There is an inevitability about sport today, regimented and very predictable.' He continued: 'Imagine today's coaches having to deal with the nonconformist, Keith Miller ... I am not convinced today's coaches would appreciate his great talent and match-winning ability, because he wouldn't conform; he would always do it his way.'

Parky first set eyes on Miller when he saw him play for the Australian Services team in the Victory Tests in 1945.

He was tall, long-legged, broad-shouldered and incredibly handsome. When he batted, he hit the ball with great power and in classic style. He bowled like the wind and caught swallows in the field. He was my hero then and was from then on.

... He became my hero and the hero of every kid in England. By 1948, when Bradman's side arrived, England was a drab, dour place. We were still on rations, the US was continuing to help resurrect Britain after the long, exhausting war years. Bradman's team lit up our summer; lit up our lives in a sense. There was Bradman himself, but also an array of super-talented players such as Miller, Neil Harvey, Arthur Morris, Ray Lindwall, Don Tallon ...

I got to know him and on one occasion, when I was working for the Daily Express *and Keith had his column with the same newspaper, we had this grudge match between the* Daily Express *and the* Daily Mail. *I was standing at second slip and Miller was at first slip. Miller was engaging with a man on the boundary, wanting to know the winner of the 2.30 pm race at Canterbury, when a snicked catch came hurtling straight to me at second slip. This figure leapt across my vision. Miller caught the ball one-handed and gave it to me, saying, 'What won that bloody race?'*

Miller saw Test cricket as a game, not as a war. Once on his show, Parky asked Miller if there was a similarity between the stress of Test cricket and war. Back came the immortal reply: 'Pressure? There's no pressure in cricket. I'll tell you what pressure is ... Pressure is when you're flying a Mosquito and there's a Messerschmitt up your arse!'

Parky concluded, 'Were I to host a dinner party to celebrate my last days on Earth, Keith Ross Miller would be at the top of my guest list.'

Parky reckons the best cricketer he ever saw was Garry Sobers. 'Bradman was the best batsman and Sobers the best all-round cricketer of them all: the complete package. I also loved watching the two Richards play, Vivian and Barry.'

However, the player Parkinson got to know from the time he was a child and 'loved until he died' was Fred Trueman. 'Growing up, he epitomised all my ambition. I wanted to be a Yorkshire cricketer. I played against him when I teamed with Dickie Bird and Geoffrey Boycott at Barnsley Cricket Club.'

Once Parky rang Fred to ask him to appear on *Parkinson* and he mentioned that Harold Pinter, the celebrated playwright, would be on the couch with him. Fred asked, 'Who's he play for?'

As an all-round bowler, he was the best I ever saw. He should have played a lot more Test matches, but he missed two Australian tours he should not have missed and never toured South Africa. He was left out of a tour to Australia after he had taken 187 wickets for Yorkshire at an average of 14 and they took a bloke named David Larter in his stead: Larter, a big bloke who couldn't bowl.

When asked whether Australians are like Yorkshiremen, Parkinson agreed, 'Yes, I think there is something in that ... When I first went to Australia it was a bit like going to a rather large, sunny Yorkshire.' The difference between cricket Down Under and in England, however, is that in Australia 'cricket has the same grip on the people that football has on the people in England. Cricket is the number two game in England, very much in the shadow of football.'

Parky has interviewed an extraordinary list of luminaries over the years. Yes, Don Bradman and Frank Sinatra were two who 'got away'.

Some of his Australian interviewees have perplexed Parky:

I spent two hours with Doug Walters on a Friday,
interviewing him for ABC TV. Next day, I played golf at
Royal Sydney and, as I walked onto the course, off came
Ian Chappell and Doug Walters. We exchanged 'G'days' –
as you do – and I overheard Doug ask Chappelli, 'Who's
that bloke?'

Miracle on Beulah Road

Miracles do happen.

On 30 January 1978, when Mr and Mrs Jeffrey Thomson arrived by taxi at Beulah Road, Norwood, a leafy suburb not far from the Adelaide CBD, they knew they were in for grand company, good food, fine wine and plenty of ice-cold beer. But they could hardly have envisaged the event the cricketing gods were about to present to them at that Sunday lunch. They were guests of Dr Donald Beard and his wife, Margaret – cricket fans and people with a generous spirit.

Dr Beard was the South Australian Cricket Association medical officer for more than 40 years. An eminent surgeon, the Doc served as an army medic in field hospitals in Korea and Vietnam. A distinguished-looking man, the Doc has been both friend and doctor to myriad state and Test cricketers.

It was Don and Margaret's pleasure to invite players from both Test sides to lunch at their home on this rest day of the Adelaide Test match. The miracle that was about to come to pass was to do with Don Bradman, as he and Lady Jessie were among the guests that day.

There was animated discussion throughout the meal and Bradman was especially happy because Australia's Test series against India was a resounding success. The series was locked 2–all, with Adelaide hosting the series decider. A close Test series was something the Establishment wanted more than anything else that summer as it fought with World Series Cricket for the hearts and minds of cricket fans.

Many of the 'Supertests' had been financial flops, with games being played on 'drop-in' wickets and before mostly meagre crowds. Curiously, Thommo was the Australian Cricket Board's star attraction in the lead-up to the series. His splendid bowling action was the image on the ACB's advertising, 'Here Come the Indians'. Ironically, Dennis Lillee, Thommo's great fast-bowling partner, was the most prominent face of World Series Cricket.

The Adelaide Test match rest day held bad memories for Thommo. It was little more than 12 months since he had collided with opening batsman Alan Turner, dislocating his shoulder, and two years since he had wrenched his shoulder playing tennis at Wyndham Hill Smith's famous Yalumba Winery in the Barossa Valley on the rest day. But today, having enjoyed a consistent bowling summer, he couldn't have been happier as he sat back in wife Cheryl's company, among good friends. 'I was sitting alongside Sir Donald and Cheryl was next to Lady Jessie. There were a couple of the Indian players there – Bishen Bedi was one and Vishy [Gundappa Viswanath] was also present. I don't think Sunny [Sunil Gavaskar] was there that day. We'd finished eating and there I was drinking a cold XXXX.

Bradman was sitting in his slacks, shirt and tie, looking pretty fit for a bloke of his age. The Doc's two sons – Matthew and Alistair – then announced that they were about to go outside and have a hit in the nets. The Doc had a grass tennis court and a turf cricket pitch in his spacious backyard. The guests watched the boys get up from the table and one of them laughingly asked, 'Would you like to come and have a bat against us, Sir Donald?' All eyes turned to Bradman and without hesitation he replied, 'Yes, lads. I'd love to have a hit.'

The guests fell silent. Any cricketer, any fan, would die to get a glimpse of Don Bradman batting. However, the guests – for a few surreal moments – were probably in shock, because Bradman simply did not give impromptu batting performances. Those Beard boys couldn't believe their luck, having lunch with

Don Bradman, cricket's greatest batsman, and Jeff Thomson, the world's fastest bowler.

Their joy increased when Thommo stood up, still clutching his can of XXXX, and announced in genuine excitement, 'If Bradman's batting, Jeff Thomson is bowling!'

Thommo's recall was clear when he recounted the miracle on Beulah Road to me in Brisbane, in 2007. My mind also turned back – to the 1960s. It was 1967 and Bradman had come into the South Australian dressing-room, as was his habit those days for matches at Adelaide Oval, at a time when he was a South Australia and Test selector. He would drop in before play on each morning of a Sheffield Shield match, have a cup of tea and chat to people nearby. He was always polite, cheery and positive.

One particular day in the 1967–68 summer, Bradman finished his cup of tea and was about to walk out the dressing-room door when he stopped. Greg Chappell was holding a bat and Bradman said: 'I'd change my grip if I were you, son.' When a cricketing god speaks, even the grass bows to his every command. Greg was very much his own man, but he was also not a person to allow an opportunity to pass by. A gem of batting advice from Bradman seemed too good an opportunity. At that stage in his career, Greg was mainly an on-side player.

Then came the magic moment. Bradman picked up a bat and played a shadow drive. Wow. It wasn't quite as life-defining a moment as it was for those who witnessed Jesus turning the water into wine, but from a cricketing point of view it was a stunning and precious moment. Bradman's bat speed was so great that the bat was a blur, like a propeller blade at full tilt – incredible.

The Don played another shadow cover drive. Again there was a blur as he swung the bat. Pure magic. Bradman was once a scratch golfer and in golf they talk incessantly of 'club head speed'. Bradman had club head speed in spades (as did Adam Gilchrist of the modern era).

More than 30 years after seeing him play the shadow drive, I wrote a book entitled *Bradman's Band*, having collected a range of comments from many ex-Test players, most of whom played in the Bradman era. Former Queensland and Test opening batsman Bill Brown said there was something very different about Bradman's batting – something he never observed in any other batsman. The standout feature? 'Bat speed,' Bill said.

So, as Thommo told me of the day he bowled to Bradman in that Adelaide backyard, I reckoned I had some idea of the wonderful event that unfolded. What could have motivated Bradman to bat that day under those circumstances, for he had nothing to prove? Why expose himself to bat against two tearaway young fast bowlers on a green pitch in an Adelaide suburban backyard? Here was the king of all batsmen: 6996 Test runs at an average of 99.94, about to face the music.

He walked briskly out of the door and headed towards the net. Thommo followed. He had to move smartly to catch up with Bradman, who was striding forward confidently, every inch the Roman centurion with the scent of victory in his nostrils. As he neared the backyard pitch, the Don confessed, 'Gee, Jeff, I don't know why I'm doing this. I haven't batted for 20 years.'

But Thommo observed that, along with the trademark confident Bradman grin, he had a gleam in his eye. There was total certainty in the way he carried himself. Instinctively, Thommo knew that this was going to be some event. He was still holding a can of beer when Bradman faced his first ball. The wicket was covered in a thick mat of grass; it was green and hard and looked as if it would bounce and seam. It was made for any fast bowler and the Beard brothers were two tearaway quick bowlers eager to make an impression on Bradman and the small group watching.

Thommo said he bowled 'a few leggies at a gentle pace'. Mind you, Thommo's idea of 'gentle pace' came at you round the speed of Dennis Lillee. He couldn't bowl a slow ball if he tried. Thommo only rolled a few balls over to the great man. He thought that, the way Bradman was shaping, he would sit back and watch.

He told me:

> *I didn't realise then that I was about to see one of the greatest events of my cricketing life. There was this little old guy in horn-rimmed glasses facing fast bowlers on a green pitch in an Adelaide backyard on the rest day of a Test match. He wasn't wearing any protection – no pads, box or gloves. He was just standing there with a borrowed bat. I couldn't keep my eyes off Bradman. He was beaming. I'm sure those two young fast bowlers were thinking, 'How good is this! We've got Bradman and Thomson playing in our backyard net.' I guess then I decided not to keep bowling; even my leg-breaks or anything at all, because I could just see the headlines if I had come in at him off my long run: THOMMO KILLS BRADMAN IN BACKYARD TEST. It really couldn't get any better than what I was seeing, so I sat back with my beer and enjoyed seeing Don Bradman in full flight. I thought to myself, 'How good is this ... it just doesn't get any better.*

Every Australian kid to play the game knows the Bradman batting record. It is so stupendous even the ABC paid tribute to the man by ensuring that its head office postbox number – 9994 – remains, a silent salute to the man's remarkable batting average of 99.94.

There have been other batsmen to score more runs than Bradman. Allan Border, for instance, hit nearly twice the number of Test runs as the Don, but no-one would seriously consider that Border, a fine Test match batsman, was a better player than Bradman.

Thommo, having watched Bradman play on Doc Beard's Adelaide backyard pitch, can easily relate to Bill Ferguson's description of Bradman. Ferguson was the man they called 'Mr Cricket' long before Mike Hussey was given the tag. Fergie was baggageman–scorer to every Australian touring side to England from 1905 until 1956 and he made this observation of Bradman's batting genius in a book he wrote in 1957:

> *Don was a phenomenon with the bat. When he was in the mood – and that was nearly all the time – he would pulverize the bowlers, indulging in what I make no apology for describing as a picturesque massacre. Like the ranks of Tuscany, who could scarce forbear to cheer, Don Bradman's pitiless punishment brought forth, so often, applause from those he punished.*

Thommo said that as he approached the wicket, Bradman's eyes lit up and

> *... you swore you could see he was thinking, 'Who are you two clowns? Do you think you are going to get me out? I've news for you.' He assumed an air of supreme confidence. Now, as he hoed into those two young fast men with relish it was as if Bradman was wearing a suit of armour; he was invincible, merciless. That little guy in glasses was suddenly transformed into Don Bradman, the human thrashing machine, belting every ball with power and precision. He did not play a false shot in twenty minutes of the most amazing batting I have ever seen. If anyone shit-bags this bloke's batting, I'll tell them the truth.*

For Jeff Thomson, the Bradman batting display was an almost-Biblical moment in his life. Here was a champion of the modern era watching more than a touch of magic from one of the gods of cricket. Thommo enthused:

*Bradman was then 70 years old, yet he belted hell out of
every ball. There wasn't a false stroke. Not one defensive
shot, and I likened the batting show to what we see of
Bradman on the old film. The old black and white films of
Bradman have him blasting every ball, not one false shot
and certainly no defensive shots. I thought those old films
were edited ... you know, the editor cuts out all the shit
shots. Now I know different. How good must Bradman have
been in his heyday?*

*I reckon if any player from then, or later on, blokes like
Viv Richards and Ian or Greg Chappell, or any star from
today, Brian Lara or Ricky Ponting, absolutely anyone,
other than Bradman, would have struggled against those
two young quicks on that green pitch. It was seaming all
over the place and those youngsters were operating at
around Glenn McGrath's pace.*

*If it was you or me, we'd be thinking of how we might get
hit, but not Bradman. How do you reckon any other man of
70 years of age would fare in similar circumstances? I don't
care if they were former Test batsmen, they wouldn't have
hit a ball, not one ball.*

Having witnessed the miracle on Beulah Road, the guests were
left pinching themselves. For they were a privileged few. That a
man – as great as Bradman undoubtedly was – could at the age
of 70 bat in such a manner defied imagination. Thommo became
an instant disciple of Bradman's batting genius.

The 12th Man

Billy Birmingham is The 12th Man – the most famous twelfth man of the cricket world. Conceived, written and performed by Billy, more than six albums and three singles have been made since 'It's Just Not Cricket' in 1984, and all went straight to number one on the charts. Billy has sold more than two million recordings. He is the ultimate star on the sidelines: cricket's king of twelfth men.

As long ago as Billy can remember, impersonating and taking the piss out of individuals and situations came naturally. He was always entertaining his friends by taking off various well-known characters. Richie Benaud, who became a big star when World Series Cricket suddenly arrived in everyone's lounge-room, was the perfect target for Billy, as he had such a unique voice that Billy couldn't resist imitating it.

By 1984, Billy had already written a monologue for the comedian he branded as Austen Tayshus. The resulting record, 'Australiana', contained a series of puns – some fair, some foul – so brilliant that it spent 13 weeks at number one in Australia and sold more than 300,000 copies, the biggest domestic-selling Australian single of all time.

As a commercial producer and creative consultant, he'd also written the famous 'How do you feel?' radio campaign for Tooheys beer, winning a truckload of awards. The time was ripe for Billy Birmingham to star in his own thing.

I was thinking about how I could capitalise on the success of 'Australiana'. I thought of Richie Benaud and the boys.

Then I hit on the idea of trying to do something with my lounge-room impersonations of them, maybe taking the piss out of the Channel Nine cricket coverage. I put down the stuff on a dictaphone. Right on cue, a few mates turned up. I pressed the 'play' button on the dictaphone and afterwards someone said, 'You've got to do something with this!'

Billy knew he was on to something special, for he had received the unanimous thumbs-up from his mates, ever the strongest of critics. He moved straight away.

I immediately shot down to EMI Records. I recall going into the boss's office and turned on the cassette. It was just the raw thing – no music, no special effects, just me taking the piss out of Richie and the Pakistanis. The EMI boss's door was open and, as we listened and he laughed, others heard the commotion. One by one, they came in until the room was full and everyone was laughing. The boss said, 'Let's go with this.'

Billy and his mate David Froggatt produced the records at Froggy's home studio in Bowral, Don Bradman's spiritual home town in the Southern Highlands of New South Wales. The EP, which had the title 'It's Just Not Cricket', ran for seven minutes and Billy was amazed that the various radio stations played it – they traditionally stuck to a musical format.

The 12th Man joked about the Channel Nine cricket commentary team generally, concentrating mainly on the key man, the late Richie Benaud, cricket legend and commentary icon. It also satirised the rest of the team: long-term stalwarts Ian Chappell, and Bill Lawry – whose passion for pigeons is almost outmatched by his manner of so overstating the ordinary that a forward defence sometimes has Bill on the edge of his seat with excitement. It also featured Tony Greig, 'who keeps leaving the fucking keys stuck in the pitch', who was one of the original Channel Nine team until his death in 2012.

The 12th Man took Australia by storm. It was different, outrageous and made fun of an icon in a fun way. The recipe was right. It fitted the mood of the Australian public and it became extraordinarily popular. In 1992, the musical single 'Marvellous', featuring 'MCG Hammer' and real rock heroes Jimmy Barnes, Glen Shorrock and Diesel, was number one. The same year, a third album, 'Still The 12th Man', became the fastest-selling Australian artist recording EMI has ever handled. All 11 albums from The 12th Man have reached number one on the Australian charts.

They are still making people laugh. People all over the world try to take Benaud off, even the female of the species and little kids. Anyone who is serious about saying 'two' in the funniest way has got to become a cult figure. Billy Birmingham simply struck the right chord – the nation's fun pulse. He got it right first time and he continues to get it right.

Billy considers himself to be a satirist, not an impressionist nor an impersonator.

I like to get the voice right, but it's hard to get it perfect. So long as the characterisation is accurate enough not to distract from the script. What the bloke says is important. How he says it is also important and that the voice is near as possible to the real thing, but the things he says, that's the really important factor for me.

It was 15 years before Billy actually met Richie Benaud and that was by chance, at The Oval in 1999. He was standing outside the BBC commentary box when he heard the distinctive voice in the background.

*I turned around and saw this bloke – the unmistakable
hair, the bottom lip. But he was somehow shorter than I
imagined and he wore glasses. He wasn't wearing the
cream, the bone, the white, the off-white, the ivory or the
beige ...*

*Just as he was about to head back to the inner sanctum,
I decided to introduce myself, jumped in front of him and
blurted, 'Hey Richie, some things you can't put off forever.'
Richie looked at me and said matter-of-factly, 'What a
strange place to be meeting you. Weren't we supposed to
play golf together some time ago? Let's do it soon.' With
that, he was off back to the combox.*

The funny thing is that Richie Benaud himself was quite adept
at taking the piss, and wasn't afraid to drop the odd 'f' word
off camera. I read somewhere that his wife Daphne said Billy
had Richie down to a T in the series. Billy told me about Richie
appearing on radio in Melbourne criticising The 12th Man for
swearing and saying he and his fellow commentators never did.
Billy went on to talk about Ian Chappell's famous on-air blunders
and how Kerry Packer banned him for a short time. Richie never
swore on camera, but who among God's male creations doesn't
swear at some stage of their lives?

Billy is right when he says the cricketers swear. 'You don't
have to be a lip-reader to interpret the expletives coming out of
disgruntled players' mouths,' he says. Nothing has changed on
that score, but television brings the players' images and voices
into our homes. What they do we see and what they say we hear.

How did Billy hit upon the persona of 'The 12th Man'?

*I was watching Stuart MacGill when he was twelfth man
in Durban. There he was – sitting back, head to one side,
a book cradled in the crook of his arm. He was filling in
time while the other eleven guys were slogging it out in the*

middle. The twelfth man has lots of time on his hands.
He can just sit there and take the piss: that's me!

Except this particular 12th Man is just a guy who
stumbled across the idea of pulling together two of
Australia's favourite pastimes – watching sport and taking
the piss. A magic combination.

The Channel Nine commentary team have had their profiles enhanced, if anything, by the antics of The 12th Man. They should be applauding him.

TJ, the lovable larrikin

In the summer of 1959, the latest recruit to our cricket club was a skinny, gangling country kid wearing a baggy brown peaked cricket hat 10 times too big for him. Fourteen-year-old Terry Jenner was leaning on the wall of our ancient wooden pavilion at Shearn Park in Mount Lawley, an inner suburb of Perth.

'I'm a wicketkeeper,' he said with a grin, 'but I plan to become a leg-spinner.' Ah, I thought, all keepers think they can bowl leg-breaks. Terry exuded confidence, as though the world was his oyster. By the time he was 16, he had grabbed a few wickets, but his main boast was scoring 60 not out, batting at number eleven. Soon Terrence James Jenner was given the label 'TJ', and the nickname stuck.

TJ and I finally teamed up in the club's A-grade team and we'd go to the Inglewood Hotel after matches, to soak up the cricket talk and down a few beers. We had a good attack and at first he was the sixth player to get a bowl and I was seventh. Despite a lack of long spells at the crease, TJ's cricket came on fast. He made the Western Australia side at the age of 18, but with Tony Lock, and sometimes Tony Mann, in the side, there wasn't much hope of lots of bowling.

One Saturday, TJ and I were batting together against Subiaco, who had in their bowling attack the raw pace of left-hander Jim Hubble. He was bowling quick and short to TJ. Each ball got progressively shorter and flew higher, eventually forcing TJ to tread on his stumps; one bail fell to the ground. TJ quickly looked at the square leg umpire, Warren Carter, who not unusually happened to be looking anywhere but at the actual play, and no fielder had seen it, so TJ nonchalantly leant over, replaced the bail and settled over his bat for the next ball. 'Jeez, TJ, you can't do that!' I blurted.

TJ and I lived for cricket. On Sundays, we played for a club called Miling, some 200 kilometres north of Perth. TJ's first attempt there at cricket coaching was a disaster. He gave the three brothers – Ray, Des and Les White – instruction on how best to defend their wickets against a big, burly fast bowler. Each of the White brothers was clean-bowled first ball. Surely this was the only time identical triplets – all clean-bowled – had featured in a hat-trick.

TJ learnt two things about becoming a spinner. You needed patience and you had to have a sense of humour. I had been twelfth man for Western Australia and TJ had played 30-odd state matches, but with Tony Lock in Western Australia we had to go elsewhere. We picked South Australia. Les Favell was an attacking captain and South Australia had no spinners. Adelaide Oval was apparently a bowler's nightmare – a flat, unresponsive pitch. However, instinctively we knew it couldn't be as tough as the flint-hard Perth wickets. We found Adelaide turned and bounced for most of the match and we figured that the side needed two spinners, certainly for home matches.

Lessons under the tutelage of Clarrie Grimmett, where the old craftsman emphasised getting the ball above the batsman's eyes, proved decisive in the development of us both as spin bowlers. Playing for Prospect against Glenelg in a one-day match also was a pointer of things to come. TJ dismissed Greg Chappell and I got Ian, so the state selectors may have been a little interested.

In my first summer of big cricket, in 1967–68, I missed the first match for South Australia with a dislocated finger, but TJ played and grabbed a five-wicket haul. He loved Favell's attitude. 'After I went for runs in my first couple of overs, I thought I'd be taken off,' TJ told me. 'But it wasn't like Western Australia. Les said, "C'mon, son, give me one good over and you're on for the session."'

Soon TJ and I were playing together and bowling in tandem and became the 'spin twins'. After a game, we'd soak up the atmosphere in the company of such luminaries as Ian Chappell, Les Favell, Barry Jarman and Neil Hawke.

We were paid $30 for the four days of a Shield game, but $7.50 was taken out for tax and if you won in three days they docked you a day's pay. Once, TJ was bowling late on day three and Queensland was 8/180-odd chasing plenty. Ross Duncan swung lustily and the ball went high in the air. Aware that the game might not go into the fourth day, Hawke yelled with a laugh: 'Drop it … drop the ball!' Of course, we would have loved to be paid big money like they get today, but we were glad we played in the 1970s, especially under the leadership of Ian Chappell.

When TJ and I bowled in tandem, there was never a need for us to stop at the end of an over and talk about which one of us wanted to bowl to which batsman. We instinctively knew, we could read one another's game so well. If TJ reckoned Ian Chappell gave me too much of a go and he was ignored, he would front the skipper at the end of play. The captain would say, 'Okay, TJ, what's the problem?' There was always a robust debate. Once, Chappelli said to TJ after he complained of not getting much of a bowl, 'Oh sorry, TJ, I forgot you were out there.'

Ian Chappell reckoned TJ would make a good coach, and Rod Marsh gave TJ some coaching at the Australian Cricket Academy in Adelaide. There he linked up with the young Shane Warne. They were alike in personality. You just knew Warne was special – he had that sparkle in his eye, much the same as TJ all those years ago.

His genius as a spin-bowling coach lay in his way of getting his message across. People know how good he was at illustrating a point or telling a good yarn, because he did that when commentating on ABC radio, giving a speech, or running his famous TJ Test match brekkies.

Spin bowling was his passion and he lived and breathed the art. He taught his protégé, Shane Warne, a lot and if you talk cricket with Warne, you'll be impressed with his great passion for spin bowling. He talks of bowling to stay on, just as TJ spoke of it. He talks of 'spinning up', again a TJ phrase. TJ maintained that O'Reilly and Mailey were something great, but statistically and realistically, Warne was the best leg-spinner of all.

Name drops

Sir Oliver Popplewell QC was used to pomp and ceremony and a sense of order in any gathering he had occasion to grace. And so it came as a bit of a shock when Australian cricketer Ross Edwards heard his learned friend bellow across a crowded room where people stood in groups at the Royal Commonwealth Society cocktail party at the Commonwealth Club in London: 'Good Lord, Edwards, who is that crashing bore smoking a pipe?'

Ever the diplomat, Edwards came to my rescue in record time; fast even for a man who lived life on the run, the human version of a pneumatic drill.

'Oh, that's our off-spinner, Sir Oliver. Not to worry. He's harmless.'

'Hmm,' the noted QC mused, 'my dear Edwards, no-one who smokes a pipe in a crowded room is harmless.'

When it came to the game of cricket, Popplewell knew his onions. From 1949 to 1951, he played first-class cricket for Cambridge University. A wicketkeeper–batsman, he scored 881 runs at an average of 20.46 including 2 half-centuries. Among his teammates was the Reverend David Sheppard. Years later (1994–96), Popplewell became president of the Marylebone Cricket Club.

Popplewell was a cricketer in the Edwards mould. Before Rodney Marsh began with Western Australia, Edwards was the team's wicketkeeper–batsman. When Marsh took over with the gloves, Edwards turned himself into a top-flight cover fieldsman.

Sir Oliver was either a masochist or intrigued by my performance that evening, for a couple of days later he invited me, along with Edwards, to his London home for a drink and a meal, so in July 1975 I accompanied Edwards to the Popplewell home. During the course of the evening, Sir Oliver introduced a tall, shy young man, sporting a huge mop of hair worn in the manner of an English schoolboy – you know, plump face with ruddy cheeks. It apparently was an important meeting for the 17-year-old Stephen Fry as, according to his photographic memory, I supposedly told him something which had some sort of profound effect on the young man, for he mentioned the incident in his stirring, if irreverent, autobiography *Moab Is My Washpot*:

> *The Popplewells had two of the Australian Test side staying with them, Ross Edwards and Ashley Mallett, whom I met in a lather of dripping excitement: cricket by now had entered my soul for keeps. Ashley Mallett told me something that I did not want to believe, something that troubled me deeply. He told me that professional cricket was ultimately hell, because the pain of losing a match was more intense than the joy of winning one. Edwards disagreed with him, but Mallett stuck fast to his belief. It was, as I see it now, simply a personal difference of outlook between the two of them, but to me it was fundamental. One of them must be right, and the other must be wrong. Was the pain of failing a deeper feeling than the joy of success? If so, Robert Browning and Andrea del Sarto were wrong: a man's reach exceeding his grasp did not justify heaven, it vindicated hell.*

I cannot recall saying that and indeed meeting the young Stephen Fry is a little foggy in the memory. I cannot fathom how I might have made the remark about losing matches. I would like to think that I liked winning and hated losing. Maybe I stressed how distasteful a loss could be compared to the joy of a win. At least, I am convinced that one learns more from a loss than a win, and that is demonstrably true in life generally.

It was in 1972 that we had struck a curious disease called 'fuserium', which strangely enough affected only a strip of turf 22 yards long and a few feet wide at Headingley, Leeds. Australia lost the Test match and the pain of that defeat weighed heavily upon us all. The memory of Headingley may have prompted my remark to Fry three years later.

Throughout the history of international cricket, a variety of celebrities – royalty, actors, pop stars, business tycoons and politicians – have been attracted to the game of cricket and its top players.

In 1972, Australian actor Ed Devereaux, who starred in that old TV favourite *Skippy the Bush Kangaroo*, would sit with the Test team at Lord's, and he also used to have a pint with us in the front bar of the Waldorf Hotel in the heart of London's fashionable West End. Often during our 1972 tour Mick Jagger, a self-confessed cricket tragic, would join our happy group for a drink. Here we were, a bunch of poverty-stricken Australian Test cricketers rubbing shoulders with the lead singer of the Rolling Stones and by that time Jagger was already rich beyond our imagination. But, despite the riches of today's cricket, I have yet to meet a player of my era who wasn't grateful, indeed glad, that he represented his country at the time he played.

There are times in your life when you really put your foot in it. In 1980, the Australian team made a brief tour of England for the Centenary Test. There were a couple of lead-up games and one was against Hampshire at Southampton. The first day saw Dennis Lillee and Len Pascoe demolish Hampshire for just over 100 – a bleak day indeed for the hosts. That evening at a local pub, the players gathered and I found myself at the bar chatting to a bloke waiting for his order.

'Did you see much of the game today?' he asked.

'Yes, I did. I wasn't in the side today, but I watched it all.'

'I guess you were disappointed with the Hampshire batting ...'

'Indeed. Hampshire batted badly, but nowhere near as bad as the bloke who batted three. It is one thing to get a duck, but to have hung around for that long, playing and missing, mistiming and generally boring everyone at the ground was dreadful. The longer he batted, the worse he got. Poor fellow. No future at all.'

There was a pause before I asked: 'Did you go to the game?'

'Yes,' he said with a wry grin, 'I batted number three.'

Mostly this fellow batted in the middle order; an attacking right-hander who played 377 first-class matches, scoring 18,262 runs at 34.39, including 36 centuries and 81 fifties and, while he didn't play Tests, he once captained England A on a tour of Zimbabwe.

The man standing beside me waiting patiently for a beer was none other than the splendid Hampshire batsman, who was destined to become the smoothest among all the modern television cricketer-presenters and commentators, Mark Nicholas.

Late in my career – it must have been in the last days of the 1981 summer – I was a member of the South Australian cricket team flying from Adelaide to Perth. I discovered that Elton John was sitting in business class. Elton and his band were on their way to a concert in Perth and he passed his personal autograph book back to where our team was sitting. We all signed Elton's book and I added my forgery of Ian Chappell, who by the summer of 1980–81 had retired and was living in Sydney.

A few minutes later, passengers were startled when Elton John stood up out of his seat and said in a loud voice: 'Who signed Ian Chappell? C'mon, own up! I know it's a forgery because I saw Chappelli at Sydney Airport and I know he didn't get on this plane.'

Charles Dickens shoulders arms

In the summer of 1861–62, when Charles Dickens rejected £7000 to embark upon a reading tour Down Under, HH Stephenson's first England cricket team toured Australia. After that highly successful cricket tour, Dickens was offered £10,000 to tour Australia in the summer of 1862–63. The offer was increased substantially, but Dickens rejected all of these advances and this great novelist was destined never to set foot in Australia.

Felix Spiers, who kept the Royal Hotel and Café de Paris in Bourke Street, and Christopher Pond, the host of the Piazza Hotel on the corner of Bourke and King Streets, were the Melbourne entrepreneurs who pooled resources to either get Dickens Down Under or bring out the first England cricket team. They had enlisted the services of an agent, Richard Mallam, who sounded out Dickens at Gadshill Place, his home in Maidstone, Kent. He had £7000 with which to lure Charles Dickens to Australia for a reading tour, or tempt the cream of England cricketers to travel to Australia.

A key member of the England touring party was Charles Lawrence, an all-rounder who, in June 1840, as a boy, walked the 22 kilometres from Merton in Surrey to Lord's Cricket Ground to watch his heroes, among them Fuller Pilch, the All-England champion bat. Round the time Lawrence was walking to Lord's, Dickens was in Ballechelish, Scotland, polishing his newest epic, *Barnaby Rudge.*

Cricket wasn't foreign to Charles Dickens. In fact, he loved the game and had a cricket pitch in his expansive backyard at

Gadshill. He may even have seen the Aboriginal team pass his house in a coach as they travelled from Gravesend, taking the main road to Strood on their way to West Malling. In *Pickwick Papers* (1836), he wrote with charm about a cricketing encounter between the fictional All Muggleton versus Dingley Dell. Dickens makes light of the game, but shows his eye for detail:

> *[Each fieldsman] fixed himself into proper attitude by placing one hand on each knee, and stooping very much as if he were 'making a back' for some beginner at leapfrog. All the regular players do this sort of thing; – indeed it's generally supposed that it is quite impossible to look out properly in any other direction. 'Play', suddenly cried the bowler. The ball flew from his hand straight and swift towards the centre stump of the wicket. The wary Dumpkins was on the alert; it fell upon the tip of the bat and bounded far away over the heads of the scouts, who had just stooped low enough to let it fly over them.*

In 2001, the fictional cricket match between Muggleton and Dingley Dell was illustrated on the back of what was then the current English £10 note.

Lawrence stayed in Australia to coach cricket and he eventually found himself as the captain–coach of the Aboriginal Australian cricket team which toured England in 1868. While he was in London, he met up with Spiers and Pond, the Melbourne entrepreneurs, who had bankrolled the 1861–62 England tour to Australia. He learnt, as they ordered more wine to share with him in their Covent Garden restaurant, that the then London-based Spiers and Pond had not collected the publicised £11,000 profit from the tour, but that their profit was a cool £19,000. After the initial Dickens knockback, the entrepreneurs had more than enough funds to tempt the famous author for a reading tour the following year.

When the offer came in the English summer of 1862, Dickens was said to have uttered: 'A man from Australia is in London, ready to pay £10,000 for eight months there. If ...'. It was an 'if' that troubled him for some time and led to agitated discussion. The Civil War having closed America, the increased offer tempted him to Australia. He tried to familiarise himself with the fancy that he would get new material for observation, and went so far as to plan *An Uncommercial Traveller Upside Down*.

On 5 October 1862, Dickens wrote:

'For the hope of a gain that would make me more
independent of the worst, I could not look on the travel
and absence and exertion in the face. I know perfectly well
before-hand how unspeakably wretched I should be. But
these renewed and larger offers tempt me. I can force myself
to go aboard a ship, and I can force myself to do at that
reading-desk what I have a hundred times, but whether,
with all this unsettled fluctuating distress in my mind, I
could force an original book out of it, is another question.'

A few days later, he wrote that 'all the probabilities for such a country as Australia are immense'.

The Aboriginal team went home and the first 'official' Australian team toured England in 1878, under the leadership of Dave Gregory. England hopeful Allan Steel had enjoyed a fabulous summer for Lancashire and he learnt that he had been picked for The Gentlemen against the Australians at Lord's. He recounted an event before that match:

they [the English public] fully expected to find members
of Gregory's team black as the Aboriginals. We remember
the late Reverend Arthur Wood 'putting his foot in it' on

*this subject before some of the Australians. One day in the
pavilion at Lord's, I was sitting beside Spofforth watching a
game in which neither of us was taking part.*

*Mr Wood, coming up, accosted me: 'Well, Mr Steel, so I
hear you are going to play against the n—s on Monday.' His
face was a picture when Spofforth was introduced to him
as the 'demon n— bowler'.*

The very first Test match had been played in March 1877 at the
MCG. Australia beat England by 45 runs, but the home side did
not grant Dave Gregory's men a Test in England in 1878. The
first Test on English soil was in 1880, at Kennington Oval, where
England, led by Lord Harris and dominated by WG Grace's 152,
beat Australia by five wickets. Then came the extraordinary Test
of 1882 at The Oval. Australia won by just seven runs, thanks
to the brilliant bowling of Fred Spofforth, who took 7/46 and
7/44 to demolish the home side. *The Sporting Times* carried a
mock obituary, stating that the body of English cricket would be
cremated and 'the ashes' taken to Australia.

The racist White Australia Policy weighed heavily against the
Indigenous people of Australia and almost certainly prevented
Aboriginal cricketers playing Test cricket. After the 1868 tour,
Aboriginal cricket fell away.

A few players, such as Jack Marsh – who Sir Pelham Warner
said in 1903 was the best bowler in the world – was hounded out
of cricket with the allegation that he chucked. (See 'Jack Marsh
– better than SF Barnes?' in this book.) Eddie Gilbert, who
(in 1931) was the only man to have knocked the bat from Don
Bradman's grasp when bowling, was also said to have thrown
and the administrators dumped him, too. Jason Gillespie is the
first acknowledged male Aboriginal Test cricketer. But how many
others had worn the baggy green before him, men who knew

that if they revealed their true background they would never have played top cricket?

In 2002, thanks to continued lobbying by former Test captain Ian Chappell, the 1868 Aboriginal cricket team was inducted into Australian Cricket's Hall of Fame.

The 1868 Aboriginal Australians were the trailblazers, the men who followed on from HH Stephenson's 1861–62 England team which toured Down Under all because Charles Dickens dismissed the lure of a reading tour in Australia.

Less than nine years after the Aboriginal team toured, Australian cricket had improved so rapidly that the first Test was played in 1877. Without Dickens having let that juicy offer fly by and his subsequent declaration not to tour Australia, Test cricket almost certainly would have taken longer to come to pass.

The gully – a different cricket world

Arguably, Australia's Jeff Thomson was the fastest bowler to draw breath, and fielding to Thommo in the gully was something else. With other fast bowlers, such as Dennis Lillee, you'd watch the bowler move in and it was not until he released the ball that your gaze shifted from its focus on the bowler's hand to a fierce focus on the edge of the bat.

It is imperative that a gully fieldsman finds a way to get a sense of timing: he needs to know almost to the split second when the ball is likely to arrive. If that sense of timing is missing, and the ball suddenly looms at you, the instinct is to grab at the ball and invariably it either goes missing or goes down. You have to combine the timing with watching the edge of the bat like a hawk.

My method for most medium and fast bowlers was to watch the ball out of the hand, then go straight to the edge of the bat. But for Thommo it had to be different, because there was no time to do as you did with the others. With Thommo, you'd watch that approach until he loaded up. A magnificent athlete, his approach was like that of a champion athlete about to throw the javelin at the Olympic Games. Momentarily before delivery, he paused to load up before releasing the ball like some magical human catapult. You knew that the ball would come at breakneck speed ... Dear moderns, imagine the velocity if you can – about two yards quicker than Shoaib Akhtar at his absolute quickest. Often in the gully I'd catch a glimpse of a red sphere flashing past my eyes on its inevitable way to Rodney Marsh behind the stumps; the ball rose like a jet, its climb stopped by Marsh's gloves, which resounded like a solid right hook to the jaw from Muhammad Ali.

To get the timing right, I suspect I would have had to employ a similar strategy when fielding in the gully to the likes of Frank Tyson and Wes Hall, both of whom possessed pace like fire.

Rodney Marsh was as tough a character as ever stood behind the stumps for Australia, but he once said: 'You'd have to pay danger money to get me fielding in the gully.' From his position behind the stumps, Marsh would have seen many shots from the likes of Garry Sobers, Viv Richards, Graeme Pollock and Roy Fredericks scream past gully at the velocity of a tracer bullet and probably wondered why in the hell anyone would put themselves in the firing line as a gully fieldsman.

I had watched some of the great gully fieldsmen, such as Richie Benaud, who made the position his own for more than a decade. Benaud fielded close to the bat, something Alan Davidson reckons he learnt from fearless gully fieldsman Ron James, who took some sensational catches at leg or regulation gully in his 45 matches for New South Wales. 'Ron got as close to the bat as he could,' Davidson recalled. 'He reckoned that the closer to the bat you were in the gully the more chances you would get, simply because the closer in you are the less of an angle is produced.'

That philosophy always made sense to me and I was amazed to see how far back Steve Waugh fielded to Glenn McGrath. The big fast bowler took 563 wickets in his brilliant Test career, but it should have been more given that a lot of edges bounced at least once before they reached the gully fieldsman. Steve Waugh, Geoff Marsh and Matthew Hayden were blessed with sure hands, but all of them stood far too deep in the gully. So too did Mike Hussey; twice in a series against India, Hussey had to dive forward at gully to catch edges which ballooned off the shoulder of Gautam Gambhir's bat. He was usually so deep in the gully that you could sneak a single to him. Hussey had brilliant hands and great anticipation, but he should have got in closer to the bat.

Nathan Lyon has been tried in the gully. He's good at backward point, but when in the gully, as with many of his predecessors, he fields far too deep. Peter Handscomb could well be the best bet. Handscomb stays low and watches the ball like a hawk. In the gully he needs to switch his gaze from the moment of the bowler's release to focus on the edge of the bat.

There are no specific physical attributes to be a gully fieldsman. Method, timing and lightning reflexes are essential to be good, but the way to success at gully is very different from standing at first or second slip. The great slip fieldsmen such as Bob Simpson, Mark Taylor, Mark Waugh, Jack Gregory, Ian Chappell and Graham Roope might have struggled to field in the gully, unless they changed their method. In the gully, you cannot succeed if you watch the ball from the bowler's hand all the way down the track until the batsman plays his shot.

Like a wicketkeeper, the gully man needs to crouch rather low on the balls of his feet, so balanced as to be able to spring to his left or his right. Staying low is essential, as many catches come low and fast, either a forward drive or a defensive push to a late outswinger. The drive usually comes hard and fast, but the defensive push can often sort of loop in the air and be on the 'down' when you move to complete the catch. Always, the key to success in the gully is to get the timing right, and with the right method you take more than you miss. By staying low, you can do as a wicketkeeper does when taking slow bowling; you come up with the ball, thus covering either eventuality – a low snick or a high slash.

Even from a close-in position at gully it was amazing how easy it was to see the ball as clear as day. When you got the timing right, the whole scene seemed to be in slow motion, even a snick from a Jeff Thomson fireball. The ball careered from the outside edge, but it was as easy as pie to watch all the way and to complete the catch. By the time the ball was within a few feet of the batsman, you had to be in good position, knees bent and hands cupped together and ready for the catch. To catch most edges in the gully you had to 'will' every ball to come to you.

Batsmen always gave clues as to how the ball might come at you in the gully. A batsman who stood with an open face of the bat always lifted your heart rate, for you knew the likes of a Roy Fredericks (West Indies) or a Ken Barrington (England) would edge square towards gully when they made a mistake in driving at a ball of full length which swung away late. So I would watch the batsman, see how he shaped. When he wasn't quite to the pitch of the ball, did it go very square? All these things helped build up a picture in the mind's eye.

More recently, batsmen such as India's Gambhir and Virender Sehwag opened the face and hit square of the wicket. Sehwag got away with a lot of lofted shots through the gully area because most gully men he played against fielded too far away from the bat.

The method of getting the timing right also applies to fielding at bat-pad. However, fielding at bat-pad and fielding in the gully are two different worlds entirely. The best bat-padders watch the bowler's hand to the point of release so they get a sense of when the ball is likely to arrive; so too those who field at leg-gully. Given that you know approximately when the ball is likely to come your way, via the edge of the bat and the pad, it usually comes like a balloon, easy to snare. Sometimes the bat is in front of the pad and the ball skips off the edge quickly, but if you are on the ball and timing is right, you accept the chance.

The best close catchers I've seen include Indian players Venkat and Solkar. These blokes stalked batsmen; seemingly moving in with the bowler, say Erapalli Prasanna, still the best off-spinner I've seen, and often catching the ball on the cut portion of the pitch. Most of the good bat-pad fieldsmen are short in stature, nimble movers who are able to get to the ball swiftly.

England's Alastair Cook had good hands, but he was slow to react, taking his eyes off the ball, and must have caused Graeme Swann much heartache when he missed or failed to make the ground to at least one chance of a catch off Swann per innings. What is similar to the method of catching in the gully is to get the timing right.

The great England left-arm spinner Tony Lock was the best leg-gully man I've seen. The method is the same as for regulation gully, the difference being that the ball would suddenly appear from behind the batsman's front pad.

I stood some seven paces back in the gully. On the bouncy Perth track, I made that about eight paces, which probably equates to near 9 metres. I was always mindful of how the edge of the bat looked to me from my position at gully. If the batsman had an open face, my heart began to race and heightened my anticipation that a catch was just around the corner.

Commonsense was a Chappell family trait. Martin Chappell taught Greg Chappell to catch a cricket ball by the time Greg was two years old. 'My way was simple,' he once told me. 'If I threw the ball to my son, his eyes would invariably look at his dad and when I threw the ball to him his eyes were on me, not the ball, making it impossible for him to catch it. So I showed him the ball, then tossed it against the wall. Greg's eyes left mine and focused on the rebounding ball, which he caught easily.' In a way, that was a simplistic version of the method of gully fieldsmen: your gaze goes from the ball release to the edge of the bat.

I boosted my hand–eye coordination by catching a rebounding golf ball off a rough wall. In my left hand I wore my baseball catcher's glove and eventually, after hours of practice, I could catch a ball, sensing its exact location, speed and direction by instinct alone. You simply didn't have to watch the ball into your hand.

Fielding in the gully had its own incalculable rewards. Once at the Adelaide Oval in the 1974–75 Ashes series, Colin Cowdrey back-cut Lillee. The ball was on the 'down', but somehow I flung myself clumsily towards it and clutched it with my left hand. Cowdrey looked at me in astonishment; then his demeanour immediately changed. He touched the peak of his cap and said cheerily, 'Well caught, master.'

KP

They call him KP, and Kevin Pietersen is world cricket's supreme egotist – a personality on and off the field with a decided cutting edge.

KP made his Test match debut against Australia at Lord's in July 2005. In the first innings, he hit 57 before Shane Warne, who he would confront in many an epic battle, had him caught by Damien Martyn. Facing just 89 balls, Pietersen hit 8 fours and 2 mighty sixes, with his trademark slog-sweep. Batting a second time, he carried his bat for 64 (6 fours and another 2 sixes) in England's paltry total of 180 and Australia won the match by 239 runs.

He immediately attracted attention with his strokeplay and equally outrageous haircuts, with the peroxide blond streak running down the middle of his head inevitably inviting cutting remarks from the Australians, such as 'a dead skunk look'. By the Australian summer of 2006–07, the Australian Test team were calling him 'FIGJAM', an acronym for 'Fuck I'm good, just ask me'.

But all the derogatory remarks and name-calling in the world didn't upset KP; he carried on, chatting away to himself in his own way and belting hell out of some of the best bowling the world has seen, especially from the likes of Warne and Glenn McGrath. Warne dismissed Pietersen a couple of times in that epic 2005 series. In the amazing Second Test at Edgbaston, he gloved the first ball he faced from Brett Lee in the second innings and the umpire turned down the appeal. Soon after, a ball from Warne hit his pad, then elbow, before popping up in the air for Adam Gilchrist to gobble up behind the stumps. Both umpiring decisions were wrong but it didn't cost the Australians dearly. Pietersen was given out on 20 after a first-innings 71.

His *pièce de résistance* of batsmanship came in the Fifth Test at The Oval. Before he had scored, Pietersen was dropped in a mix-up between Matthew Hayden at slip and Gilchrist. When he reached 15, Warne dropped a sitter off him at slip and when on 60, Shaun Tait turfed one. His innings of 158 finally ended when McGrath bowled him. While others about him bumbled and fought, Pietersen hit out with gay abandon, smacking 7 sixes, a feat which broke Ian Botham's record for the most number of sixes by an English player in an Ashes innings. In the five Tests, Pietersen scored 473 runs at an average of 52.55.

In the field he was less successful, dropping six catches, a point he wryly brought into the conversation when questioned about the Australians dropping him three times on the final day. Pietersen was also honoured as one of the five Wisden Cricketers of the Year, alongside teammates Matthew Hoggard and Simon Jones. And along with the rest of the England team, Pietersen was decorated in the 2006 New Year Honours list, awarded the MBE for his role in the successful Ashes series.

Pietersen scored 8181 runs in 104 Tests, including 23 centuries. He also hit more than 4000 runs in ODIs, but as a character he always divided opinion. On one hand, he was a brilliant stroke-maker, who took ludicrous risks to destroy attacks. On the other hand, he struggled to fit into the England team environment.

Over the years, there have been players who are considered dangerous because if they hit a purple patch they can change a game by themselves in a session's play. In my time, the game-changers included Doug Walters, Ian Botham, West Indians Viv Richards, Clive Lloyd and Roy Fredericks, and South Africans

Graeme Pollock and Barry Richards. More recently it was the likes of VVS Laxman, Sachin Tendulkar, Brian Lara and Adam Gilchrist. And Kevin Pietersen is right up there with the best of them.

Often Pietersen began an innings all a dither, floundering in survival mode until he got into his strokes; something akin to a champion swimmer who had forgotten what to do when first entering the water, then suddenly grabbing the moment by swimming strongly. On occasion he would be batting magnificently, opposition bowlers wringing their hands in despair, then suddenly, as if the lights were switched off, he would play a wild shot and be walking off the field. In the wake of his 444-run World Cup batting performance in 2007 (at an average of 55.5), Pietersen was described as shining in the England team 'like a 100-watt bulb in a room full of candles'.

He was seemingly at odds with the England team rules and had a fractious relationship with England coaches Peter Moores, then Andy Flower. It is said that he could be intolerant of fellow players, especially less-experienced teammates. While his ability was never questioned, there were other aspects of his character which haunted the English cricket establishment.

When both Test captain Michael Vaughan and ODI skipper Paul Collingwood resigned at the same time, Pietersen was appointed captain of both teams. Following England's disastrous ODI tour of India in 2008 where Pietersen's men lost 5–nil, the media reported in January 2009 that Pietersen had asked the England and Wales Cricket Board (ECB) to hold an emergency meeting to discuss coach Peter Moores's role with the England team. The pair were apparently at loggerheads over a number of issues, particularly the team's training regimes.

After a public falling out with England team head coach Peter Moores, the ECB acted swiftly. Moores was sacked on 7 January 2009 and, surprisingly, Pietersen resigned the same day.

Pietersen was captain of England for three Test matches and 10 ODIs when Andrew Strauss was appointed as his replacement. His career continued with brilliant form one day, ordinary the next. His batting could verge on the genius, or a chump. Sometimes he caught well, but usually he could be guaranteed to drop a sitter.

Social media was not the best bedfellow for Pietersen, for it served only to highlight his impetuous nature; he was almost Donald Trump–like in shooting off at the mouth before sitting down and giving the matter due consideration. In 2010, he was fined for a foul-mouthed outburst on Twitter after being omitted from the England squad for a series against Pakistan. In 2012, he was again punished when he used social media to criticise a pundit. He was axed from the final Test match against South Africa at Lord's in 2012 when it was discovered he had been sending provocative texts to opposing players.

Pietersen's career stagnated for a time, but in October 2012, the ECB confirmed that they had put in place a process which could lead to his return to the England cricket team. In less than a month, Pietersen was back in the Test side and in the team which completed a successful tour of India. He scored 338 runs in four Tests, including a century and 2 fifties. The highlight was his masterly 186 in his second Test back in the fold. Ex-England teammate Andrew Flintoff said: 'When Kevin's got a point to prove, he usually proves it with the bat.'

External conflicts aside, KP seemed to be forever fighting an inner demon. Even when he talks about his own character, there seems to be a degree of inner agony. Perhaps the supreme ego we see on the Pietersen face as he flays the bowling is in continual turmoil with how he is actually feeling.

KP says, 'I'm very much an introverted person. I like my own company, my own family. I don't really go out much. I'm not as confident as everyone thinks. I think what confidence I have has grown from what I achieved on the cricket field.'

The ECB eventually ran out of patience with Pietersen, announcing on 4 February 2014 that he had not been selected for the upcoming tour of the West Indies. The decision was 'unanimous'. The media immediately stated that Pietersen's England cricket career was over.

Pietersen released a statement which read: 'Although I am obviously very sad the incredible journey has come to an end, I'm also hugely proud of what we, as a team, have achieved over the past nine years.'

Born to an Afrikaner father, Jannie, and an English mother, Penny, Kevin Peitersen has three brothers, Tony, Greg and Bryan. He had a strict and disciplined upbringing. 'Discipline is good,' he says. 'It taught me that I didn't always have to have what I wanted: that what I needed was different from what I wanted.'

At 17, KP made his first-class debut for Natal's B team in 1997. He was mainly then an off-spinner and hard-hitting lower-order batsman. After two seasons, he moved to England for a five-month stint as an overseas player for the Cannock Cricket Club and his all-round talent helped his team win the Birmingham and District Premier League in 2000. He lived fairly rough, in a room above a squash court, and during the week worked pulling beers in the club bar.

Then fate took a hand. Clive Rice, the great South African all-rounder, saw Pietersen play at a school cricket festival and he invited him to sign for the Nottinghamshire County Cricket Club and KP had no hesitation in accepting the offer.

In 1999, playing for the newly named KwaZulu Natal in a tour match against Nasser Hussain's England side, KP impressed with four top-order wickets and, batting at number nine, he belted 61 not out in 57 balls, including 4 towering sixes. Despite praise from the England players, Pietersen claimed he was dropped from the Natal first team because of

South Africa's quota system, in which provincial sides were required to have at least four black players in the eleven. He believed, as many other cricketers in that country believe, that all players should be judged on merit and he has never changed his stance.

However, the experience made him determined to play for the country of his mother's birth: England. He copped a lot of flak from South Africans, especially the long-time Proteas captain Graeme Smith, who was quoted as saying of KP: 'I am patriotic about my country, and that's why I don't like Kevin Pietersen.' That rant came after KP, who believes the quota system forced him out of South Africa, said of Smith: 'An absolute muppet, childish and strange.'

Pietersen had to spend four years in England before he was eligible for Test selection. While playing back in his homeland with England A, Pietersen was subjected to a barrage of abuse from the South African crowd, who regarded him as a 'traitor'. Typically, KP reacted in this manner:

> *I expected stick at the start of the innings, and I'm sure it will carry on through the whole series. But I just sat back and laughed at the opposition, with their swearing and 'traitor' remarks ... My affiliation is with England. In fact, I'm starting to speak too much like Darren Gough ... In fact, I'm going to get one of Gough's tattoos with three lions and my number underneath ... No-one can say I'm not English.*

KP let his bat do the talking for the rest of that tour. At East London, he scored an unbeaten 100 off 69 balls, the fastest century by an England batsman in a one-day match. At Centurion Park, Pietersen came to the wicket with his team tottering at 3/32 and he scored 116. While England lost the series 4–1, Pietersen was far and away the best batsman on either side. He scored 454 runs in five innings and the Player of the Series award. Thanks to his batting brilliance, by the end of the series the South African crowds had shrugged off all hostility towards him. There was a renewed respect, reflected by his receiving a standing ovation for his last-match century.

Sadly, we won't see KP play a Test match again, but we can look forward to his cricket commentary. KP had TV commentary experience, with the odd stint behind the microphone in England, before he joined Mark Nicholas, Ian Chappell, Shane Warne, Michael Slater, Mark Taylor, Michael Clarke and Ian Healy on the Channel Nine team for the three Tests between Australia and South Africa in the 2016–17 summer, KP proved an instant success. He was articulate, informative and entertaining. Like his widespread appeal as a cricketer, KP's laughter was infectious. His banter with Shane Warne was as much a treat for viewers as his epic on-field battles with the spin legend.

KP played over differing formats for a lengthy list of teams and hit his highest first-class score (355 not out) for Surrey in May 2015. Months before that epic knock, which was soon after he learnt of his permanent split from the England team, KP told *The Telegraph*:

People say you're bitter. I've answered this question in my book. There are some days when I go – 'I should be playing cricket for England. Why am I not?' And then there's most of the other days I wake up and I go – Kevin, you came to England as a bowler, you played 104 Test matches, you've scored more runs than anyone else who's ever played for England, you've got more Man of the Matches for England than anyone's ever got. Be happy, be proud.

A day of two knights

It was the Saturday before the Fifth Test against the West Indies at the SCG in February 1969. That afternoon I was batting for Prospect against East Torrens on Norwood Oval. A typical Adelaide February day – hot and dry, not a breath of wind – and there I was at drinks ripping my right glove off with my teeth. I felt a strange sensation in my mouth and there on the top of my glove lay one of my two front teeth. The tooth had snapped off cleanly at the gum line and sat there, a glint of the gold filling sparkling in the sunlight.

As I had to be in Sydney to prepare for the Test the following Monday afternoon, I had to arrange for a tooth to be fitted to a temporary dental plate in time to catch the flight to Sydney. By the time I boarded the plane, my tooth was in place. All was well with the world except that on match morning I was named twelfth man for the fourth successive Test match.

West Indian captain Garry Sobers won the toss and invited Bill Lawry's team to bat on what looked like a magnificent SCG batting strip. Australia began poorly. Keith Stackpole (20) was clean-bowled by Wes Hall, Ian Chappell (1) fell lbw to Sobers, and Ian Redpath (0) also became a Sobers victim. Australia was a precarious 3/51 when Doug Walters joined Lawry at the crease. At lunch, Lawry and Walters were still there. In fact, they were at the start of a record fourth-wicket partnership of 336, Lawry finishing with 151 and Walters with a magnificent 242 in an Australian total of 619.

When Lawry came from the field at lunch, he said to me, 'Rowdy, I want you to don your blazer and become Bill Lawry at lunch. You'll be sitting at the top table with the Governor and the board chairman. Good luck.'

I knew the Australian Cricket Board chairman was Sir Donald Bradman and I soon learnt that the New South Wales Governor was Sir Roden Cutler. I knew Bradman's remarkable story, but didn't then know of Sir Roden's extraordinary life journey. In mid-1941, in an action in Syria against the Vichy French forces, Roden Cutler came under heavy machine-gun fire and was badly hit. He lay in no-man's-land for 26 hours before he could be rescued, and his right leg was amputated. Awarded the Victoria Cross, he was invalided home to a hero's welcome in Sydney. In 1946, he was appointed Australian High Commissioner in New Zealand, then Consul-General in New York and, from 1965 to 1981, was state Governor. A tall, handsome, dignified man, Sir Roden loved sport and epitomised Australians' fighting spirit.

So there I was that day in February 1969, sandwiched between two knights – two great Australian heroes – but they made me very welcome and we engaged in enjoyable conversation. I settled for roast beef tenderloin, garlic mashed potato, mushroom ragout, spring onions, beef reduction – the same dish Sir Roden selected. Inwardly I thanked the cricket gods for making the lunch a happy occasion. I also thanked my dentist, under my breath, for the brilliant job he'd done with the one tooth attached to a plate. It was such a good fit, so snug and comfortable, that I hardly noticed it was in my mouth at all.

After dessert (fruit salad and ice cream), I happily grabbed a red apple and took a bite, but didn't have time to finish it because I was needed back in the Australian dressing-room. It was never good form for the twelfth man to be away for any length of time. (Lawry would notice my absence; Walters couldn't have cared less, for he would be, at that precise moment, sipping tea between drags on a Rothmans filter-tipped cigarette.)

I shook hands with Sir Roden Cutler and Sir Donald Bradman, both men obviously sensitive to the nervous plight of the young Australian cricketer substituting for the Test captain at the top table in the Members' Dining Room at the SCG.

Twenty minutes after lunch, the score raced past 100. As the ovation subsided, I heard a faint knock on the dressing-room door. I opened it and there, standing with a bread plate, its contents covered by a linen serviette, stood a small waitress. She said with a wry smile, 'Young man, I think this is yours.' I thanked her and went inside. All the players were outside the dressing-room watching the game, so I was alone.

I removed the serviette and there before my eyes was my temporary dental plate, its one tooth firmly embedded in the remnants of a shiny red apple.

Allan Border's best shot

For all his heroics on the Test cricket field, Allan Border reckons his best shot in cricket happened when he was barely nine years old. He lofted a ball from his brother Brett straight through a neighbour's bathroom window. It was not the elderly spinster who loved the sound of the children playing and didn't mind the odd breakage; this was an entirely different window. Gingerly, Allan climbed over the fence and peered through the broken window to be confronted by a young woman who had just stepped out of a shower. Allan always regarded that hoick to leg as the best shot of his career.

Born in Cremorne, a suburb of Sydney, on 27 July 1955, Allan lived with his family opposite Mosman Oval. He loved to sit on a step leading to the front door of their home and watch the players on the oval across the street. He dreamt of the day when he would be old enough to play cricket and baseball for Mosman. Allan was the second of four sons to John and Sheila Border. Mark was born in 1946 and after Allan came John (1958) and Brett (1962).

The Border boys played the inevitable backyard Tests. On occasion their parents had to intervene in the odd dispute, for the games were hotly contested and at times tempers became a little frayed. At the back of the house, there was a large concrete area providing the boys with a good, true batting surface. A row of fruit trees formed the boundary line and a garbage bin served as the stumps. Initially, the boys used a tennis ball and a home-made bat cut from an old paling.

It didn't take long for them to seek a greater challenge, because they found batting too easy with the paling bat, so they 'procured' a stump from the Mosman Cricket Club nets and that became their new bat. The boys experimented with a practice golf ball made of plastic, which they found they could spin and curve easily. This proved a real test for the boys and Allan, especially, honed his early footwork against spin and curve on the Border backyard concrete pitch.

The boys soon gravitated to using the hard cricket ball. However, when the bill for broken windows became excessive, John and Sheila Border banned hard-ball Tests. Yet even with a soft ball, the neighbours' windows suffered. One day the owner of a nearby block of flats asked John Border if he would pay the insurance premiums on his windows. In addition to the special insurance spent on the neighbours' windows, John and Sheila had a handyman friend on standby to replace broken windows, 'at any hour'.

At the age of 15, Allan was the Mosman Baseball Club's A-grade first-baseman. He was also a good outfielder and a solid batter. For the best part of a century, baseball was a winter sport in Australia. Many good cricketers played baseball, among them Vic Richardson, Neil Harvey, Les Favell, Norm O'Neill, Bill Lawry and Ian Chappell. By the late 1960s, baseball had become a summer sport and cricketers such as Allan Border had to make a decision.

At the age of 16, Allan retired from baseball to concentrate on his cricket and in his A-grade debut for Mosman took 0/67 with his left-arm spinners and scored an unbeaten 40. But all the hard work did not suit Allan. By the time he had turned 19, he was going through the motions as a cricketer, keener on lazing on the beach, lapping up the sun and chatting up the girls.

Then a mentor came into Allan's life – former England all-rounder Barry Knight, who had played 29 Tests for England. He was then playing for the Mosman club and running a cricket coaching school in Mosman. Knight had a good eye for talent. While he saw tremendous potential in young Border, he was concerned that the youngster was not applying himself. For two years, he worked hard on Allan, helping him with grip, stance and mental approach. Young Border benefited greatly from Knight's coaching and enjoyed batting against him in the nets.

On Knight's advice, Allan went to play for Downend in England's Western League, then East Lancashire the following year. He learnt first-hand how tough a player had to be to succeed as a professional cricketer. There was added pressure in the Lancashire League because Border was the sole professional in the side, the only one in the eleven who was being paid. That meant the pro simply had to perform.

Between 1977 and 1979, world cricket was in turmoil because World Series Cricket had split the game. Kerry Packer's troupe wanted to win the crowds over and the Establishment wanted to prove that their way was the only way. They banned WSC players from Test and first-class cricket.

Having impressed as a state player for New South Wales, Allan made his Test debut against England at the MCG in December 1978. Batting number six, he scored just 29 in the first innings and was run out in the second for a duck. But it was in the next Test against England at the SCG that Border first made his mark in big cricket. England off-spinners John Emburey and Geoff Miller exploited a dusty, turning track, but Border, showing the sort of grit which characterised his cricket in all his 156 Test matches, top-scored in both innings with 60 not out and 45 not out.

In the First Test against Pakistan at the MCG in March 1979, Australia were chasing 382 in the second innings for an improbable win. Border, now number three in the order, scored his maiden Test century (105) and Australia were 3/305, but when he was out the team lost seven wickets for five runs to be all out for 310.

In 1979, Kerry Packer had won the television rights to broadcast the cricket, WSC was wound up and many of the players were back in the official Test team for the 1979–80 season. Stalwarts such as Dennis Lillee, Greg Chappell, Doug Walters and Rod Marsh were chosen to play the series against the West Indies; so too was Lennie Pascoe and even, for a time, yours truly. When I was picked in the Third Test at Adelaide Oval, I met Allan Border for the first time.

During the Pakistan tour which followed the Australian summer, Border batted brilliantly on a treacherous turner in Karachi and scored 150 not out and 153 at Gaddafi Stadium, a magnificent double which was a first in Test history.

As the seasons passed, Border continued to bat consistently; however, when Lillee, Greg Chappell and Rod Marsh hung up their boots in 1984, Australia under the captaincy of Kim Hughes struggled, especially against the might of the West Indies. After a string of huge defeats at the hands of the West Indies in the Caribbean and in Australia, Hughes, in a flood of tears, announced he was quitting the Test captaincy. Hughes led Australia in 28 Tests for a dismal record of 13 losses, 4 wins and 11 draws. He blamed criticism from former players as the catalyst for his resignation.

He eventually was picked up as captain of the Australian rebel team to play in South Africa, flouting the international agreement against Apartheid. In April 1985, seven players originally selected for the Ashes tour had signed for the Hughes-led team and withdrew from the squad. Among these were John Dyson, Terry Alderman, Carl Rackemann, Steve Rixon and Rodney Hogg. They all got a truckload of Krugerrands; rumour has it that the average contract was worth 200,000 rand, with the senior players collecting as much as 300,000 rand. (The rand was then on parity with the Australian dollar.)

The players, through a large and lucrative loophole in the system, reputedly paid only one cent tax on the money they received each South African summer. Prime Minister Bob Hawke moved to change the taxation laws and the Minister for Sport urged the Australian Cricket Board to take punitive action against players who went to South Africa. Bruce Francis, the South African Cricket Union's Australian agent, described this as the most obnoxious request ever put to a sporting organisation. The ACB thought they had a good case, but they eventually agreed to a settlement whereby the South Africans paid all legal costs the board had incurred.

On the England tour, Border scored 196 at Lord's to inspire Australia's only win of the three-Test series. He hit 8 centuries on the tour, including 2 in the Tests, but lacked support. Border was pretty much a reluctant captain.

The board was concerned about the incredible stress Border was under. Because of Australia's decided lack of quality batsmen to support Border he became the batsman all Australia's opponents targeted. The West Indians were best at that caper; bowlers such as Joel Garner, Malcolm Marshall and Curtly Ambrose came at him in waves of unrelenting hostility. Former Australian captain Bob Simpson was sounded out to help. The ACB knew there was no obvious replacement for Border if he quit and they believed Simpson was the man for the full-time role of team coach. Simpson joined the team for the tour of New Zealand in 1986, the start of a successful partnership in which Simpson looked after the practice sessions and Border the on-field captaincy. Training became more professional and specialised. The players responded with great enthusiasm and soon the hard work started to pay off.

Simpson clearly saw the need for Australia to pick players of strong character. Tasmania's David Boon and Western Australia's Geoff Marsh became ensconced as openers; Victorian Dean Jones batted at three. Mark Taylor, Steve Waugh and Ian Healy came into the side.

Winning the Fifth Test against England in 1987 was only Australia's third win in 23 Tests, but later that year Australia unexpectedly won the World Cup in India. Border's men then regained the Ashes in England in 1989. Steve Waugh returned Bradman-like figures and Border scored 6 half-centuries, but, more importantly, he led Australia to a famous 4–nil Ashes victory.

Allan Border epitomised all that is pugnacious, determined and stoic in Test cricket. As a batsman, he had a good, tight technique and a never-say-die attitude which bordered on an obsession to make Australian cricket strong again. His Test record is outstanding, with 11,174 runs at 50.56, including 27 centuries and a highest score of 205.

Allan Border had the passion, skill and an inherent stubbornness to never give up which appealed to the Australian public. Leading Australia to World Cup victory in India in 1987 and regaining the Ashes in England in 1989 he regards as highlights of his lengthy reign as the nation's captain. Australian cricket owes AB much for his tireless contribution to the game and, since 2000, the best Australian international player of the year is awarded by Cricket Australia with the Allan Border Medal.

Once upon an all-run nine

In 1868, it was just four years since the cricket lawmakers had allowed a bowler to operate with his bowling arm at a height above the shoulder. Sporting long hair and a slinging action, Twopenny (Murrumgunnarin, also know as Jarrawuk) was a fast round-armer – the Lasith Malinga of the 1868 Aboriginal Australian cricket team.

Twopenny played 46 of a possible 47 matches on tour, but team captain Charles Lawrence was reluctant to bowl Twopenny for any decent spells until late in the tour. When he did, he collected 35 wickets at an average of 6.9, off just 704 balls, a strike rate of a wicket every 20.11 balls. Against East Hampshire, Twopenny proved a sensation with match figures of 15/16 (9/9 and 6/7).

Lawrence's reluctance to bowl Twopenny early on the tour was due to his fear that his fast bowler might be called for throwing. His fear was unfounded, because his action had never been queried in Australia and, when he did get to bowl in England, critics marvelled at his skill and applauded his performances.

His greatest claim to fame on the 1868 England tour was, however, with the bat, not the ball. He was a terrific hitter, but the kind of lower-order batsman who hits across the line, so it wasn't the sheer number of runs he hit, for that was a lightweight 589 at an average of 8.29. His fame was a result of batting in the match against Sheffield at Bramall Lane over the two days of 10–11 August 1868.

Twopenny achieved with his bat something which eluded WG Grace, Don Bradman, Ricky Ponting or Sachin Tendulkar.

In his score of 22, Twopenny hit a ball so high and so far that he completed *nine* runs before the ball was returned to the wicket. That is, an all-run (no overthrows to swell the tally) *nine*. The cricket correspondent for the *Sheffield Independent* was present to record the event for posterity:

> *Twopenny made the sensational hit of the match,*
> *accomplishing a feat which has no parallel on Brammall*
> *Lane, and we should say on no other ground, and Mr*
> *Foster, who was well up, did not offer for some time to go*
> *for the ball, and when started it was at a slow pace, the*
> *result being that nine was run for the hit amidst vociferous*
> *cheering.*

Poor Mr Foster. Short of being built like a 104-year-old elephant with lumbago, he must have been very slow off the mark in his efforts to retrieve the ball and get it back to the wicket. Little did he know that the enthusiastic Aboriginals struggled in their judgment of a run and in their 47 matches they suffered 60 run-outs.

The 1868 Aboriginal Australian team played 47 two-day matches in England, winning 14, losing 14 and drawing 19 games. This was Australia's first international sporting tour of England and the team delighted crowds with their cricket, athletic prowess and the throwing of spear and boomerang.

The Aboriginal players were given sobriquets because their pastoral landlords could not pronounce their tribal names. This is the popular theory, although there is a condescending tone in some of the nicknames. Apparently, cricket scorers were relieved. Instead of Murrumgunarrin or Jarrawuk the player was called Twopenny; Brimbunyah was Redcap; Unaarrimin was Johnny Mullagh.

All the Aboriginal players were expert in either throwing a boomerang or spear or both, or wielding a stockwhip. After the match, spectators were treated to a display of athletics, whip-cracking, and spear and boomerang throwing. Charley Dumas (Pripumuarraman) was the team's star boomerang man. He brought 15 of his best boomerangs with him to England and he blew the crowd away at The Oval with his throwing, which had a boomerang soar the entire length of the ground, past the famous gasholders and back to a position where the ancient aeronautical marvel hovered 'obediently' for its master and landed gently between Dumas's feet.

The team's keeper, Bullocky (Bullchanach), won 'the mighty toss' (the long throw) by heaving the ball a distance of 105 yards 6 inches. Charley Dumas, discarding his boomerang, ran second with a throw of 100 yards 9 inches.

After the presentations were completed, a young man emerged from the Members' Stand. It was WG Grace, then 19 and immensely strong and athletic. He challenged the Aboriginals to replay the long throw. In three goes, Grace threw a cricket ball distances of 116, 117 and 118 yards. Then he hushed the crowd by throwing 109 yards one way and 104 the other.

Although Grace's throws easily beat the best by Bullocky and Dumas, they came in the wake of the official presentation, so the acknowledged 'official' chronicler of the time, *Bell's Life*, only recorded the throws of Bullocky and Dumas.

Mosquito (Grongarrong) and Peter (Arrahmunyjarrimin) were experts with the stockwhip. Johnny Cuzens (Zellanach), whose action was catapult-like in the Jeff Thomson mould, could also run like the wind, and Redcap, at Mote Park in Kent, nailed a squirrel scampering up a tall oak tree with a boomerang. Red Cap possessed the skill and the deadly accuracy of Viv Richards throwing down the wicket.

A few years back, Twopenny's boomerang turned up at an auction house. There was some doubt about its authenticity, but on the back were autographs of county cricketers who had played against the 1868 Aboriginal tourists.

Back in Australia, Twopenny played one first-class match for New South Wales against Victoria in the summer of 1869–70. He was the first man of Aboriginal descent to play top cricket, but his one game produced just eight runs in two completed innings and figures of 0/56 off 30 fruitless overs.

However, Twopenny's all-run nine on the 1868 tour is a batting record that will stand forever.

Fergie's wagon wheel

They called him Mr Cricket more than 60 years before Mike Hussey was born. On umpteen cricket tours from 1905 to 1954, scorer–baggage master Bill Ferguson, affectionately known as 'Fergie', carted luggage for such flannelled gods as Victor Trumper, Don Bradman, Bill O'Reilly, Wally Hammond and Jack Cheetham.

But his greatest claim to fame was having created cricket's wagon wheel. During lulls in play or as a creative aside to his main function of recording the score, Fergie gave the cricket world its first official wagon wheel on 17 May 1912. That day he charted Jack Hobbs's shots in his 81 for Surrey versus Australia at Kennington Oval. Hobbs hit 1 six, 13 fours, 2 threes, 3 twos and 11 singles.

Fergie's wagon wheels were drawn in pencil or ink from an ancient dipped nib with meticulous, loving care. Over the years, he recorded many great and famous innings, including Bradman's 334 for Australia versus England at Leeds in 1934 (46 fours, 6 threes, 26 twos and 80 singles), and Wally Hammond's 336 in 318 minutes for England versus New Zealand at Auckland in April 1933.

Today on television we see all manner of graphics, but the wagon wheel still catches our eye. It reveals where a batsman scores the bulk of his runs, his strengths and where he can be contained. Once, before World War I, a journalist tried to patent Fergie's charts, but soon realised that they were by then as much in the public domain as the game itself.

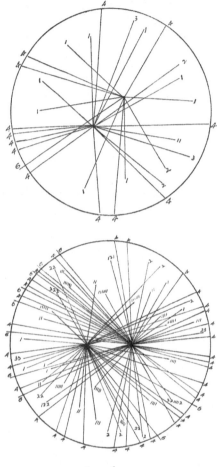

Fergie's first wagon wheel, featuring Jack Hobbs, who hit 81 for Surrey versus Australia, at The Oval, 12 May 1912.

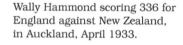

Wally Hammond scoring 336 for England against New Zealand, in Auckland, April 1933.

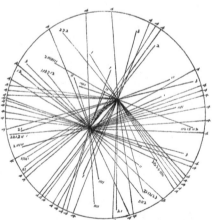

Don Bradman's amazing range of scoring shots in his 334 for Australia versus England, at Headingley, Leeds, July 1934.

Bill Ferguson hailed from Sydney. At the age of 24, he worked for the *Sydney Directory*, filing the names of householders, streets and districts – which he called 'the most monotonous task known to man'. In his lunch break, he'd stroll down to the waterfront and gaze longingly at the ships from all nations and dream of distant, exotic places. How could he realise his dream to travel?

In the early summer of 1904, the answer came as swiftly as a Tibby Cotter yorker. Cricketers were great travellers. The Aussies were due to sail for England in January 1905, the Ashes tour. They'd need a scorer. Fergie reasoned that a formal application might be lost among the rush for such a plum job. Even if it reached the desk of tour manager Frank Laver, Fergie's chances were zero. He had never scored in his life.

Fergie's only opportunity to win a tour spot was to endure lots of pain for lifetime gain. He decided to put his future in the hands of the future Test captain, Monty Noble, a leading Sydney dentist. Fergie was willing to have every tooth in his head filled, capped, polished or extracted if it meant the chance to talk to Noble about the Ashes tour job. No extractions were necessary, but Fergie bought enough gold fillings to last a lifetime. The pair struck up a friendship. Fergie was subtle in his approach to the subject of cricket and then the tour. Noble was impressed with Fergie's passion and earmarked the little *Sydney Directory* clerk for great things. Fergie was introduced to two of the game's heroes, Trumper and Laver, and sensed a real chance of an England trip.

When the team left Australia, Fergie had missed the boat. In February 1905, a letter arrived from Laver, informing him that he had been appointed to the job at a salary of '£2 a week and to pay your train fare to the various grounds upon which we play'. From his life savings of £25, Fergie paid his own fare to England – £17 one way – on the White Star line's SS *Suevic*. How times have changed.

In his 1957 book, *Mr Cricket*, Fergie noted:

*England was a very sedate country in those days.
Manners, etiquette and breeding were the paramount
virtues, and, wanting to be taken for a gentleman of
distinction, our manager, Mr Frank Laver, followed the
English fashion of the day by appearing frequently in
top hat and frock coat. The players, and I, had no liking
for the universally popular bowler hat, so we all wore
straw hats – the players sporting green and yellow bands
bearing the Australian coat of arms, the baggage master
an undistinguished plain band.*

Victor Trumper was Fergie's favourite player. He said of him:

*Probably the neatest and most elegant bat in the world at
that time, Vic was anything but neat when in the dressing
room, or at a hotel. He was the despair of his charming
wife, and the not-so-charming baggage master, because he
simply refused to worry about the condition of his clothes
or equipment. Any old bat would do for him, whether there
was rubber on the handle or not, and I can still see him
now, after slaughtering the best bowling in England, taking
off his flannels in the dressing room, rolling them in a ball
and cramming them into an already overloaded cricket bag
– there to remain until they were worn again the next day.*

Fergie's first scoring duty was at Crystal Palace, London, where
he recorded the 'demise' of WG Grace, out for five. His last tour
was with New Zealand in South Africa in 1953–54. He carted
baggage and scored for Australia, England, New Zealand,
South Africa, India and the West Indies and made the job the
fascinating career he'd dreamt of. In 1957, he was awarded the
British Empire Medal for his services to the Commonwealth.

Despite cricket being interrupted by two world wars, Fergie made 41 tours with international teams and scored in a total of 204 Test matches and his travels covered 614,000 miles (916,800 kilometres). He said the South Africans and the Marylebone Cricket Club (MCC) were the most generous of employers, both giving him a £25 bonus at the end of the respective tours. As for the Australians, 'they sent me a letter of thanks'.

An interview with Don Bradman

In March 1974, an interview I conducted with 65-year-old Sir Donald Bradman was published in the now-defunct Australian magazine *Cricketer*. The interview was carried out in Q & A fashion, providing readers with a further insight into this complex legend of cricket.

Q. Do you think the players of today are as good generally as those who played in your era?

A. It is terribly difficult to be specific because there are good and bad in any era. Cricket is unlike sports such as swimming, athletics etc., where a direct comparison of time is possible. It is a team game wherein rules and playing conditions vary. A batsman sometimes gets out because he is so good he touches a ball a less skilful player would miss. I find it difficult to believe that sport has improved in other areas but not cricket. From observation, I can see and appreciate the talent of modern players. As a generality, I believe today's first-class performers play as well or better than their forebears would have done under today's circumstances.

Q. Have you lost any zest for the game now that your cricket administrative duties have lessened?

A. Having shed the responsibilities attached to Chairmanship of the Selection Committee, the Board of Control and the South Australian Cricket Association, it is understandable that my involvement has lessened. But as an active committee-man still, and as a great lover of the game, I retain my interest and enthusiasm at my present level and am sure I always will.

Q. Sickness has followed you and your family throughout your married life. Do you consider this to be a major reason why you have valued physical fitness so highly?

A. No, I don't think sickness had anything to do with it. I just believe that no player can do himself justice unless he is truly fit. I believe there is considerable scope for improvement in the fitness of most cricketers and if only they were prepared to dedicate themselves to the cause, results would amply repay their efforts.

Q. I understand that at the conclusion of the 1934 English tour, illness nearly ended your cricket career and that your wife made a hurried trip to England to be at your side. What happened?

A. Actually, I had been very off colour throughout 1932–33, 1933–34 and the whole tour of England in 1934. It all culminated in an emergency appendix operation in England just before the 1934 team sailed for home. My wife came to England under somewhat dramatic circumstances because it was reported when she was en route that I had died. She rang London and fortunately found the report to be exaggerated. I was convalescent for seven months and was not able to play at all in Australia in 1934–35 or go to South Africa in 1935–36.

Q. Do you still play squash and golf?

A. I am too old for competitive squash but still play social golf. I find it a great mental relaxation.

Q. What is your golf handicap?

A. Seven – but I have great difficulty in playing to it.

Q. Would you consider attempting anything, in the way of sport or business, that you had any reservations about not being sure of succeeding in?

A. At my age, I'm a bit beyond attempting new ventures so the question is theoretical. But as a generality may I reply that no man can be certain, in advance of trying, that he will succeed in anything – sport or business. He may be confident, but he can't be sure. I had successes. I had failures, and was certainly not successful in everything I tried. If a young man won't try anything unless he has a built-in guarantee of success, he won't try much and won't get far.

Q. You have been described as having had a 'killer instinct'. Do you think this paramount for a batsman or a bowler for him to become a really good player?

A. The so-called 'killer instinct' is merely a term coined by journalists. I was never conscious of possessing it and frankly don't think I did. However, to be successful one must have a degree of determination. A boxer who shrinks from knocking out his opponent when he gets the chance is unlikely to become a champion. The bowler who 'eases up' when he is on top won't achieve maximum success. I prefer to call it a strong competitive spirit.

Q. How would you rate Ian Chappell as a captain in comparison with Richie Benaud?

A. It is far too early to make meaningful comparisons. Richie was a great captain. That is undeniably true, as an historical fact, after his career had ended. Ian is in the middle of his career and events yet to unfold may have a big bearing on the place history will allot to him.

Q. Are you or have you ever been superstitious? I ask that because your office number is Room 87 (the Australian cricketer's dreaded number).

A. No. Frankly, I think it is so much bunk. In my playing days, the so-called dreaded 87 didn't exist. Going by the stars, not walking on cracks on the pavement, unlucky 13, not walking under ladders – they all come under the same category – *rubbish*.

Q. The present lbw law was obviously designed to do away with excessive pad play. Do you think umpires should be invested with greater power to dismiss batsmen who pretend to play shots to balls coming in from outside their off stump, but really are not making a genuine attempt to play the ball?

A. By this question, you are really castigating the umpires. They are charged with deciding whether the striker has made a 'genuine' attempt to play the ball and their verdict is to be given accordingly. They need no more power. They only need to exercise what they have. You are obviously questioning their judgment – or their courage – or both. That's all.

Q. Do you think cricket imports should be restricted to Australian players (e.g. Greg Chappell) except for circumstances where great players such as Garry Sobers and Barry Richards have contributed a great deal to our cricket?

A. I am not prepared to pass arbitrary judgment on the many facets of the issue. Clearly men like Sobers and Richards were of great value to South Australian cricket. By this, I'm not just speaking of first-class cricket, but of their worth in the fields of propaganda, incentive, coaching, inspiration and example. Their greatest value could well have been at schoolboy level where their influence was enormous.

I have no criticism of states which won't have imports. But if there is a blanket ban, it must operate both ways and Australians would not be welcome elsewhere. Some Australian XI players have learnt much from playing English domestic cricket.

Certainly, too, many imports could cause problems, as in fact has happened in England. As with most things, balanced judgment appears best.

Q. You have a reputation for answering all your fan mail. Do you still receive a lot of mail? If so, how many fan letters a week would you get on average?

A. Yes, I've always dealt generously with fan mail. On an English tour, when it once reached 600 letters a day, it was a real problem.

Thank goodness it has dwindled to negligible proportions, but there is never a week even now when I don't get some large proportion of it from India. Some event, like the opening of the Bradman Stand recently, always sparks off an increase.

Q. Limited-over cricket has been well received by the Australian public. Do you think that Test cricket will reach the stage where to virtually ensure a result, a compulsory declaration after say 85 overs on each team's first innings will come about? Would you like this to take place or would you rather Test cricket remain in its present form?

A. For the time being at least I would prefer Test cricket to remain in its present form. It is certainly not beyond the bounds of possibility that your suggestion will eventuate. But any artificial limitation would clearly alter the concept of a Test as we know it.

Q. Do you think the days when Australia toured England for 5–5½ months are numbered and that short tours will become the 'in thing'?

A. Short tours are likely to become more frequent but the precise nature of them will vary from year to year according to circumstances. This will be evident by the new adventure of playing the 'World Cup' and the side issues from that. Air travel and economics will tend to dominate more and more.

Q. What would you say to the idea of sending an Australian umpire away with our touring side to England to participate in county matches and in Tests? The arrangements could work both ways, with an English umpire coming to Australia and officiating here in state and Test matches. It might mean Australia taking one less player on a tour of England to cover expenses – but it could prove valuable experience for one of our top men, who could pass on his experience to others in Australia.

A. The idea makes little appeal to me. For all practical purposes, laws operate identically in all countries and any man can become 100 per cent proficient in his knowledge of them just by study.

The practical application of that knowledge depends on eyesight, hearing and judgment. Take the lbw law. An umpire must, on every single occasion, determine whether the ball would have hit the stumps.

A trip overseas would not assist him one bit to say whether that would be so in Adelaide six months later. Nor would it help his eyesight or his hearing if they were defective.

To leave an extra player behind for the sake of sending over an umpire for experience is ludicrous. There just isn't the scope for passing on umpiring knowledge, as there is with playing knowledge and the heavy and unproductive expenses must be considered.

I prefer to think the umpires of a home country are given the maximum encouragement in their own environment. We did in fact have two English umpires here on a scholarship but suggestions that they might officiate in first-class matches whilst here found no support from our umpires or administrators.

Q. What business interests have you now? In how many companies do you hold rank as a director?

A. My professional work is that of a company director. I am on the boards of about a dozen public companies and some private ones. It is a full-time occupation and gives me a wide variety of interests.

Q. If you saw a first-class or Test player doing something wrong technically in his batting or bowling, would you approach him and tell him, or would you let his captain know and let him learn that way?

A. In my playing days, as captain, I certainly took the initiative in trying to help players.

As an administrator, my policy is that I do not interfere in matters outside my jurisdiction. I would never go to a player with gratuitous advice. Conversely, I would be delighted at any time to assist a player who sought my advice, whether through his captain or otherwise.

Who am I to say a boy is doing something wrong? His modern captain may say he is doing it right – might even have told him to do it that way.

In any case, advice has great limitations. The best teacher is the hard school of experience. I made plenty of mistakes as a youngster and my best lessons were my failures. Life won't change in that respect.

I am always ready to help if wanted, but I won't butt in.

I had a rather strange relationship with Bradman. There was little use in my getting hold of his silent telephone number, because he changed it frequently and those in power at the Australian Cricket Board or at the South Australian Cricket Association would never have released his telephone number to anyone outside the inner circle of cricket administration, let alone a member of the press. My strategy was to write him a letter and I discovered that, if I asked him a question, he always replied.

My 1974 Bradman interview was mentioned in Christine Wallace's 2005 book, *The Private Don*, based upon exchanged letters between Bradman and Rohan Rivett, who was appointed in 1951 by Rupert Murdoch's father, Sir Keith Murdoch, as editor-in-chief of *The News*, Adelaide's afternoon tabloid. The two corresponded regularly and I found that Rivett had told Bradman how much he enjoyed my interview with him. Bradman was relieved at Rivett's assessment, saying, 'I confess I was a little dubious.'

However, publication of the interview proved a rod for my own back, because years later, long after Rivett had left the newspaper, I was chief cricket writer for *The News* and, whenever there was a cricket controversy – be it in Australia, the West Indies, India, England or Timbuktu – my editor hounded me to get Bradman to comment. When I explained that the only way was to write to him and wait for a written reply, the chief-of-staff, Doug 'Stainless' Steele, eyed me quizzically and grunted. After half a dozen attempts to get Bradman to say something about whatever, Doug and the others reluctantly drew stumps on the issue.

If you didn't need to meet a deadline, my strategy for getting a Bradman comment worked a treat. I would write and ask a question – sometimes it might be an outlandish question – but it was all aimed at getting a reply, in the hope that he might volunteer information on something newsworthy which was quite apart from the actual question posed.

In July 1981, I wrote to him about South Africa and whether he would welcome that nation's return to the world stage. There was nothing subtle in his reply about what he thought of my questions:

Dear Ashley,

I don't know why it is, but you seem always to ask me questions that can't be answered, are sub judice, that I don't want to answer, or which must be qualified.

The latest is no exception.

What is the use of my, for instance, saying I would like South Africa to be in the World Cup if South Africa doesn't want to – if the other countries think it is unwise – if logistically and financially it cannot be done, etc etc.

This is a matter entirely for the people organising the event. Of course I would be HAPPY to see South Africa in the Cup PROVIDING it suits all the parties concerned. But not otherwise.

I am told (with what validity I cannot say) that in fact South Africa prefers her first re-introduction to the International scene to be a home Test series against India. As the latter country (I understand) nominated South Africa to be readmitted to the ICC, and as India was violently opposed to apartheid, I can see some sense in that idea.

In any event, cricket does not have to be the first instance of South Africa being readmitted to sporting contests.

It is much easier, for instance, to stage a rugby football match than a cricket match (especially when there may be protesters). It makes good sense that South Africa may first of all participate in the truly international Olympics.

There are so many aspects to the proposition.

I am very insistent that any public remarks that I make are sensible and relevant and I am very sensitive to saying anything otherwise.

So you see my answer to your query cannot be a yes or no, but I hope it makes sense to you.

Kind regards.

Yours sincerely,

Don

I found no real solace in the fact that most men and women in the media also found Bradman stubbornly blocked all their attempts to get one past his guard. Bradman knew when to speak out and when to remain silent.

By hook or by cut – Les Favell

Fearlessly, Les Favell hooked the Wes Hall thunderbolt off his head and before the ball cleared the fence he yelled to his partner, Neil Dansie: 'That's six. Get in fer yer chop, Nodda!'

Favell's batting was always outrageous. He hooked and cut his way through 202 first-class matches for 12,379 runs at 36.62 with 27 hundreds and 67 fifties. In 19 Tests, his record is modest – 757 runs at 27.03 with 1 century, against India at Madras in 1959.

He hailed from St George in Sydney, but decided to transfer to South Australia to get a game. In his first match – against New South Wales on the Adelaide Oval – the 22-year-old Favell scored 84 and 168; some debut.

It wasn't the runs he scored that made Favell my favourite cricketer; it was the way he made them. All-out attack was his motto. His total disdain for any type of bowler most definitely ate into his average, but Favell wasn't interested in averages.

Once, in Melbourne, Favell was not out at tea on the last day. South Australia was five down and, to Favell, we had an excellent chance of denying Victoria victory. There he was, padded up, cup of tea in hand, speaking in turn to the remaining batsmen in the shed. 'Keep your head down, son, I'll be there at stumps,' was the theme. First ball after tea was taken by the ebullient Johnny Grant. As he bounded in, Favell was down the track, his bat raised à la Victor Trumper. The outcome was as inevitable as was our laughter as we witnessed all three stumps being scattered to the four winds. We were all out within half an hour from the interval.

Although he was deadly serious in his total commitment to the game of cricket, Les Favell was one of the funniest characters to have played first-class cricket. In the first over of a match against New South Wales at Adelaide, Dave Renneberg's first four deliveries were cut to the point boundary by the confident Favell. The fifth ball was almost out of reach, but Favell managed to get a toe of his bat to it and keeper Brian Taber took the catch between third and fourth slips. After five balls, South Australia was 1/16. Favell c Taber b Renneberg 16.

The South Australian captain walked forlornly from the arena and quietly sat down in the dressing-room. The players at Adelaide Oval sit facing the ground and Favell was sitting behind the adjoining wall.

'Jesus Christ, seeing 'em like a football,' he said.

Neil Hawke waited for the right moment. He was taking off the veteran commentator and writer Johnny Moyes, 'Well, we all know Favell. Sometimes he gets them and sometimes he doesn't. Today, he didn't ... but tomorrow's another day.'

Favell loved his players and South Australia, and he also had an abiding respect for the game of cricket and possessed a sense of fair play. In 1969, South Australia was in a commanding position to bowl New South Wales out a second time to secure the 1968–69 Sheffield Shield trophy. New South Wales was 5/173 in its second innings when John Wilson was felled by a Kevin McCarthy bouncer. The ball struck his forehead and blood began to gush before the stricken batsman fell all over his stumps. Instantly the umpire raised his index finger in the wake of a lone appeal. Wilson was out, hit wicket bowled McCarthy for a duck! Having been dismissed for 110 when it batted first, New South Wales was still 30 runs short of the South Australia total of 307 when Wilson was hit.

An outright victory was on the cards, yet as Wilson was being taken by stretcher from the field, Favell sidled up to the umpires and said: 'We withdraw the appeal. If Wilson is fit enough to return later, I'd like to see him bat on.' Wilson returned, all right. He scored 114 – the only century he ever scored in 12 first-class matches for New South Wales. His side scored 335 and South Australia had to bat frantically to win the match and secure the Shield. The greatest winner of them all was Favell.

The devil's number in Australia is 87 and one day Favell had reached that figure at the SCG when New South Wales player Norm O'Neill approached him and said: 'Hey, Favelli, you're on 87!' Favell laughed it off, but next ball he was out. When Favell walked out to open the batting the second innings, Normie said: 'Hey, Favelli ... you are *still* on 87!' Favell was out for nought, so he had been dismissed twice for a total of 87.

He loved to give a running commentary when he batted. When he was extremely confident, he would sing 'Happy Birthday', presumably to himself but always within earshot of his enraged opponents. One day in Perth, Western Australia captain Barry Shepherd threw the ball to young leggie Terry Jenner. Favell was at the batting end and, as Shepherd set the field, the batsman began to sing 'Happy Birthday to me!' First ball, Favelli charged down the wicket and hit the ball one bounce over the cover boundary. Shepherd immediately put John Parker on the cover fence. Second ball, still singing at the top of his voice, Favell charged down the track, again meeting the ball on the full. This time, the ball went one bounce to Parker on the fence. Non-striker Ian Chappell rushed through to complete the run, but Favell had his back turned to him. His skipper had not budged.

'Piss off, Chappelli. It's my birthday, not yours!'

My part in Packer's war

In 1977, I was working for News Limited and had retired from cricket. News of Packer's World Series Cricket (WSC) had no sooner hit than I rang Ian Chappell. Actually getting paid to play the game resonated with me and I thought, 'Why not?'

'Chappelli, I want a contract with World Series.' Chappell sounded a little lukewarm.

Little did I know that the Australian captain of the new WSC, had argued for his off-spinner, only to be countered by Packer, who apparently told him: 'I'm not offering a contract to that fucking straight-breaker. Couldn't get me out!'

Chappell told me, 'Rowd, about a contract ... I'll need to talk to the boss. See what he says. I'll get back to you within seven days.'

A day later, *The News* chief-of-staff, Geoff Jones, received a phone call. 'Don Bradman here ... Can I please speak with Ashley Mallett?' Ordinarily, Jones would have said something like, 'If you're Don Bradman, I'm Spiderman,' but no, he transferred the call.

'Ah, Ashley, I'll get to the point,' he said in that unmistakable squeak. 'We want you to come back to play for Australia.'

I thanked Sir Donald for his offer. The prospect of playing Tests again against the Indians was tempting, given that I'd taken 28 Test wickets at 19 against them in India in 1969, but in this year of 1977 money was a huge issue. I'd come from an environment which provided $30 for a four-day Shield match, less $7.50 tax, and you were docked a day's pay if you won in three days. For most of the Tests I played, we received $200 a game.

So I asked him, 'Does that mean I will play every Test match?'

'Oh, no. You'd have to make yourself available and take your chances like everyone else.'

'Hang on, you've guaranteed Bobby Simpson every Test.'

'Ah, he's different. He's the captain.'

Mind you, Simpson was one of Australia's cricket greats; myself a good Test bowler, but not a great one. There was another catch. Simmo was said to be a bit like Bill Lawry as a captain: dour and not given to taking chances. Maybe he was also like Lawry regarding spin bowling. Bill appeared to think spin was something to do with the quick-drying function on a washing machine.

I told Bradman that I was a chance to play WSC and that I would need to seriously consider an offer that would guarantee a lump sum for the entire summer. For two days I sweated it out, then Chappelli got back to me with an offer ... of sorts.

'Kerry's willing to give you a contract, but only if you agree to fly to Sydney and bowl against him for one over. If you get him out twice in six balls, he'll make you an offer.'

I did not hesitate. 'Chappelli, tell Mr Packer to get fucked!'

I got a contract. Some 30 years later, I asked Chappelli if he had relayed our conversation verbatim to Kerry. He said, 'No, Rowd ... I didn't think it would be in your best interests.'

Signing for WSC meant we were ostracised by the Establishment. We were banned from playing for our club or state, and even stopped from training on certain grounds. I picked up 4/54 in our first hit-out practice match at Moorabbin and, to my surprise, Packer sat down beside me at lunch.

'A few wickets, eh, son?' he said, stubbing out a cigarette.

'Yeah, Kerry. Not bad for a bloke who can't bowl!'

But you couldn't help liking the big bloke. He was hard but fair. You always knew where you stood with him. I never bowled to Kerry, but I did hear that he spent time batting at the Alf

Gover Cricket School in England in 1977. Maybe he wasn't that confident after all. His heart was very much for his players and you got the feeling he would do anything to help them.

Everyone knew his plan was to get the television rights, but here was a chance to get the players a better deal and stick it up the Establishment, who thought they could screw Packer like they had screwed the players for generations.

Playing WSC was a financial boon for me, for I had come from a background of struggling to make ends meet to play big cricket. I then went on a number of Test tours where we were treated badly by the Australian Cricket Board in terms of pay and accommodation.

During a seven-month tour of Ceylon (Sri Lanka), India and South Africa in 1969–70, we were paid peanuts, and although we batted and bowled out of our skins to beat a very good Indian outfit 3–1 in India, eventually we played like monkeys in losing 4–nil to the Springboks.

In India, there were some good hotels, but we stayed in many which could only be described as hovels, with dreadful food. A slice of toast, half a banana and a swig of scotch was often a hearty breakfast for some of our bowlers in India, where Delhi-belly reigned supreme. We also later learnt that our lives were insured for $400 per man.

Then came South Africa, where the hotels were good, the Springboks were terrific, the umpiring was horrendous and we were deservedly thrashed 4–nil. There was to be a Fifth Test, but we made a majority decision to opt out. The Australian Board of Control for International Cricket wanted us to play the extra Test for a sum of $200 extra each man. We refused. The South Africans said they'd throw in an extra $300 per man to make it up to $500. However, we again refused, the argument being that our board should have made that offer, not the host nation.

To his credit, Bill Lawry took the blame and it cost him his Test spot a few months later. Defying the board was a no-no. In

1980, after a golfing four at Pennant Hills with Ian Chappell, Brian Taber and Graeme Watson, Neil Harvey told Chappelli that it was he, Harvey, who had convinced his fellow selectors that the time had come for Bill Lawry to go and Ian Chappell to take over.

'Don wasn't too keen on the idea,' Harvey recalled later. 'He believed that Ian wasn't the right bloke for the job, but he became the captain and Bradman was wrong.'

That tour was the catalyst for WSC getting off the ground. While Packer's WSC did not come to pass until 1977 – seven years after the 1969–70 tour – many of the tourists (men such as Ian Chappell, Doug Walters, Ian Redpath, Graham McKenzie and yours truly) were so incensed with the board's attitude towards them that all that was needed was a hook for the 'us' to take on the 'them'.

A year before Packer's WSC started, then ACTU boss Bob Hawke was in talks with Chappell, Bob Cowper and others with a view to starting up a players' union, but it didn't get off the ground. Hawke, of course, went into federal politics and became Prime Minister in 1983.

By then, WSC had come and gone and Packer had got his way. He wanted the much-prized TV rights and that aspiration fitted perfectly with the players who were after a better deal. Packer's timing was perfect for him and for us.

Being paid good money to play top cricket was a revelation. I just wanted to be part of it. It was Kerry Packer who provided that opportunity and his Channel Nine televising Test and one-day cricket was the start of the big money for top cricketers the world over. It is thanks to him that the money is there for the players.

There are many aspects of Packer's compassionate side, some of which have been reported. In the second year of WSC, Australia was about to leave for a tour of the Caribbean. All the players were on $16,000 for an eight-week stint against

Clive Lloyd's terrific side. Ian Chappell was called in to Packer's Park Street, Sydney, HQ. Packer asked Chappelli if he was happy with his team and it emerged that the fixed sum of $16,000 was less than the daily rate stipulated under their WSC contract.

Packer turned to his executive Lynton Taylor and asked, 'Aren't we paying according to the contract?'

'No, Kerry, but Ian's sorted it out with the players. It's all fixed.'

'Aren't we paying according to the contract?'

Taylor said, 'No.'

Packer bellowed, 'Then fucking pay 'em according to the contract!'

Chappell interjected: 'This is ridiculous, Kerry. You're not going to make any money out of this tour to the Caribbean. Our blokes are going to make more money on this tour than they'd earn at home.'

But Packer was determined. He turned to Taylor. 'How much more would it cost if we pay according to the contract?'

Taylor did his sums quickly and replied, 'Double – about $340,000.'

Packer hardly drew a breath before he said, 'Well, pay 'em according to the contract.' He explained, 'Son, I'll tell you something: $340,000 is about the price of a B-grade movie for my TV station. That's not going to break me. What will fucking-well break me is not sticking to the word of my contracts. Lynton, pay 'em.'

These days, television is the financial lifeblood of the game. And the players are getting huge money for their efforts. In my time, the boards ran the game and were the veritable landlords lauding it over the players, the serfs. There has been a big turnaround, for today it is the players who call the tune. They dictate what form of the game they play. Some decide to opt out of Test cricket and play just one form of cricket – T20 or the 50-overs format.

That in itself is a big worry, for it is degrading the only true test of an elite cricketer's mettle: Test cricket.

You cannot blame the likes of Shane Warne, Matthew Hayden, Brad Hodge and Brett Lee for a time and more recently Brad Hogg, who's in his mid-40s, for playing the wham-bash-crash T20 stuff, because they have given a great deal to all forms of cricket at the elite level and this is a chance for them to further cash in on what they have given to Australian cricket. However, others, including South Australia's Shaun Tait and Western Australia's Mike Hussey, should really have been available to play the longer form of the game.

If dozens follow Tait's choice, Test cricket Down Under will be threatened. Cricket Australia should insist that all current players make themselves available for all forms of cricket or be axed. Today, Cricket Australia seems happy to allow the players to pick and choose what form (or forms) of the game they play.

Perhaps we should not leave things to the ICC, for that august body might struggle to organise a piss-up in a brewery.

Our first Aboriginal Test player

Faith Thomas (née Coulthard) was Australia's first Aboriginal Test cricketer. I met her in Canberra in April 2001, where she was invited to present the inaugural Johnny Mullagh Trophy in the Prime Minister's XI versus the ATSIC (Aboriginal and Torres Strait Islander Commission) Chairman's XI match at Manuka Oval. My role in writing the story of the 1868 Aboriginal cricket tour of England saw me involved in the match. The ATSIC Chairman's XI won and Faith was there to present the trophy to the winning skipper, Jason Gillespie. Here was the first female Aboriginal Test player presenting the winning trophy to the first acknowledged male Aboriginal Test cricketer.

I bowled a few overs for the PM's XI, but was forced to field for 28 overs after one guy went off with a pulled hamstring and Steve Waugh left the field with a migraine headache. Though I tripped and fell a few times, and swear I missed four balls at mid-on by 25 years, the spirit of the match overshadowed all else.

It was a moment to savour. Denial of Aboriginal heritage has been part of the sad story of the clash of cultures between white and black in this country since the Union Jack was first raised at Botany Bay more than 200 years ago. Faith Thomas doesn't deny her heritage. She is proud of it and is in no way angry or resentful, despite hardship through the years. Aboriginal women have had an even tougher row to hoe than their male counterparts, for they have been ignored on the one hand and maltreated on the other.

Women's cricket had begun in Australia in the 1920s and, in the 1934–35 summer, a visiting English women's team played a Queensland XI which included two Aboriginal women – Mabel Campbell and Edna Crouch. Edna's niece, Thelma Crouch, became a prominent player, representing the Australian junior cricket team against the English women in 1949. There were some early gains in women's cricket for Aboriginal people, but only one made the big time: Faith Coulthard.

Faith was born in 1933 at Nepabunna Mission in the Flinders Ranges of South Australia, the daughter of an Adnyamathanha woman. Faith was not cast aside, but as a babe in arms she was taken to the Colebrook Home in Quorn. Her mother kept in contact with Faith through the years and she has never considered herself to be a 'stolen child'. Faith recalled:

Colebrook Home was a real home away from home. Mum took me there because she knew that I would be well cared for and have lots of children about me. The people I grew up with at Colebrook were (and still are) my extended family.

Among Faith's Colebrook 'family' is noted Aboriginal leader Lowitja Lois O'Donoghue.

Cricket folklore has the legend of Don Bradman with his golf ball and stump. The Aboriginal kids at the Colebrook Home in Quorn played a form of cricket which Faith reckons was more a cross between cricket and rounders, with a stick for a bat and a stone for a ball. They also had fun chucking stones at electricity poles. The kid with the fastest, most accurate throw could easily knock out a light. The games with the sticks and the stones helped hone remarkable skills and extraordinary hand–eye coordination.

When Faith and her mates moved from Quorn to Eden Hills, they found they could play the same games, but equipment was provided, so the stick was replaced by a real cricket bat and the stone gave way to a real cricket ball. However, they still managed to play with stones. The game was simple. One kid threw stones at another kid, who protected himself with a tin. It was a game which helped forge the legend of the 1868 cricketer Dick-a-Dick (Jungunjinanuke), whose skill in dodging harks back to the Aboriginal 'game' of dodging spears. (See 'The Artful Dodger of the 1868 team' in this book.)

Faith learnt to duck and weave and to develop a strong throwing arm. Cricket was never something she yearned to do until Fay Beckworth, night duty nurse at the Royal Adelaide Hospital, invited Faith to practice, explaining that they were keen, but needed players.

She recalled, 'We trained in the North Parklands in Adelaide. It had large trees and lots of grazing cows – We had to shoo the cows away from the joint and get out there with a shovel to get rid of the dung off the pitch before we started applying ant powder at each end of the pitch.'

She bowled in the manner of Jeff Thomson – a few shuffles in and then let fly. Bowling came naturally. The kids had watched people play cricket and copied their bowling styles. Faith insists that they bowled and didn't throw when they played their impromptu games of cricket. Faith got a hat-trick in her second match. That same year, she took 6/0 to demoralise the Adelaide Teachers College team.

As a bowler, Faith was, as they say in cricket-speak, a 'natural'. The few shuffling paces in her approach did not impress Vic Richardson, the former South Australia and Test captain. Faith got no formal coaching, but Vic suggested to her that she add a few paces to her run. He told her, 'You need to take a run and point your feet where the ball's going or you'll rip your cartilage to pieces. You need more balance.' Faith accepted Vic's advice and added six paces to her approach. She found the new approach an improvement, in that she was able to better utilise her body at delivery, instead of relying almost exclusively on shoulder power.

Faith also loved, like all fast bowlers, to knock down the stumps:

No-one ever told me about the subtle things like swinging away for catches in the slips. I always tried to bowl them out, that if you've got a ball in your hand, try and knock the stumps over and that was it. Then they encouraged me to bowl to the slips, but no-one explained the positions on the ground. They'd say, 'Go to cover' and where they pointed I went. If they said they'd set a field and wanted me to bowl to it, it didn't mean a thing to me.

The extraordinary upshot of all of this is that when Faith Thomas played for Windsor (Adelaide), for South Australia and for Australia she did not know all the fielding positions. 'They had it all worked out, but no-one ever told me. I only began to get the idea of all the field placings years later when watching cricket on the television.'

In 1952, Faith began training for a nursing career, worked at Queen Victoria Hospital from 1954 to 1956, and completed her midwifery training there in the years 1957–58. This was the time of her best years in cricket. In the summer of 1956–57, Faith scored 28 for South Australia against the visiting New Zealanders, then took a remarkable 9/15. Three of the South Australian players in 1957–58 had medical backgrounds. Ruth Dow was a qualified doctor of medicine, Barbara Orchard was studying medicine and Faith was nursing.

That summer, the national championships were held in Adelaide and New Zealand also took part, with South Australia the only undefeated side. In 1958, delegates from England, Holland, South Africa, New Zealand and Australia met in Melbourne to form the International Women's Cricket Council.

Faith was selected for the Test series and on the train to Brisbane she recalls having to lie in the pack-rack to get some sleep. At the Gabba, her spirit soared, for there were three Aboriginal men clapping her every move. 'I literally played for those three old fellows,' she recalled. How they cheered when Faith cleaned-bowled the England captain, Mary Duggan, with a searing yorker which sent her leg stump actually flying high over the wicketkeeper's head.

The Australian captain was Joyce Christ, and when Mary Duggan saw the name 'J. Christ' on the scoreboard, she exclaimed, 'How in the hell are we supposed to win? Look at that on the scoreboard!'

Faith played two Test matches against England, then, just half an hour or so before the first ball was bowled, was made twelfth man in the match at Adelaide. Faith was more than a bit peeved about having to carry the drinks and decided upon a plan of non-cooperation. She would spill the drinks, accidentally on purpose. As she told me:

> *I was so disappointed in not playing. All my family were down for the match. I walked onto the Adelaide Oval carrying a wooden tray with low sides. When I got about halfway to the wicket, I tripped and fell headlong over a blade of grass, and every time I walked onto that field I fell over that same blade of grass. I hung on to the saltshaker. Ruth Dow used to get us to take a handful of salt instead of salt tablets, but there was nothing to wash it down.*
>
> *My fall was on purpose, not like you in Canberra, where you must have fallen over the blackfella's flag!*

Faith was never again selected for Australia in Australia, although she was offered a place in the touring side to England and New Zealand in 1960. She reluctantly withdrew from the selected side because she had completed nine months of a year-long midwifery course and did not wish to repeat the year. That was how Faith rationalised withdrawing from the tour. In reality, that was one factor, but, 'I was afraid of the travel. We would go by ship, second-class cabin. I was afraid I would have been claustrophobic. I simply hate being closed in. There I was, a girl from the desert, about to sail the ocean.'

When Faith Coulthard was first selected for Australia, the press moved in like feeding sharks. They saw Faith as a 'novelty' and were after every conceivable angle. Team management closed ranks and protected Faith from the press. 'I'd run away every time I saw a reporter,' Faith said.

> *We were referred to as 'natives'. It was 'native nurse' this and 'native nurse' that. This goes back to the days of being under the control of the Protector of Aborigines. We were natives, the protected Aborigines.*
>
> *There was a song on the hit parade called 'Freight train, freight train, going so fast'. Well, the opposition used to try and put me off by singing it. Racist, no doubt – a freight train being big and black. But it had the reverse effect. It resulted in things flying everywhere. I got my ire up a bit and bowled faster and more accurately than I thought I could.*
>
> *As far as the press were concerned, the management told reporters that they were supposed to be reporting on the cricket, not 'novelties'.*

Recently Faith became one of five female and 18 male cricketers (including the yours truly) to be included in the South Australian Cricket Association Avenue of Honour.

Jason Gillespie: a stallion, stayer and workhorse all rolled into one

Jason Gillespie was the warhorse of the cricket world: once the tearaway yearling, then the stallion and finally the workhorse of the Australian Test team.

Born to Neil and Vicki Gillespie at Darlinghurst Hospital, Sydney, on 19 April 1975, Jason's ethnic background was interesting and diverse. Neil had a mix of Scottish, German and Indigenous Australian heritage and Vicki was of Greek descent. Neil Gillespie's paternal great-grandfather was a warrior of the Kamilaroi, one of the largest groups of Aboriginal people in eastern Australia. Charles Greenway, son of the famous early convict architect Francis Greenway, spoke of the Kamilaroi's impressive physique: 'a well-formed, agile and enduring race ... many of the men six feet in height'. At another time, he could have been describing fast bowler Gillespie at his peak – the first man of acknowledged Aboriginal descent to play Test cricket for Australia.

By the time his family moved to Adelaide in 1985, Jason was already a keen all-round cricketer with the Illawong Menai Cricket Club (situated some 27 kilometres southwest of Sydney) and in 1984–85, his last season for the club, Jason was Junior Cricketer of the Year. (That same year, former Test batsman Doug Walters was persuaded to turn out for one A-grade match with Illawong and, although long retired, Doug dusted off his gear and hit a glorious 144 not out.) Current Test captain Steve Smith also had a long association with Illawong, playing 11 seasons with the club from the Under-8s to the Under-16s.

By the time he was in his teens, Jason was doing okay in grade cricket for the Adelaide club, playing C-grade one week, D-grade the next. His C-grade coach, Shane Bernhardt, told Jason:

I'll be perfectly honest. You have a good defence and I think batting is your best bet to play at a higher level. If you concentrate on bowling alone, I can't see you going beyond B-grade.

That brought Jason down to earth. From the age of six, he had dreamt of playing Test cricket as a bowler and that was his ambition. Then came the day at Bayley Reserve when a few of the boys from the Adelaide lower-grade teams were sitting on the grass chatting casually about their futures. When 16-year-old Jason Gillespie came to tell the group his ambition – 'Well, I'm going to play Test cricket for Australia' – they all fell over laughing.

Somehow, that was the light-bulb moment of my cricketing career. I had made the statement and I was determined to make it happen. I had and have always had belief in myself and my abilities.

I went home, went out for a run, determined to get fit and strong and show them. There was no way I wanted to remain a powder-puff medium-pacer, I wanted to bowl fast. At the nets, I marked out a long run and charged in to bowl as fast as I could every ball. That was the turning point in my thinking about the game and where I sat.

He was not invited to the state nets to bowl in the under-age squads until the 1992–93 season when, in one inspired selection, he was plucked from the relative obscurity of C-grade into the A-grade team. There he bowled with pace and fire and his speed and stamina impressed. He was chosen in the South Australia Under-19 team for the national carnival and selected in the Australian Under-19 team to tour India.

Adelaide captain Paul Nobes spoke to state coach Jeff 'Bomber' Hammond about the promising Gillespie and Jason was quickly brought into the fold, bowling against the state players in the Adelaide Oval nets.

I found Bomber a terrific influence. He took me under his wing. When I got to work with Dennis Lillee, I'd go back to the nets and Bomber would ask how he could stay in touch with what Lillee was saying and how he could embrace the great fast bowler's philosophy in helping me.

Jason said Lillee helped smooth out his action and worked towards improving the rhythm of his approach.

I was one of three South Australian selectors when Gillespie made his Sheffield Shield debut in the summer of 1994–95. It was round that time he was attending the Australian Cricket Academy under head coach Rodney Marsh. Gillespie was young, fit, strong and willing. He played three Sheffield Shield matches, then the final against Queensland in Brisbane. South Australia got into the Shield final again the following summer, taking out the 1995–96 trophy in a tightly fought match at Adelaide Oval.

On 29 November 1996, Gillespie made an inauspicious Test debut against the West Indies at the SCG, taking 2/62 and 0/27 and scoring 16 not out. But he was destined to fit in brilliantly as the back-up go-to man when either Glenn McGrath or Shane Warne was having a rest. Soon he was wowing fans and foe alike on the Test stage. He ran through England at Headingley in 1997 to the tune of 7/37, but he maintains the greatest thrill was to play in winning teams.

*In 1997, we played South Africa in Port Elizabeth. I was
holding up an end and had negotiated eight Jacques Kallis
deliveries without mishap. Then came the time to win the
game. Ian Healy was facing, only a ball or two to go. We
needed six. A wayward delivery and Heals whacked it
over the fine leg fence for six. I raced down the track to
give Heals a high five and stood there looking at him as he
continued to ignore me and wave his bat to the crowd.*

Jason was a key member of the Australian team which won the
Test series against India in 2004. This was the first Australian
series win against India in India since Bill Lawry's Australians
beat India 3–1 there in 1969.

Throughout his career, Gillespie was plagued with injury,
suffering strains to his feet, stress fractures to his back, hip
twinges, side strains, shoulders, torn calves, aching hamstrings,
groin complaints and a terrible leg injury in Sri Lanka.

During the 1999 Australian tour of Sri Lanka, he was involved
in an infamous and sickening outfield collision. In the First Test
at Kandy, Australia was out for 188 in the first innings and Sri
Lanka lost Sanath Jayasuriya early, then Russel Arnold off the
last ball of the first day. Marvan Atapattu fell early the second
morning and Sri Lanka was 3/139 when the horrific accident
derailed Australia's big-hearted comeback.

Off-spinner Colin Miller tempted Mahela Jayawardene to
sweep. He top-edged the ball, seemingly too high and out of
reach for Steve Waugh at backward square leg and threatening
to drop between Waugh, running at breakneck speed, and
Jason Gillespie, galloping in from deep square leg. The noise of
the crowd would have drowned out any sound of warning to the
men racing headlong into a collision. Waugh appeared to see
Gillespie at the last moment and both men instinctively ducked,
but it was too late. The crowd fell silent as the pair crashed
sickeningly to the ground, Gillespie grabbing his right shin and

Waugh lying motionless on his back in the wake of his head hitting Gillespie's foot.

Waugh sustained several fractures to his nose and extensive bruising to his eye sockets, nose, forehead and cheeks. Gillespie suffered a broken right tibia. They spent the rest of the Test match lying in adjoining beds in Colombo Hospital nursing their wounds. Gillespie returned to Australia, but Steve Waugh remarkably played in the next Test.

Shane Bernhardt, the coach who suggested Dizzy concentrate on his batting, is still one of his closest mates and perhaps felt some justification after Jason's 71st and last Test match, against Bangladesh at Chittagong in April 2006. In the Bangladesh first innings he took 3/11 off five overs.

Skipper Ricky Ponting often asked Gillespie to pad up late in the day, in case a key wicket fell close to the scheduled time for stumps. The big fast bowler was a natural as a nightwatchman for he had a limited repertoire of shots, but his defence was as impenetrable as Fort Knox. With the Australian score standing at 67, Matthew Hayden fell and Gillespie walked to the wicket.

He went on to share a fourth-wicket stand of 320 with Mike Hussey (182). On his 31st birthday, 19 April 2006, and wearing the biggest grin in the world, Gillespie was 201 not out when Ponting called a halt to the slaughter at 4/581. His double century was the highest score made by a nightwatchman in Test cricket history.

Exactly one year after his amazing double century against Bangladesh in his final Test match, he scored his debut first-class hundred for Yorkshire against Surrey at The Oval. The day he turned 32, he hit an unbeaten 123 and in doing so, with Tim Bresnan, set a ninth-wicket record for Yorkshire. They compiled 246 and Jason made the highest-ever score for a Yorkshire batsman batting number ten.

As an ethical vegan, Jason has been critical of the dairy farming industry and the use of leather cricket balls. While coaching Yorkshire, the club's sponsor, a dairy, came under the Gillespie gaze. He said, 'Yes, they are a sponsor, but it doesn't mean I agree with what they do. It's out of my control; just like the reality that cricket balls are made from leather.'

Despite the late batting achievements, through his bowling career for Australia Dizzy not only proved Shane Bernhardt wrong, he proved to himself that with great belief one can move mountains. Since his statement to his teenage peers at Adelaide Cricket Club, Dizzy has proved a lot of people wrong; but his great belief in himself was unwavering.

Acknowledgements

My thanks to the following people for their help in my compiling myriad stories, some of which appear in this book: John Arlott*, Dr Ali Bacher, Dr Donald Beard, Richie Benaud*, Daphne Benaud, Billy Birmingham, *The 12th Man*, Sir Alec Bedser*, Geoff Boycott, Sir Donald Bradman*, Mike Brearley, Greg Chappell, Ian Chappell, Michael Clarke, Alan Davidson, Ross Edwards, Les Favell*, John Fordham, Stephen Fry, Gary Gilmour*, Jason Gillespie, Clarrie Grimmett*, Neil Harvey, Bob Hawke, Rangana Herath, John Inverarity, Terry Jenner*, Elton John, Duleep Mendis, Rodney Marsh, Mark Nicholas, Kerry O'Keeffe, Bill O'Reilly, Kerry Packer*, Sir Michael Parkinson, Len Pascoe, Sir Timothy Rice, Graeme Swann, Anura Tennekoon, Jeff Thomson, Max Walker*, Doug Walters, Shane Warne, Sunil Wettimuny.

Special thanks to John Fordham, whose expertise in the media helped me find the right publisher, ABC Books; and Sir Donald Bradman*, who (from 1974–1995) generously gave his time to answer my questions, whether face to face or by carefully typed letter.

Thanks to Bob Hawke for his invitation to interview him at his home, and to Sir Michael Parkinson for generously giving his time to chat about his involvement in cricket and his illustrious television career.

I fondly recall Ross Edwards inviting me in 1975 to the London home of Sir Oliver Popplewell QC, a one-time president of the Marylebone Cricket Club, where I was introduced to a shy, ruddy-faced plump schoolboy, Stephen Fry. The young Fry and I engaged in cricket speak and the meat of our discussion appeared in Stephen Fry's autobiographical best-seller, *Moab Is My Washpot*. Further thanks, Rosco, for your organising a night at the Hampshire home of John Arlott*. The Australian threesome comprised Rosco, Max Walker* and yours truly. It proved a night for this writer to sup and savour.

Thanks to friend and fellow wordsmith Trevor Gill for his encouragement to have a gathering of my cricket writings compiled into a reader-friendly book.

During my convalescence in the wake of surgery, Greg Chappell buoyed me with these words: 'We need you writing ...'

My thanks to Sir Ron Brierley, former Cricket Australia chairmen Jack Clarke and Creagh O'Connor, and ex-teammate, later chairman of the Australian selectors, John Inverarity, for their encouragement of the craft I pursue. So, too, Rodney Cavalier; writer, a minister in the Wran and Unsworth New South Wales Labor Governments, cricket tragic extraordinaire and life member of the SCG Trust.

The people at ABC Books – Brigitta Doyle, James Kellow, Jude McGee, Barbara McClenahan, Mark Evans and Matthew Howard – provided a formidable and helpful team. Thank you all.

Any writer worth his salt needs a top-flight team about him. My fiancée, Patsy Gardner, former television executive, provided feedback on the stories that appear in this book. There is no doubt that where a writer tries to paint a vivid picture in words, TV people have a particular image in mind. Patsy's insights were invaluable and enlightening. We are a good team.

Ashley Mallett
Adelaide, 2017

*deceased

Some stories in this book have appeared (in part or in full) previously.

An adapted version of 'A bat, a ball and a pen' appeared as 'My life in cricket and writing' in *Cricinfo* on 18 December 2016. 'That first Boxing Day classic' appeared in *Cricinfo* on 27 December 2014. 'Backyard Test matches' first appeared in *Cricinfo* as 'Legends in their own backyard' on 17 April 2013. 'Bradman versus Warne' was first published in *The Age* and *Sydney Morning Herald* on 21 January 2012. 'Mandela breathed life into Test cricket' first appeared in *Cricinfo* as 'Mabiba and the Godfather' on 16 December 2013. 'Bradman caught and bowled Bob Hawke' first appeared as 'The tragic who bowled Bradman' in *Cricinfo* on 23 April 2014. 'Five great quicks' first appeared as 'The five best fast bowlers I've seen' in *Cricinfo* on 10 June 2012. 'Mr Mendis, do you wish to press charges?' first appeared as 'Do you want to press charges against a Mr Jeff Thomson?' in *Cricinfo* on 9 February 2015. 'The Tiger and the Fox' first appeared in *Cricinfo* on 8 May 2013. 'Swann in full flight' first appeared as 'England's best since Laker' in *Cricinfo* on 23 December 2013. 'Rangana Herath: sings a song of spin' first appeared in a different form as 'Spin 'em hard Herath' in *Cricinfo* on 13 December 2013. 'Five great all-rounders' first appeared as 'Five to do it all' in *Cricinfo* on 10 July 2012. 'Alec Bedser: cricket colossus' first appeared as 'When Bedser bowled the Don for a duck' in *Cricinfo* on 1 September 2014. 'Keith Miller, superstar' first appeared as 'The swashbuckling flight lieutenant' in *Cricinfo* on 3 November 2014. 'The "baby" of the 1948 side' first appeared as 'The "baby invincible" who always stood tall' in *Cricinfo* on 18 October 2014. 'Davo, the great all-rounder' first appeared in a longer version as 'Big hearted, broad-shouldered Davo' in *Cricinfo* on 26 November 2014. 'Doug Walters: a touch of Bradman' first appeared as 'A touch of Bradman' in *Cricinfo* on 14 September 2014. 'Gary Gilmour, the last amateur' first appeared as 'A glimpse of genius' in *Cricinfo* on 12 June 2014. 'Boycott's genius on a black pudding' first appeared as 'Boycott on a black pudding' in *Cricinfo* on 4 July 2013. 'Parky on Bradman and company' first appeared as 'Parky and the stars' in *Cricinfo* on 23 June 2014. 'Miracle on Beulah Road' first appeared in Ashley Mallett's book *The Diggers' Doctor* (2014). 'TJ, the lovable larrikin' appeared as 'Terry, my twin' in *Cricinfo* on 1 June 2011. 'Name Drops' first appeared in a longer version as 'A shy Stephen Fry, an irate Elton John' in *Cricinfo* on 16 August 2014. 'Charles Dickens shoulders arms' first appeared as 'When Charles Dickens shouldered arms' in *Cricinfo* on 19 February 2012. 'The gully, a different cricket world' first appeared in a longer version as 'The art of the gully man' in *Cricinfo* on 16 April 2012. 'Once upon an all-run nine' first appeared in *Cricinfo* on 12 August 2012. 'By hook or by cut: Les Favell' first appeared in a longer version as 'Attack and revel' in Cricinfo on 25 December 2011. 'Fergie's wagon wheel' was first published in *The Age* and *Sydney Morning Herald* on 21 December 2012. 'My part in Packer's war' first appeared as 'What Kerry did' in Cricinfo on 25 December 2011. 'An interview with Don Bradman' first appeared in the now-defunct *Cricketer* magazine, edited by Eric Beecher, in 1974.

Index